Defending American Religious Neutrality

Defending American Religious Neutrality

Andrew Koppelman

Harvard University Press

Cambridge, Massachusetts

London, England

2013

Library of Congress Cataloging-in-Publication Data

Koppelman, Andrew.
Defending American religious neutrality / Andrew Koppelman.
p. cm.
Includes bibliographical references and index.
ISBN 978-0-674-06646-5 (alk. paper)
1. Church and state—United States.   2. Freedom of religion—United States.
3. Ecclesiastical law—United States.   I. Title.
KF4865.K67 2013
342.7308'52—dc23   2012008382

Contents

Defending American Religious Neutrality

Introduction

The American law of freedom of religion is in trouble, because growing numbers of critics, including a near-majority of the Supreme Court, are ready to cast aside the ideal of religious neutrality. This book defends the claim, which unfortunately has become an audacious one, that American religious neutrality is coherent and attractive.

Two factions dominate contemporary discussion of these issues in American law. One, whom I'll call the radical secularists, tend to regard the law of the religion clauses as a flawed attempt to achieve neutrality across all controversial conceptions of the good—flawed because it is satisfied with something less than the complete eradication of religion from public life. The other, whom I'll call the religious traditionalists, think that any claim of neutrality is a fraud, because law necessarily involves substantive commitments. They believe that there is thus nothing wrong with frank state endorsement of religious propositions: if the state is inevitably going to take sides, why not this one? One side regards religion as toxic and valueless; the other is untroubled by the state's embrace of an official religion. Neither sees much value in the way American law actually functions.

Yet America has been unusually successful in dealing with religious diversity. The civil peace that the United States has almost effortlessly achieved has been beyond the capacities of many other generally well-functioning democracies, such as France and Germany. Even if the American law of religious liberty were entirely incoherent, it might still be an attractive approach to this perennial human problem. There is, however, a logic to the law that its critics have not understood.

1

Prominent scholars of religion have ridiculed President-elect Dwight Eisenhower's 1952 declaration: "Our form of government has no sense unless it is founded in a deeply felt religious faith, and I don't care what it is."[1] Eisenhower nonetheless revealed a deep insight into the character of American neutrality. This book aims to recover that insight.

Contrary to the radical secularists, First Amendment doctrine treats religion as a good thing. It insists, however—and here it parts company with the religious traditionalists—that religion's goodness be understood at a high enough level of abstraction that the state takes no position on any live religious dispute. It holds that religion's value is best honored by prohibiting the state from trying to answer religious questions.

American religious neutrality has over time become more vague as America has become more religiously diverse, so that today (with the exception of a few grandfathered practices) the state may not even affirm the existence of God. This is not the kind of neutrality toward all conceptions of the good that many liberal political theorists have advocated, but it is the best response to the enormous variety of religious views in modern America. It is faithful to the belief, held by the leading framers of the First Amendment, that religion can be corrupted by state support.

Many aspects of present American law in this area are puzzling. Some kinds of official religion are clearly impermissible, such as official prayers and Bible reading in public schools. Laws such as a ban on the teaching of evolution are struck down because they lack a secular purpose. Yet at the same time, "In God We Trust" appears on the currency, legislative sessions begin with prayers, judicial proceedings begin with "God save the United States and this Honorable Court," Christmas is an official holiday, and the words "under God" appear in the Pledge of Allegiance. Old manifestations of official religion are tolerated, while new ones are enjoined by the courts: the Supreme Court held in 2005 that an official Ten Commandments display is unconstitutional if it was erected recently, but not if it has been around for decades. There is confusion about faith-based social services, public financing of religious schools, and the teaching of "intelligent design."

All this, I will argue, makes sense. The key is understanding the precise level of abstraction at which American law is neutral toward religion.

This book offers new answers to three questions: What conception of neutrality is relied on in the interpretation of the Establishment Clause of the First Amendment? Is it coherent? Is it defensible?

THE FIRST AMENDMENT of the United States Constitution says "Congress shall make no law respecting an establishment of religion, or abridging the free exercise thereof." The interpretation of this provision has been controversial for a long time, and indeed may be ripe for revolution. A growing number of writers, including several Supreme Court justices, have argued that religion clause doctrine is both incoherent and substantively unattractive. They propose to replace it with a new set of rules that are far friendlier to official endorsement of religion.

If these proposals are adopted, the result would be heightened civil strife, corruption of religion, and oppression of religious minorities. One proposal, for example, is to permit states to endorse general principles of Abrahamic monotheism. Official religious pronouncements not only brand as outsiders anyone whose beliefs do not conform to the official line; they tend to produce religion of a peculiarly degraded sort. If the state gets to discern God's will, we will be told that God wants the reelection of the incumbent administration. Another proposal is that religious activities should be eligible for direct funding so long as there is a plausible secular reason for doing so. Such funding for religious entities, particularly when those entities are relied on to provide public services such as education, aid to the homeless, prison rehabilitation, or drug treatment, can easily lead to a situation where the only option is a religious one, and people are bullied into religious activities. The most radical proposal would discard the requirement that every law have a secular purpose. Some religious justification is available for nearly anything that the state wants to do to anyone. Permitting such justifications would devastate many constitutional protections that have nothing to do with religion.

And this exorbitant price will have been paid for nothing. Present doctrine already allows for what the doctrine's critics most value: state recognition of the distinctive value of religion. The law treats religion as something special in a broad range of legislative and judicial actions. What the state may not do—what the doctrine properly forbids it to do—is declare any particular religious doctrine to be the true one, or enact laws that clearly imply such a declaration of religious truth.

Religious liberty in American law has for decades been understood in the language of neutrality. The decision barring official Bible readings in the public schools is only the most prominent example.[2] Neutrality is a ubiquitous theme in Establishment Clause decisions spanning more than half a century.[3] One prominent scholar has concluded that neutrality is "[p]erhaps the most pervasive theme in modern judicial and academic discourse on the subject of religious freedom."[4] For a brief period, in the 1970s and early 1980s, it appeared that the idea of neutrality would be a master concept both of the constitutional law of religion and of liberal political philosophy more generally.

Its reign was short, however. It quickly came under attack, on two grounds. First was the charge of incoherence: political theorists objected that any government must necessarily rely upon and promote some contestable scheme of values, so neutrality is impossible.[5] The charge of incoherence was also raised against the idea of neutrality in the Supreme Court's religion jurisprudence. This objection focused on a deep tension in the Court's position, between the idea that religion ought to be accommodated and the idea that government should be neutral between religion and nonreligion.[6]

The idea of neutrality was also blamed for substantively bad results. A neutral state would be disabled from pursuing real goods, and so its citizens' lives would not be as good as they could be.[7] Moreover, the requirement of state neutrality was deemed hostile toward religion, producing a "naked public square" in which the public is deprived of urgently needed moral resources.[8]

Today the constitutional law of religion is in disarray, because a growing number of legal scholars and Supreme Court justices are impressed by these claims. Steven D. Smith concludes that the quest for a neutral theory of religious freedom "is an attempt to grasp an illusion."[9] Thomas Hurka declares that in political theory, "it is hard not to believe that the period of neutralist liberalism is now over."[10]

These criticisms grow out of a larger consensus that the American law of religious liberty makes no sense. It has been called "unprincipled, incoherent, and unworkable,"[11] "a disaster,"[12] "in serious disarray,"[13] "chaotic, controversial and unpredictable,"[14] "in shambles,"[15] "schizoid,"[16] and "a complete hash."[17]

This book will argue that the critics are mistaken. Neutrality is a valuable and useful idea. It works well as a master concept in the theory of the religion clauses. If the concept of neutrality is properly understood, it can resolve the deepest puzzles in contemporary religion jurisprudence.

The critics of neutrality are right that the concept is indefensible when it is understood at the highest possible level of abstraction. Yet neutrality has a persistent appeal. Even the most sophisticated critics of neutrality acknowledge that modern political life requires some degree of abstraction away from controversial conceptions of the good. Almost no one regrets the state's refusal to take a position on the metaphysical status of the Eucharist. Neutrality's continuing power demands explanation.

The answer is that neutrality is available in many forms. The First Amendment stands for one such specification. That specification has done its work well.

There is, indisputably, a deep coherence problem in First Amendment law. The Court has interpreted the First Amendment to mean that "[n]either a state nor the Federal Government can set up a church. Neither can pass laws which aid one religion, aid all religions, or prefer one religion over another."[18] But the Court has also acknowledged that "the Free Exercise Clause, . . . by its terms, gives special protection to the exercise of religion."[19]

Accommodation of religion as such is permissible. Quakers' and Mennonites' objections to participation in war have been accommodated since colonial times. Other such claims are legion. Persons whose religions place special value on the ritual consumption of peyote or marijuana (or wine, during Prohibition) seek exemption from drug laws. Landlords who have religious objections to renting to unmarried or homosexual couples want to be excused from antidiscrimination laws.[20] Churches seeking to expand sometimes want exemption from zoning or landmark laws. The Catholic Church wants to discriminate against women when ordaining priests. Jewish and Muslim prisoners ask for Kosher or halal food. These scruples have often been deferred to, and religious objectors have frequently been exempted from obligations that the law imposes on all others.

There is considerable dispute about whether the decision when to accommodate ought to be one for legislatures or courts, but that debate rests on the assumption, common to both sides, that *someone* should make such accommodations. The sentiment in favor of accommodation is nearly unanimous in the United States. When Congress enacted the Religious Freedom Restoration Act (RFRA), which attempted to require states to grant such exemptions, the bill passed unanimously in the House and drew only three opposing votes in the Senate.[21] After the Supreme Court struck down the act as exceeding Congress's powers, many states passed their own laws to the same effect.[22] Many of those opposed to judicially administered accommodations, such as Supreme Court Justice Antonin Scalia, think that it is appropriate for such accommodations to be crafted by legislatures.

Each of these measures raises the same dilemma. If government must be neutral toward religion, then how can this kind of special treatment be permissible? It is not logically possible for the government both to be neutral between religion and nonreligion and to give religion special protection. Some justices and many commentators have therefore regarded the First Amendment as in tension with itself. Call this *the free exercise/establishment dilemma*.

This apparent tension can be resolved in the following way. Begin with an axiom: the Establishment Clause forbids the state from declaring religious truth. A number of considerations support this requirement that the government keep its hands off religious doctrine. One reason why it is so forbidden is because the state is incompetent to determine the nature of this truth. Another, a bitter lesson of the history that produced the Establishment Clause, is that the use of state power to resolve religious controversies is terribly divisive and does not really resolve anything. State involvement in religious matters has tended to oppress religious minorities. Finally, there is a consideration that is now frequently overlooked, but which, I will show, powerfully influenced both the framers and the justices who shaped modern Establishment Clause doctrine: the idea that establishment tends to corrupt religion. These considerations mandate a kind of neutrality. The state may not favor one religion over another. It also may not take a position on contested theological propositions.

It is, however, possible, without declaring religious truth, for the state to favor religion at a very abstract level. *Texas Monthly v. Bullock*, for example, invalidated a law that granted a tax exemption to theistic publications, but not atheistic or agnostic publications. Justice William Brennan's plurality opinion said that a targeted exemption would be appropriate for publications that "sought to promote reflection and discussion about questions of ultimate value and the contours of a good or meaningful life."[23] Justice Harry Blackmun thought it permissible for the state to favor human activity that is specially concerned with "such matters of conscience as life and death, good and evil, being and nonbeing, right and wrong."[24] What is impermissible is for the state to decide that one set of answers to these questions is the correct set.

But the state can abstain from endorsing any specification of the best or truest religion while treating religion as such, understood very abstractly, as valuable. That is what the state in fact does. That is how it can accommodate religion as such while remaining religiously neutral. The key to understanding the coherence of First Amendment religion doctrine is to grasp the specific, vaguely delimited level of abstraction at which "religion" is understood.

What in fact unites such disparate worldviews as Christianity, Buddhism, and Hinduism is a well-established and well-understood semantic practice of using the term "religion" to signify them and relevantly analogous beliefs and practices. Efforts to distill this practice into a definition have been unavailing. But the common understanding of how to use the word has turned out to be all that is needed. Courts almost never have any difficulty in determining whether something is a religion or not.

The list of reported cases that have had to determine a definition of "religion" is a remarkably short one. The reference I rely on here, *Words and Phrases*, is one of the standard works of American legal research, a 132-volume set collecting brief annotations of cases from 1658 to the present. Each case discusses the contested definition of a word whose meaning determines rights, duties, obligations, and liabilities of the parties.[25] Some words have received an enormous amount of attention from the courts. Two examples, "abandonment" and "abuse of discretion," drawn at random from the first volume of this immense compilation, each exceed one hundred pages.[26] "Religion," on the other hand, takes up less than five pages.[27] The question of what "religion" means is theoretically intractable but, as a practical matter, barely relevant. We know it when we see it. And when we see it, we treat it as something good.

This vagueness has much to be said for it. This book is not an essay in comparative law, but here I will merely note two regimes that have tried a different approach. France's insistence on a more uncompromising secularism has produced the notorious and apparently unending headscarf controversy, which has bitterly alienated not only Muslims, but also Jews and Sikhs.[28] Italy's attempt to evenhandedly fund all religions requires that each religion have some official leadership to receive and disburse the money. Because Italian Muslims are in fact diverse and fragmented, the government finds itself in the embarrassing predicament of either refusing recognition to Islam or recognizing the largest faction, which represents only a small minority and is associated with anti-Semitism and violence.[29] By refusing all official recognition of specific religions, either positive or negative, America has avoided these difficulties.

THIS BOOK STRADDLES TWO FIELDS OF STUDY: law and political theory. When each of these disciplines addresses the law's treatment of religion, it cannot do its work well unless it is informed by the other. The difficulties that ensue from a failure to grasp the particularity of American practice are revealed in the work of two leading thinkers on opposite sides of the political spectrum, philosopher John Rawls and Justice Scalia. Neither of them appreciates the unique kind of neutrality instantiated in American law.

Rawls is the best-known exponent of a liberal theory that aims at neutrality toward all controversial conceptions of the good. He claimed that the "intuitive idea" of his theory was "to generalize the principle of religious toleration to a social form."[30]

A well-ordered society, for Rawls, "is a society all of whose members accept, and know that the others accept, the same principles (the same conception) of justice."[31] The aim is a stable basis for mutually respectful political life in a society that is profoundly divided about the good life. Political liberalism is first and foremost a response to a problem: "How is it possible for there to exist over time a just and stable society of free and equal citizens, who remain profoundly divided by reasonable religious, philosophical, and moral doctrines?"[32]

Rawls's well-known answer is the original position and the decision procedure modeled in A Theory of Justice. That procedure generates a conception of justice that is designed to exclude from the outset controversial conceptions of the good. "Systems of ends are not ranked in value"[33] in the original position, because the parties do not know their conceptions of the good. Those conceptions of the good simply do not figure into reasoning about the justice of the basic structure of society.

Rawls evidently thinks that abstracting away from all controversial conceptions of the good life is the only reliable path to social unity. In modern societies, there is so much normative pluralism that the only overlapping consensus that is consistent with respectful relations is that constructed without any reference to the actual normative views of members of society. Political liberalism, he argues, should be free-standing, so that it "can be presented without saying, or knowing, or hazarding a conjecture about, what [comprehensive] doctrines it may belong to, or be supported by."[34] "[T]he political conception of justice is worked out first as a freestanding view that can be justified *pro tanto* without looking to, or trying to fit, or even knowing what are, the existing comprehensive doctrines."[35]

Rawls aspires to "civic friendship," in which we the citizens exercise power over one another on the basis of "reasons we might reasonably expect that they, as free and equal citizens, might reasonably also accept."[36] Reasonable people understand that others won't accept their comprehensive views. "Putting people's comprehensive doctrines behind the veil of ignorance enables us to find a political conception of justice that can be the focus of an overlapping consensus and thereby serve as a public basis of justification in a society marked by the fact of reasonable pluralism."[37] The path to actual civic friendship leads through reasonable terms of cooperation.[38]

This approach may possibly work under certain circumstances, but they are likely to be as unusual as the circumstances in which it is safe to drive a car while blindfolded. If you want civic friendship, you need to learn what your fellow citizens think before you propose terms of cooperation. T. M. Scanlon explains why the strategy of surveying actual comprehensive views would not be satisfactory to Rawls. "It would be impossible to survey all possible comprehensive views and inadequate, in an argument for stability, to consider just those that are represented in a given society at a given time since others may emerge at any time and gain adherents."[39] This book will show, however, that a consensus built around the convergence of a contingent set of actual views may last a long time.

Rawls is right that we should generalize from the practice of religious toleration. But before we can do that, we must understand the practice of religious toleration. A political philosophy informed by this history will be better able to think about how to achieve the aspiration that Rawls articulates so well.

Justice Scalia is also concerned about the terms of cooperation in a pluralistic society. He thinks that the answer is a generalized monotheism: "[N]othing, absolutely nothing, is so inclined to foster among religious believers of various faiths a toleration—no, an affection—for one another than voluntarily joining in prayer together, to the God whom they all worship and seek." Such a broad monotheism is also a solution to the free exercise/establishment dilemma. The way out of that dilemma is to relax the requirements of disestablishment: "[O]ur constitutional tradition . . . ruled out of order government-sponsored endorsement of religion . . . where the endorsement is sectarian, in the sense of specifying details upon which men and women who believe in a benevolent, omnipotent Creator and Ruler of the world are known to differ (for example, the divinity of Christ.)"[40]

This revision would free the Court's reading of the religion clauses from self-contradiction. But it does not work, because it discriminates among religions. Scalia frankly acknowledges that ceremonial theism would entail "contradicting the beliefs of some people that there are many gods, or that God or the gods pay no attention to human affairs."[41] Yet he once wrote: "I have always believed, and all my opinions are consistent with the view, that the Establishment Clause prohibits the favoring of one religion over others."[42]

Not all religions believe in "a benevolent, omnipotent Creator and Ruler of the world." The Court held long ago that the Establishment Clause forbids government to "aid those religions based on a belief in the existence of God as against those religions founded on different beliefs."[43] The membership of the latter has been steadily growing in the United States. Scalia is driven to this thin state-sponsored religious discrimination because he thinks that there is no other coherent answer to the free exercise/establishment dilemma, no other way to foster civic unity. His desire to bring coherence to this area of the law is admirable. But he does not appreciate the fluidity of neutrality.

The civic friendship to which Rawls aspires, the reconciliation of free exercise and establishment to which Scalia aspires, can be, indeed already is being, achieved, but on different terms than either of them imagines.

MY ANALYSIS OF MODERN RELIGION CLAUSE DOCTRINE goes only part of the way toward answering the critics. I have thus far addressed the incoherence objection, but there remains the allegation of normative unattractiveness. Here there are two sets of objections from different directions. One objection is that this conception is hostile to religion and opposed to its flourishing. The other is that this conception is *too* friendly to religion, and that it is unfair for the state to give religion as such special treatment. The answer to both is that the First Amendment is not hostile to religion, because it treats religion as a distinctive human good. And because it is not unreasonable to treat it as such a good, it is not unfair to single it out for special treatment.

This analysis has doctrinal implications. The most pressing controversies in the courts revolve around three questions. First, should religiously based exemptions from generally applicable laws be determined by the courts or the legislatures? Second, may government directly fund religious activity, so long as the principle that determines who gets the funding is not itself religious? And third, is it appropriate for citizens to seek to enact laws based on their religious beliefs? The analysis offered here has something to contribute to all three debates.

The first question presupposes (what hardly anyone doubts) that it is appropriate for *someone* to enact exemptions. Exempting Quakers from the draft, or Native Americans from the criminalization of peyote, is uncontroversial; the arguments are about who ought to draw those lines. The question also presupposes that it is possible to distinguish those cases in which special treatment of religion is required, as in church governance cases, from those in which it is forbidden. But how can these accommodations have a secular purpose? They seem flatly to contradict the secular purpose requirement. Such accommodations are therefore always susceptible to a charge of favoritism toward religion, while any failure to accommodate—or even judicial deference to legislative decision making about accommodation—is susceptible to a charge of callous indifference to religion.

Religious exemptions can, however, easily be consistent with the support of religion-in-general so long as the government does not discriminate among religious views when it provides such exemptions. The decision whether to treat religion specially involves balancing the good of religion against whatever good the generally applicable law seeks to pursue. That balancing is a matter of judgment, not reducible to any legal formula. The argument for giving these judgments to the judiciary is that courts hear cases one at a time and so are confronted, as legislatures usually are not, with concrete situations. On the other hand, the contestable nature of the value judgments that are involved suggests that courts should not have the last word on these matters. The regime we now have is one in which, with respect to federal law and the law of more than half the states, courts are instructed by legislatures to balance on a case-by-case basis, but the results that courts reach can be revisited and overridden by legislatures.[44]

The second question, that of neutrally allocated government funding for religious activities, is now urgently relevant, because in *Mitchell v. Helms*,[45] a four-justice plurality of the Supreme Court suggested that a valid secular purpose can validate a program that directly aids religious activities. The argument is that equal access is as neutral as anything can be. But there is a danger that such programs will lead to religious oppression, by in effect creating a union of church and state that oppresses nonadherents of the majority creed. Thus, for example, a school voucher program, such as that which the Court upheld in *Zelman v. Simmons-Harris*, could lead to a situation in which the only good schools in a given area are pervasively religious, thereby forcing parents who want a decent education for their children to accept a religious education from a denomination whose doctrines they reject. Forced religious indoctrination is one of the core evils that the Establishment Clause is aimed at preventing. The Court declared that the program it approved in that case provided "genuine opportunities . . . to select secular educational options,"[46] but it did not make clear that this was a constitutional requirement.[47]

Here the requirement of religious neutrality reaches its limits. Because the requirement is so weak, the *Mitchell* plurality is wrong to think that this requirement could provide the answer to, for example, the school voucher question. The requirement can do only limited (albeit important) work. To make that requirement the center of Establishment Clause analysis would in practice nearly read the clause out of the Constitution altogether. But whether more is necessary depends on the impact upon religion of whatever funding program is put in place. Assessing the significance of impact is, once more, a matter of discretion that does not lend itself to general rules. The account offered here explains why some aspects of Establishment Clause law are unavoidably fuzzy. The peculiarly religion-friendly kind of neutrality that characterizes American law is not an algorithm that can resolve all disputes. It sets the bounds and terms for those disputes, and so limits the range of answers that are possible.

The third question addresses what seems to be an irresolvable tension between the right of religious citizens to participate in politics and the right of religious minorities to be free from religious domination. Believers claim that they will be disenfranchised if they are forbidden to seek to have laws enacted on the basis of their religious beliefs. Religious minorities claim that laws with religious purposes exclude them from full citizenship.

The reformulation of religious neutrality that I develop offers a way out of this impasse. Because religious neutrality focuses on *what* government is saying rather than on *who* supported any particular law, the participation of the religious is unimpaired. The courts should monitor legislative output, not inputs. Citizens may make whatever religious arguments they like in favor of a law, so long as the law that is ultimately passed is justifiable in nonreligious terms. Because government may not take a position on religious truth, a law that can be justified only in religious terms is invalid. The requirement that a law have a secular purpose will, of course, prevent some people from getting what they want in the political process, but any meaningful constitutional restriction will do that.

The book describes and then defends present American law.

Chapter 1 explains why neutrality is fundamentally a fluid concept, with many possible specifications, and how American law's idea of neutrality has become more abstract as the nation has become more religiously diverse.

Chapter 2 examines the history of a classic but neglected basis for religious neutrality, the idea that religion can be corrupted by state involvement with it.

Chapter 3 shows how this understanding of religious neutrality can explain the American law of religious liberty.

Chapter 4 responds to the objection that it is unfair to single out religion in this way.

Chapter 5 argues that contemporary law, if properly understood, has the potential to attract the allegiance of even the most opposed factions in today's culture wars.

American religious neutrality is studiedly vague about the good that it is promoting, and this may be a source of frustration to its admirers. But there is wisdom in this vagueness. Citizens do need to share an understanding of what is valuable. But when the details of this particular Valuable Something are so hotly disputed, the most effective way for the government to pay it reverence is just to shut up about it.

— 1 —

The American Specification of Neutrality

What is neutrality? In this chapter, I will clarify the concept, and show that it is susceptible to many specifications. Then I will examine the particular kind of neutrality that has come to prevail in American law.

The Fluidity of Neutrality

One of the many ways that government can go wrong is to take a position on some question that it should abstain from deciding. The classic example is the question of which (if any) religion is true. The idea of neutrality holds that government ought to avoid this pathology. Claims for neutrality will always be claims that the state ought to abstain from purporting to authoritatively answer certain questions. There is probably an infinite number of ways in which the field of abstinence might be specified. Given the range of possible reasons and combinations of reasons for any particular specification, there is a lush profusion of possible neutralities.

The neutrality question has divided philosophers into two opposing camps: those who endorse it in its most abstract form as a principle of political morality, and those who reject the idea categorically.

The basic neutralist liberal claim is that no exercise of political power can legitimately be justified by "perfectionism," the view that some ways of life are intrinsically better than others, and that the state may appropriately act to promote these better ways of life.[1] Rawls, for example, claims that his theory does not "try to evaluate the relative merits of different conceptions of the good," and he argued that in a just state,

15

"[e]veryone is assured an equal liberty to pursue whatever plan of life he pleases as long as it does not violate what justice demands."[2] Rawls and other neutralists thought that their move to neutrality was a generalization from the idea of freedom of religion, and as we have already seen, religious liberty itself has increasingly been conceptualized in the language of neutrality.

Neutrality theory emerged in the 1970s simultaneously with controversies over abortion, gay rights, funding for the arts, child-care policy, the roles of the sexes, and the place of traditional values in education and especially in sex education. Neutrality claimed to provide impartial prescriptions on these issues, while prescribing policies that progressivists (who dominated the university faculties where these theories were devised) found congenial. The tendentiousness of that trick has long since been exposed. Yet the continuing power of the idea makes it worth asking: what is living and what is dead in the ideal of neutrality?

Neutrality is a vague idea that needs further specification before it can produce any determinate result. Once one abandons the exceedingly high level of abstraction proposed by the antiperfectionists, the idea of neutrality can stand for so many different political conceptions that standing alone it cannot resolve any actual controversy, about religion or anything else. But it does not follow that the language of neutrality has no value.

To see how neutrality can at once be vague and valuable, consider the analogous idea of equality. Equality is a trivial entailment of almost any moral and political theory. Once a theory offers a complete statement of what is relevant regarding some issue, it necessarily implies that nothing else counts. It will then be egalitarian in the sense that all cases with respect to which the relevant considerations are the same are to be treated the same, and all other considerations are excluded.[3] On the basis of a similar argument, Peter Westen concludes that the idea of equality is "an empty vessel with no substantive moral content of its own."[4] But this analytic point does not entail, as Westen claimed,[5] that the language of equality ought to be abandoned. The aspiration to equality is one of the classic themes of American public life. In this context, at least, "equality" means more than the abstract and formal claim that people who are alike should be treated alike. It also stands for the substantive claim that certain alleged bases of unlikeness, classically race, sex, religion, and national origin, are not appropriate reasons for treating some people worse than others.[6] An allegation of unjust inequality is hardly empty. It is a claim that some people's interests are wrongly being regarded as mattering less than others'.[7]

Neutrality is another formal idea with practical implications. Like equality, it has rhetorical power because it signifies an ideal with real value, one that is vague but which nonetheless can be and often is violated. When it is violated, we need a name for the wrong that has been done. When I say that the law ought to be neutral between Catholicism and Protestantism, I am saying that the difference between them is a difference that ought not to count in political decisions. Neutrality, like equality, claims that some considerations ought not to be operative. It does not specify what those considerations are, or what is problematic about reliance upon them.[8]

Religious neutrality has been denounced as an illusion. Frank Ravitch, for example, claims that "neutrality does not and cannot exist, at least not in the Establishment Clause context."[9] This is because neutrality necessarily depends on the baseline it is defined against, and "there is no superbaseline to determine whether a given baseline is neutral."[10] But this obscures a term that is in many contexts coherent and useful. Compare the following exchange:

> *A:* That umpire is scrupulously neutral. He calls balls and strikes reliably and without being biased toward either team.
>
> *B:* No, neutrality is an illusion. You say he's neutral, but I happen to know that he's a registered Republican. What's more, he loves his children more than anyone else's children. He's not even neutral about baseball. He cares intensely about making his calls accurate.

Speaker B has missed the point of neutrality. The umpire does not need to be devoid of any human commitment in order to be neutral in the pertinent sense. He just has to aim at a certain kind of fairness as defined by a determinate set of rules. If he does that, he is neutral in the only way in which neutrality makes any sense. Any possible agent, collective or individual, that intentionally adopts any possible policy of neutrality, will do so for reasons, and so cannot be neutral with respect to those reasons. The notion of a policy of neutrality all the way down is conceptually incoherent. Put another way, you can be an agent, or you can be neutral all the way down (in the manner of rocks and oceans), but you can't be both at once.

So it is quite possible for neutrality to exist in the context of the Establishment Clause. The problem is not that neutrality is impossible. It is that there are too many ways of being neutral, depending on the baseline you establish. That baseline does not have to be justified in terms of some superbaseline, whatever that might mean. It simply has to be justified, in the way that any other social practice is justified.[11]

The Fluid Justification of Neutrality

The range of possible justifications for any version of neutrality is broad. The following is a crude taxonomy of typical strategies of argument. It probably does not exhaust the possibilities,[12] and arguments for neutrality typically rely on more than one of these strategies. *The argument from moral pluralism* holds that there are many good ways of life and that the state should not prefer any of these to any other. *The argument from futility* holds that some perfectionist projects are doomed to failure. *The argument from incompetence* holds that the state should be neutral about things that it is likely to get wrong. *The argument from civil peace* proposes that some issues be removed from the political agenda in order to avoid destructive controversy. *The argument from character* argues that neutrality is necessary, either because deviations from it will damage the character of state actors, or because a regime of freedom with respect to the issue in question will be good for the character of citizens. Finally, *the argument from dignity* argues that some political projects fail to properly respect citizens' capacity for free choice. None of these can be defended at the level of abstraction that the antiperfectionists propose. But each can be formulated in many less abstract ways.

Different formulations of these arguments have persuaded different people. Conceptual analysis cannot, of course, say whether or in what form you ought to accept them. Neutrality is not a fixed point, but a multidimensional space of possible positions. As (or, more precisely, if) one's normative commitments and empirical beliefs shift, one moves through the space. Neutrality is, in short, fluid.[13]

Richard Arneson observes that liberals distinguish three versions of "neutrality," one of which they repudiate.[14] *Neutrality of effect,* under which no way of life would be advantaged over others, is impossible, because no society can possibly be equally congenial to all forms of life. The other two versions are *neutrality of aim* and *neutrality of justification*. Neutrality of aim, understood at the highest level of abstraction, holds that state policies ought not to aim at the promotion of any particular conception of the good. Neutrality of justification, also in the most abstract sense, holds that state policies ought not to be justified on the basis of the presumed superiority of any conception of the good life. An establishment of religion solely for the sake of civil peace would satisfy neutrality of justification but not neutrality of aim. A policy of nonestablishment with a theological justification would satisfy neutrality of aim but not neutrality of justification. Contemporary Establishment Clause doctrine requires both neutrality of aim and neutrality of justification, albeit only with respect to religion.

The Argument from Moral Pluralism

One basis for neutrality is moral pluralism, the idea that there are many ways to live well. Government ought not to discriminate among equally good ways of life. The argument supports both neutrality of aim and neutrality of justification. Government ought neither to promote nor to act upon false moral beliefs, and moral monism is one kind of false moral belief.[15]

Moral pluralism entails nothing about the boundaries of the set of equally good ways of life. It certainly does not entail that the state must be neutral between *all* competing conceptions of the good. There are as many possible moral pluralisms as there are sets of ways of life, a plurality of which may be thought by someone to be equally good. Any set with more than one member can be neutral among its members. But the idea of moral pluralism itself will not tell us which ways of life are appropriately placed within the set of possible good lives. The fact that a set includes members A through W does not entail either the inclusion or the exclusion of X.

Thus, for example, Locke was arguing for a kind of neutrality based on moral pluralism when he claimed in his *Letter Concerning Toleration* that the religious divisions of his time concerned "frivolous things . . . that (without any prejudice to Religion or the Salvation of Souls, if not accompanied with Superstition or Hypocrisie) might either be observed or omitted," and that such matters ought not to divide "Christian Brethren, who are all agreed in the Substantial and truly Fundamental part of Religion."[16] Locke, of course, falls well short of the abstraction of modern liberal theory or even of modern religion law. His neutrality applies only to different varieties of Protestant Christianity, not to religion in general. But this is still a kind of neutrality, supported by a kind of moral pluralism.

The Argument from Futility

It is sometimes argued that violations of neutrality will not accomplish what they seek. Locke thought that law could not compel religion, because "true and saving Religion consists in the inward perswasion of the Mind, without which nothing can be acceptable to God. And such is the nature of the Understanding, that it cannot be compell'd to the belief of anything by outward force."[17] Futility arguments are made by modern liberals with respect to many issues, for example when they argue that homosexual orientation is immutable and that efforts by the state to induce conversion are therefore useless.

The futility argument presupposes some limit to neutrality of justification, since it takes its bite from the fact that the state has already decided that some end, say maximizing the number of sincere Anglicans, is an end worth pursuing. This point is often obscured by the binary oppositions that constitute the perfectionist/antiperfectionist debate. The futility argument offers a perfectionist basis for specific forms of operational antiperfectionism. It says that, even if your purposes are not neutral with respect to a given end, your practical aim ought to be, because it is just futile or self-defeating for the state to pursue that end. On the other hand, once the argument has been accepted, it supports neutrality of justification as well. Once you've decided that a goal is unattainable (or unattainable by certain means), it makes sense to stop pursuing it (or pursuing it by those means) even if it is very desirable. Most relevantly for this book, one basis for state abstention from adjudicating religious questions is the claim that such abstention will produce better religion, while state support corrupts religion. That claim presupposes that religion is a good thing.

The strength of the futility argument depends on its field of application. Futile means should not be pursued, but analysis cannot say which means are futile for which ends. At the level of abstraction proposed by the antiperfectionists, the argument would be ridiculous, because obviously the state has sometimes been efficacious in promoting conceptions of the good.

The Argument from Incompetence

Another argument for neutrality is that, while there may be a fact of the matter about what way of life is best, the state is not competent to determine what it is. "The one only narrow way which leads to Heaven is not better known to the Magistrate than to private Persons," Locke wrote, "and therefore I cannot safely take him for my Guide, who may probably be as ignorant of the way as my self, and who certainly is less concerned for my Salvation than I my self am."[18]

The incompetence argument dictates neutrality with respect to whatever it is that the state is incompetent to determine. The point applies to both justification and aim. You should not base your decision making on propositions that you have inadequate reason to think are true, and you should not try to lead others to accept such propositions. Like the moral realist claim, the incompetence claim has a nearly infinite range of possible fields of application, depending on which questions government is incompetent to decide.

The Argument from Civil Peace

The classic argument for religious neutrality is, of course, that such neutrality will provide civil peace. "It is not the diversity of Opinions, (which cannot be avoided)," wrote Locke, "but the refusal of Toleration to those that are of different Opinions,(which might have been granted) that has produced all the Bustles and Wars, that have been in the Christian World, upon account of Religion."[19]

Both Larmore and Rawls emphasize the divisiveness of any state departure from neutrality. Larmore writes that "the terms of political association must now be less comprehensive than the views of the good life about which reasonable people disagree."[20] Rawls aims for a deeper civil peace than Locke: the aspiration is for "a constitution the essentials of which all citizens as free and equal may reasonably be expected to endorse in the light of principles and ideals acceptable to their common human reason."[21]

The virtue of neutrality, then, is that it removes potentially destructive issues from politics. The civil peace argument might dictate neutrality of justification or neutrality of aim or both, depending on what is needed for peace. If you think that decisions will not be regarded as legitimate if the process by which they were reached was contaminated by illegitimate reasons, then you will want neutrality of justification. If, on the other hand, you think that civil peace requires that government not signal its endorsement of views that some strongly reject, then you will want to avoid government decisions that have that result. That will dictate neutrality of aim.

The civil peace argument, like the others, can have many possible fields of application. How much and what kind of neutrality we need depends on the range of our disagreement. "Where everyone agrees about some element of human flourishing," Larmore concedes, "the liberal should have no reason to deny it a role in shaping political principles."[22] It may be that we are so divided that no agreement is possible, at any level of neutrality. On the other hand, there is an infinite number of ends, defined at an infinite possible number of levels of abstraction, that we (or a sufficiently large majority of us) might agree upon.

The Argument from Character

A classic formulation of the argument from character, one with deep roots in Protestantism, was John Milton's pamphlet *Areopagitica*, which argued for the abandonment of licensing of the press. This, Milton admitted, would allow the proliferation of heretical religious doctrines, but even correct religious doctrine would not bring about salvation if it was the consequence of blind conformity rather than active engagement with religious questions. "A man may be a heretic in the truth; and if he believe things only because his pastor says so, or the Assembly so determines, without knowing other reason, though his belief be true, yet the very truth he holds becomes his heresy." Religious salvation was to be achieved only by struggle against temptation. "Assuredly we bring not innocence into the world, we bring impurity much rather: that which purifies us is trial, and trial is by what is contrary."[23] Genuine virtue is achievable only through the encounter with evil.

Milton's argument is in part an argument from futility. The attempt to shield citizens from temptation is like "the exploit of that gallant man who thought to pound up the crows by shutting his park gate." But the futility of censorship is derived from his central claim that what the state should aim at is good character. What matters is not outward conformity, but adherence to the inner light. Coercion can produce no more than "the forced and outward union of cold and neutral and inwardly divided minds."[24]

Milton's defense of free speech depended crucially on his religious views.[25] It is, however, possible to make a similar argument from character without relying on Protestant premises. An argument that is structurally similar to Milton's, but is relentlessly secular, is made in John Stuart Mill's *On Liberty*. For Mill, good character is valuable, not as a means to salvation, but for its own sake. Freedom of thought and conduct is necessary to the development of valuable characters: "It is not by wearing down into uniformity all that is individual in themselves, but by cultivating it . . . that human beings become a noble and beautiful object of contemplation." Milton's claim that one may be a heretic in the truth reappears in Mill: true belief, if held without understanding of its grounds, is "but one superstition the more, accidentally clinging to the words which enunciate a truth."[26] For both Milton and Mill, virtue consists centrally in the ability to cope with morally distressing ideas. The pursuit of truth is more important than the harm caused by error. What ultimately matters is the development of character, which is possible only in an atmosphere of freedom.[27]

The argument from character is a persistent theme in liberal political philosophy. Notably, it has played a large role in the development of free speech law.[28] But, as with the argument from futility, it presumes that there is a limit to neutrality of justification, because the ideal of character it relies on is itself contested. To the extent that these arguments for neutrality have been effective, neutrality of justification is an obstacle to the justification of neutrality.

The Argument from Dignity

Finally, it is sometimes argued that neutrality is required by respect for human autonomy and dignity. Ronald Dworkin, for example, claims that government fails to treat citizens with equal concern and respect whenever it justifies its actions on the ground that one citizen's conception of the good life is better than another's.[29] But there is a gap between the premise of equal concern and respect and the conclusion of neutrality. Preferences based on *who* people are violate equal concern and respect; views of *how* people ought to behave do not.[30]

People's preferences are inevitably shaped in nonrational ways by their environment.[31] This is why the argument from futility fails, and this fact is similarly troublesome for the dignity argument. George Sher asks, "[E]xactly what is disrespectful about taking (benign) advantage of a causal process that would occur anyway?"[32] Liberal theorists have yet to specify just how dignity is violated by the state's doing what it can to promote what it understands citizens' well-being to be.

It is, to be sure, insulting for the state to proclaim a comprehensive view, and thus to denigrate the comprehensive views of some citizens, without adequate warrant. Thus understood, the argument will support both neutrality of aim and neutrality of justification. But the argument's force will depend on the state's lack of adequate warrant for its policies. In other words, it will be parasitic on the argument from incompetence. The argument from dignity, standing alone, is a powerful constraint on legislative means, but an unpersuasive basis for neutrality of aim or of justification.

The Fluid Application of Neutrality

The upshot of our survey is that the exceedingly abstract neutrality advocated by the antiperfectionists is unsustainable, but that neutrality may be appropriate at a more modest level of abstraction. Once the antiperfectionists' ambition is abandoned, many possible neutralities present themselves. The number of possible meanings of neutrality approximates the number of reasons one might have for seeking abstraction in the definition of political ends.

Like equality, neutrality has a conventional meaning. The invocation of neutrality in conversation is typically a shorthand gesture toward the generally understood value of removing some issues from political consideration, together with the arguments in favor of this removal. Thus, for example, religious neutrality takes at least some religious questions off the agenda. Such linguistic conventions are useful. The vague term "neutrality" may either introduce substantive argument or serve as a meaningful slogan in the many contexts in which it is impossible to develop arguments in a careful and systematic way.

What practical consequence follows from the fluidity of neutrality? In the strictest sense, none. One cannot logically derive conclusions about what ought to be done from premises that merely state what is the case. Even if my analytical conclusion enlarges the menu of practical possibilities, each of these must be defended on its merits. The analytical point merely calls attention to rival possibilities that ought to be considered and rejected on their own merits. When it is alleged that American religious neutrality is incoherent, the key questions are, first, whether *any* of the many possible specifications of neutrality could consistently justify the various components of present doctrine, and second, whether the arguments for that specification of neutrality are persuasive.

Understanding the fluidity of neutrality will not tell you what to do. It will, however, alert you to the breadth of your options. That awareness can have practical consequences. There are many ways to address the "culture wars" issues beside absolute state neutrality or the official embrace of an orthodoxy. Government could recognize both same-sex and opposite-sex marriages, while continuing to give marriages special treatment withheld from other relationships. It could support the arts while remaining neutral between avant-garde and classical art. It could support the preservation of species while remaining scrupulously neutral between cute and repulsive species. It could leave citizens free to pursue a broad range of gratifications while disfavoring dangerous and addictive activities such as gambling and heroin use. It could accommodate eccentricity without creating a population of homeless mentally ill. It could also tolerate some activities without being neutral toward them. For example, it could legalize recreational drugs while restricting their advertising and trying to minimize the harm they cause. Of course, some of these positions are already public policy. That suggests that the notion of a culture war is an overstatement.[33] Political theorists need to catch up with, or at least understand, their fellow citizens' more moderate views on these issues.

If Locke's proposal, that the state abstain from adjudicating controversies in Christian theology, is a kind of neutrality, then it would be most surprising if neutrality were impossible for contemporary doctrine. In deciding to treat religion as a distinctive human good, even defined in a very inclusive way, the state is taking sides on fundamental matters. Some people think that religion is always worthless and harmful, and the state rejects their views when it accommodates religion. American law is not and has never been neutral in the sense advocated by antiperfectionist liberals. But that does not mean that it is not neutral at all.

The idea of neutrality will survive the death of antiperfectionism. But it will be a chastened and vague neutrality. One can never tell, without further specification, just what it is that neutrality requires. The very flexibility of neutrality means that both sides of a dispute will often be able with equal justification to claim neutrality.[34] But neutrality is also important. The danger will always be with us that the state will be insufficiently attentive to the virtues of plurality. There can be no good society without neutrality.

American Neutrality

Neutrality's fluidity means that it can vary in both its conceptual scope and its field of application. Religious neutrality, for example, could mean neutrality among varieties of Protestantism, or varieties of Christianity, or varieties of monotheism, or something even broader and vaguer. Whatever conceptual scope is attributed to it, the obligation of neutrality could be held to apply only to judges, or to judges and legislators, or to citizens when voting.

American law has always treated religion as a distinctive human good. Its neutrality toward different religious forms, however, has shifted over time, becoming vaguer and more inclusive. Its inclusivity has been uneven and at times altogether bogus, most notably in the treatment of Native American religion. It competes with unapologetic tendencies toward religious triumphalism and a Christian conception of American identity. But there is an ecumenical tradition that has at least been part of American law, and it is the source of modern religious neutrality.

Which specification of neutrality we actually adopt will depend on our substantive reasons for adopting neutrality in the first place. Those reasons should guide the effort to operationalize neutrality. It is not possible to be blind to an issue with respect to which one has resolved to remain neutral. Race is an example. David Strauss observes that, because race does correlate with some other characteristics, a norm banning racial discrimination does not treat race as an irrelevant characteristic. Either people will notice the correlations and discriminate on that basis, or they will alter their usual patterns of generalizing about people and consciously exclude race from their decision making.[35] Similarly, religious neutrality entails singling out religion for special treatment in some way.

Public secularism takes different forms in different regimes.[36] France and Turkey, for example, aggressively strive to purge the public sphere of any trace of religion. The United States isn't like that. The salient difference is that in America, there was no danger that an old local monarchy would reestablish itself on a religious basis. Secular rationalists therefore did not, for the most part, become anticlerical or antireligious. Rather, they worked together with religious believers toward a regime of religious liberty acceptable to both.[37]

The aim could not be to eliminate alienation—that cannot be done— but to improvise strategies to cope with it. Bonnie Honig has observed the pervasiveness of the assumption "that the task of political theory is to resolve institutional questions, to get politics right, over, and done with, to free modern subjects and their sets of arrangements of political conflict and instability." Honig argues, on the contrary, that "every politics has its remainders, that resistances are engendered by every settlement, even by those that are relatively enabling or empowering." Because theorists who aim to settle political questions do not take responsibility for those who do not fit their mold, they tend to "adopt a not terribly democratic intolerance and derision for the other to whom their democratic institutions are supposed to be (indeed, claim to be) reaching out." The proper response to alienation and even criminality, Honig argues, is "not . . . to deny or dissolve it or to reconcile ourselves to it but to politicize it, to engage the fact that we are implicated in it, indeed, constituted by it, too."[38]

In America, as new minorities have emerged or immigrated, they have in time managed to renegotiate the terms of religious pluralism and disestablishment. One of the benefits of democratic contestation is that it makes the size of the remainder matter. The history of American disestablishment is a history of neutralities that shifted over time in order to cope with newly emergent remainders.

Scholars of the early history of American church-state relations have tended to fall into two polemical factions, the conservatives who want closer church-state relations and the liberals who want an even broader separation than is now required. "Each side claims," Douglas Laycock observes, "that it won the late twentieth century culture wars and took over the government—two hundred years ago."[39]

Each has its own proof-texts. Conservatives note the references to God in the Declaration of Independence, the overtly religious elements in Madison's defense of religious liberty, and the long history of public prayers and ceremonial acknowledgments of religion. Liberals observe the absence of any reference to God in the Constitution, Jefferson's refusal to issue Thanksgiving proclamations, his letter to the Danbury Baptists describing "a wall of separation between Church and State," and the 1796 Treaty of Peace and Friendship with the ruler of Tripoli, declaring that the United States government "is not in any sense founded on the Christian religion."

Both sides are right. There has been a public religion in America, but it has evolved. The early establishment of Protestant denominations at the time of the founding, the semiestablished nondenominational Protestantism of the nineteenth century, the establishment of monotheism in the 1950s, and the vague favoring of religion-in-general of contemporary American law each is more inclusionary than the form that precedes it.

Generic Protestantism

At the time of the American founding, nearly everyone was Protestant, and the law reflected this. This was not understood to amount to establishment. On the contrary, virtually every church that came to America in the seventeenth and early eighteenth centuries was, in one way or another, a dissenting church.[40] Sophisticated thinkers of that time, Thomas Curry observes,

> did not oppose a particular religion to religion in general in the sense of Protestantism, Catholicism, Judaism, or any other faith. Rather, they opposed a particular Protestant denomination to Protestantism in general, which latter they did not equate with an establishment. . . . [T]he notion of prayer and worship based on the Bible that was accepted by all Protestants did not amount to a general establishment, but constituted an essential foundation of civilization. Such others as Catholics or Jews did not impinge sufficiently on their lives to challenge that assumption.[41]

By the American Revolution, ecumenism had broadened so that, when there were official references to God in public pronouncements, they did not mention Christ or any specifically Christian doctrines. God goes unmentioned in the Constitution. There were even public ceremonies that conspicuously included Jews.[42] The level of abstraction varied from one state to another, depending on the level of religious diversity that was present. Diversity was at a maximum at the national level, but it increased in the states, and as it did, the common denominator was increasingly watered down.

This watering down was a response to by then familiar religious divisions. An immediate consequence of Luther's objections to the Roman Catholic Church's religious authority was a growing, and eventually obsessive, focus on doctrinal disputes. Elaborate theological edifices such as Calvin's *Institutes of the Christian Religion* and the pronouncements of the Council of Trent brought about an understanding of religion that was based less on piety and ritual than on intellectual assent.[43]

Religious persecution during the Reformation was based centrally on the victims' refusal to accept specified philosophical claims. Diarmaid MacCulloch observes that thousands of Protestants in sixteenth-century Europe were burned at the stake for denying the essence-accident distinction posited by Aristotle, who never heard of Jesus Christ.[44] Besides the frightful carnage this produced, such persecution also insulted the Protestant ideal of a genuine personal connection with God. This pathology was not presented by state endorsement of propositions that no reasonable person disputed and upon which civil society depended for its moral foundation, such as the existence of God.

The ratification of the First Amendment was no obstacle to this general endorsement of religion, in part because the Bill of Rights did not apply to the states and in part because it is uncertain whether, at the time, the amendment was understood to accomplish anything more than to bar the establishment of a national church.[45] (That will strike some readers as a very big deal. But it does not settle the question of what the amendment should mean today. That question will be taken up in Chapter 3.)

The dominance of generic Protestantism can be clearly seen in two now-obsolete areas of the law: religious qualifications for office holding, and the prohibition of blasphemy.

In 1787, non-Christians were officially barred from public office almost everywhere in the United States, and most states barred Catholics as well. Delaware restricted office holding to Trinitarians.[46] This discrimination was at the same time a kind of neutrality, as for example New Jersey's 1776 constitution, which made eligible for office "all persons, professing a belief in the faith of any Protestant sect."[47] Compare English law of the same period: no one who was not a member of the Church of England could hold public office, and those who denied the Trinity could be imprisoned on the second offense.[48]

The struggle to eliminate these restrictions went on for decades.[49] Even the absence of reference to God and Christ in the Constitution provoked protest, and a futile crusade to Christianize the Constitution began at the Constitutional Convention and persisted into the twentieth century.[50]

The ecumenists who prevailed did not advocate antiperfectionist neutrality, merely a broader inclusion, to embrace everyone who believed in God. The Maryland "Jew bill," enacted by a one-vote margin in 1825 after decades of debate, amended the preexisting requirement that officeholders be Christians (itself a reflection of Maryland's atypically powerful Catholic minority), to provide that "every citizen of this state professing the Jewish religion" would be eligible for public office upon declaring "his belief in a future state of rewards and punishments."[51] The Jew bill perpetuated the idea that the common denominator was assent to religious propositions. Those propositions had simply become broader than generic Christianity. Maryland retained its religious test for public office until the mid-twentieth century.[52]

Blasphemy laws were understood to be similarly nonsectarian, while favoring Christianity in general. The limits of public neutrality were made clear in *People v. Ruggles*, an 1811 New York Court of Appeals decision, affirming the conviction for blasphemy of a man who had declared that "Jesus Christ was a bastard, and his mother must be a whore." Chancellor James Kent acknowledged a right of religious liberty, but held that "to revile, with malicious and blasphemous contempt, the religion professed by almost the whole community, is an abuse of that right." Christianity's privileged place in the law had a secure basis in the beliefs of the American people: "Nor are we bound, by any expressions in the constitution, as some have strangely supposed, either not to punish at all, or to punish indiscriminately the like attacks upon the religion of *Mahomet* or of the grand *Lama*; and for this plain reason, that the case assumes that we are a christian people, and the morality of the country is deeply ingrafted upon christianity, and not upon the doctrines or worship of those impostors." Kent was untroubled by the implication that, if the nation's demographics were to change, then the scope of the law's prohibition might need to be adjusted. A similar potential adjustment was implied by his claim that the state's interest lay, not in any particular religious truth, but in whatever promoted morality: "Though the constitution has discarded religious establishments, it does not forbid judicial cognisance of those offences against religion and morality which have no reference to any such establishment, or to any particular form of government, but are punishable because they strike at the root of moral obligation, and weaken the security of the social ties."[53]

The *Ruggles* decision was widely cited and reprinted throughout the nineteenth century. The law of blasphemy was cited by courts and casebooks as a recognized body of jurisprudence as late as the 1940s.[54]

Religious qualifications for office and blasphemy laws both protected a minimal set of religious propositions upon which the public weal was thought to depend. The more specific doctrines upon which sects divided were not important to most Americans. American religion in the nineteenth century tended to be broadly latitudinarian. The Puritans' Calvinism was increasingly supplanted by a broad Arminianism: the unmerited, surprising visitation of the holy spirit, in the First Great Awakening of the early 1700s, was replaced by the will to repent of sin and claim salvation in the Second Great Awakening in the early 1800s.[55]

The voluntary character of religion tended to make the free consent of the individual take priority over divisive considerations of doctrinal soundness. This tendency was accentuated by the importance of the mission enterprise and revivalism as means of recruitment. Revivalism, Sidney Mead observes, "tends to produce an oversimplification of all problems, both because the effective revivalist must appeal to the common people in terms they can understand and because he must reduce all the complex of issues to a simple choice between two clear and contrasting alternatives."[56]

Religious qualifications for office never made much practical difference, since almost no one was actually excluded from office under them.[57] The function of religious tests, Gerard Bradley observes, was "to identify the shared religious commitment of the people, thereby defining them as a community."[58] Blasphemy prosecutions were noteworthy in part because they were so rare.

A broadly ecumenical Protestantism has an obvious remainder. In early nineteenth-century America, however, that remainder was small. Atheists were conspicuously excluded, but that meant nothing in practice, since there were hardly any real atheists in the United States until the late nineteenth century.[59] Other excluded absentees were Muslims, Buddhists, and Hindus, who were thought of, if at all, in the most derogatory terms.[60]

The one piece of religious stereotyping that mattered was the tendency to view Native Americans as barbarous heathen or proto-Christians.[61] The Establishment Clause was no obstacle to the use of federal funds to coercively evangelize them throughout the nineteenth century.[62] Their treatment reminds us that there is a different way of dealing with remainders than that of broadening inclusion.

The Disintegration of Generic Protestantism

In the nineteenth century, the most important manifestation of the understanding that disestablishment meant nonsectarian Protestantism was the public school curriculum. Free, publicly funded common schools emerged in the early 1800s. From the beginning, it was assumed that their role was in part to teach children to be moral, and morality was founded in the Bible.

Religious pluralism, Noah Feldman observes, posed a problem for public education. "If religion were not taught, morality would disappear and the schools would fail; if religion were introduced into the curriculum, many parents would object that it was not the right religion and might pull their children out, causing the schools to fail for a different reason."[63] The answer was, once more, a generic Protestantism.[64]

Protestantism-in-general as a mode of neutrality was entrenched most consciously by Horace Mann, secretary of the country's first board of education, in Massachusetts. Mann fought efforts to inject specific religious doctrines into public education. Instead, he instituted Bible reading, without any commentary at all. As he put it in 1849, "[O]ur system earnestly inculcates all Christian morals; it founds its morals on the basis of religion; it welcomes the religion of the Bible; and, in receiving the Bible, it allows it to do what it is allowed to do in no other system—*to speak for itself*."[65]

Mann's compromise might have been brilliant a generation earlier. The idea that true religion consisted in an unmediated communion with the Bible was, of course, a cornerstone of Protestantism, and so could be a basis for common ground between liberal and conservative Protestants (though some ministers resisted the watered-down religion that Mann advocated).

Unhappily, Mann's approach began to unravel immediately, because the nation was already becoming more religiously diverse. As a consequence, what was intended as a nonsectarian compromise soon and increasingly became directed against a growing religious minority, the Catholics.

At the time of the Revolution, barely 1 percent of the population was Catholic, about 30,000 people. That number grew to 600,000 in 1830, 1.5 million by 1850, twice that many ten years later, and 12 million by 1900.[66] By 1890, urban Catholics outnumbered all other urban denominations combined.[67]

The Protestant majority regarded the newcomers, who were mostly poor and Irish, with deep suspicion. They feared "the church's authoritarian institutional structure, its long-standing association with feudal or monarchical governments, its insistence on close ties between church and state, its endorsement of censorship, and its rejection of individual rights to freedom of conscience and of worship."[68] Anti-Catholic suspicions were exacerbated by the Vatican's 1864 publication of the Syllabus of Errors, which denounced the freedom of conscience and disestablishment.

Protestant responses sometimes took violent form. Catholic students were beaten or expelled for refusing to read from the Protestant Bible.[69] There were anti-Catholic riots, including one in Louisville, Kentucky, in 1855 in which nearly one hundred Catholics were killed and scores of houses burned.[70] The anti-Catholic Know-Nothing Party was a major precursor of the Republicans.[71]

The reason why Bible reading did not violate nonestablishment, Protestants reasoned, was because the Bible was not the property of any particular church, and so did not reflect the dominance of any particular church. "The position of the Bible in the schools is not the result of any union between Protestants and the state; nor was it secured by the political action of one denomination, or of all combined," one Baptist, George C. Lorimer, explained in 1877. "The Church, as such, did not put it there, and the Church, as such, cannot take it away."[72] Catholics, on the other hand, allegedly sought support for their religion not as free individuals, but as servants of their Church.[73]

Protestants also thought that Bible reading served a crucial secular purpose: the inculcation of morality. The Rev. Josiah Strong, in a widely read book, defended the teaching of the existence of God, the immortality of the soul, and rewards and punishments after death. He asked rhetorically, "[D]oes not the teaching of religious doctrine which is undenominational violate the rights of agnostics as much as inculcating the dogmas of one sect wrongs the adherents of others?" The answer was no, because "the teaching of the three great fundamental doctrines which are common to all monotheistic religions is essential to the perpetuity of free institutions, while the inculcation of sectarian dogmas is not."[74]

The consequence of the aggressive Protestantism of the public schools was to drive Catholics into what became a massive system of private education. Their efforts to secure public funding for their schools were universally rejected. For much of the nineteenth century and into the twentieth, "the Protestant position was that the public schools must be 'nonsectarian' (which was usually understood to allow Bible reading and other Protestant observances) and public money must not support 'sectarian' schools (which in practical terms meant Catholic)." A revealing manifestation was the Blaine Amendment, which came within a few votes of congressional approval in 1876. The amendment would have barred all funding for religious schools, but added that nothing in it should "be construed to prohibit the reading of the Bible in any school or institution." By 1890, twenty-nine states had amended their constitutions to impose some limitation on private school funding. On the other hand, Catholics did score some early victories in their efforts to ameliorate the Protestantism of the public schools. In 1869, Cincinnati banned Bible readings in the schools, and other urban centers with large Catholic populations, including New York and Chicago, soon did the same.[75]

The late nineteenth century also saw the emergence of the first antireligious secularists.[76] In 1875 a group of them formed the National Liberal League, which demanded that church property be taxed, that chaplains in the military and prisons be abolished, and that all public religious observances be abandoned. The organization was short-lived, and soon broke apart. It never had much influence.[77]

The Supreme Court was not a major participant in the nineteenth-century struggles over the place of religion in the polity, but the implicit Protestantism of American religious neutrality was manifest in the few opinions in which it was relevant. In 1844, it referred to the Bible as a "divine revelation," and asked, "Where can the purest principles of morality be learned so clearly or so perfectly as from the New Testament?"[78] In 1890, the Court invoked "the general consent of the Christian world" as a legitimate basis for banning Mormon polygamy.[79] In 1892, it declared that "this is a Christian nation."[80]

By the beginning of the twentieth century, however, the Protestant consensus had begun to collapse. The growing number of Catholics were joined by increasing numbers of Jews and atheists, and Protestants were less united around an official religion than they had been. In 1800, there were fewer than three thousand Jews in America. That number steadily rose, then exploded in the late nineteenth century. Between 1870 and 1914, nearly 2 million Jews arrived from Europe.[81] The Jewish population had been a few thousand in 1800. By 1917, it was 3.5 million, rising to 5.5 million in 1964.[82] Jews were strong supporters of secular education.

Beginning in the nineteenth century, a European, secularist social science was increasingly influential in the American elite. Social scientists were drawn to the view that religion would wither with the advance of civilization, and natural scientists were increasingly persuaded that religion was incompatible with Darwinian evolution. Protestant moralism and censorship was also a barrier to new professionals such as teachers, writers, journalists, artists, and businesspeople. These groups combined to found secular universities, spread European secular science, and supported John Dewey's humanist approach to education.[83]

A new ideology of pluralism was emerging. In the 1893 World's Parliament of Religions, held in Chicago, American Protestants for the first time openly welcomed Jews and Catholics to a conference on religion, and even invited Buddhists, Hindus, and Muslims. In 1927, the National Conference of Christians and Jews was founded.[84]

The Protestant coalition came together for a last time to win Prohibition and block Al Smith's 1928 presidential campaign, but Prohibition was repealed in 1933, discrediting Protestant legal moralism. Eventually, the mainline Protestants broke with the evangelicals to support state secularism, a move that culminated in the founding in 1947 of Protestants and Other Americans United for Separation of Church and State.

Nonsectarian Monotheism

In the early twentieth century, Kevin Schultz has shown, a coalition of Protestants, Catholics, and Jews (which eventually became the National Conference of Christians and Jews) worked together in a movement to refashion national identity so that all three faiths were understood as equally American. The idea was devised in the 1910s and 1920s, first in response to the newly revitalized Ku Klux Klan, then in reaction to European totalitarianism in the 1930s. By the time World War II began, it was incorporated into official government war material that was disseminated to millions of servicemen.[85]

In the 1950s, it became clear that the new neutrality was not one of indifference to religion. Rather, the old generalized Protestantism was replaced by a broader, generalized monotheism. The older order was manifestly anti-Catholic and ignored Jews. By 1955, the sociologist Will Herberg observed, American society had come to see Protestantism, Catholicism, and Judaism as "three diverse, but equally legitimate, equally American, expressions of an over-all American religion, standing for essentially the same 'moral ideals' and 'spiritual values.'" The consensus he described troubled Herberg, who regarded it as a kind of idolatrous self-worship. But he did not think it excluded many people. On the contrary, he cited a 1955 Gallup poll showing that 96.9 percent of Americans identified themselves as belonging to one of the three denominations.[86] "Religion has become part of the ethos of American life to such a degree that overt anti-religion is all but inconceivable."[87]

There were many legal manifestations of the new nonsectarian monotheism. In 1952, Congress declared that each year there would be a National Day of Prayer. In 1954, it added the words "under God" to the Pledge of Allegiance—a phrase, one congressman explained, that was "inclusive for all religions."[88] In 1955, it mandated that the words "In God We Trust" appear on all currency. (It had previously appeared only on certain coins.) In 1956, it made these words the national motto of the United States.[89] The Supreme Court joined in this new consensus, declaring in 1952, "We are a religious people whose institutions pre-suppose a Supreme Being."[90] That was the same year that Eisenhower made his famous statement. By the 1960s, the recently popularized idea of "Judeo-Christian America" was available for appropriation by the movement for racial equality, an issue that its pre–World War II proponents had carefully avoided. (The phrase frequently appears in the speeches of Martin Luther King Jr., for example.)[91]

But the second disestablishment also created modern Establishment Clause law. That body of law began in 1947 when the Court held for the first time that the states were constrained by the Clause. Within a few years, the Court held that government may not "aid those religions based on a belief in the existence of God as against those religions founded on different beliefs."[92] At the behest of a suit by two Unitarians and an atheist,[93] it invalidated Bible reading in the public schools.[94] It also struck down state-composed, generic prayers.[95]

The recognition of nontheistic religion was a turning point in Establishment Clause jurisprudence. It meant that there was no set of propositions that all religions converged upon. Religion would henceforth have to be understood in a different way.

The funding of religious schools remained divisive, with both sides offering their own account of neutrality. Catholics continued to argue that neutrality required equal funding for religious and nonreligious education. But their efforts failed in the Supreme Court. They continued to be resisted by almost all Protestants and Jews, along with public secularists.[96] Jews continued to regard the Catholic Church as the primary source of religious intolerance. Secularists tended to oppose any restructuring of funding that they thought would hurt public education.[97]

On the other hand, during this period the Court was friendly toward state accommodation of religion in one crucial respect: it held, for the first time, that religious exemptions from generally applicable laws were constitutionally mandated unless the state could show a compelling interest against it.[98] It had never before read the Free Exercise Clause so broadly.

Throughout the 1960s and 1970s, the law of the religion clauses was largely consolidated. The new regime is in some ways friendly toward religion and in some ways eager to keep religion separate from the state, and the simultaneous holding of these two positions is the basis of the charge of incoherence that is leveled against the doctrine.

The New Diversity

The biggest shift that has taken place under the present regime is the explosion of even greater religious diversity. Protestants declined from nearly 80 percent of the population in 1900 to 60 percent in 2000.[99] In 1948, 91 percent of Americans identified themselves as some kind of Christian. That number dropped to 77 percent by 2008.[100]

Throughout American history, religious diversity has increased because of both immigration and new domestic religious movements. Recent developments are no exception. The immigration reforms of 1965 ended a system that sharply restricted the eligibility of non-Europeans to immigrate to the United States. Since then, millions of Muslims, Hindus, and Buddhists have come to America. The "New Age" movement of the late 1960s and early 1970s increased interest in non-Christian religion among millions of people who never met an immigrant. Even among Christians, the meaning of their religion has been affected by the new pluralism. One survey found that 37 percent of Americans said that Native American, New Age, or holistic health practices had had an important effect on their thinking about religion or spirituality, while 18 percent said that about Buddhist, Hindu, or Muslim teachings.[101] "The United States," Diana Eck observes, "has become the most religiously diverse nation on earth."[102]

Robert Wuthnow observes that increasing numbers of Americans have become "spiritual shoppers," drawing from a broad array of religious options to construct a spirituality that fits their particular needs. In this category he places about 31 percent of the American population. They regard all religions as equally true, and do not privilege Christianity. Another 23 percent privilege Christianity, but in an inclusive way: they think Christianity is best, but somehow manage at the same time to think that all religions, including Hinduism and Buddhism, are equally valid. Only 34 percent think that Christianity is the one true religion.[103] Thus, individual religious experience, rather than doctrine, is the touchstone of religion for a growing number of Americans.

One of the best things about American religiosity is its ecumenism. In 2000, 75 percent of Americans said "yes" when they were asked, "Do you think there is any religion other than your own that offers a true path to God?" and more than 80 percent of those said that such paths were equally good as their own.[104] In 2006, 84 percent agreed that "religious diversity has been good for America."[105] These people discern a common denominator that cuts across their theological differences.

Even for religious traditionalists, experience is increasingly important. When one survey asked Catholics why they attended Mass, the largest group, 37 percent, pointed to "the feeling of meditating and communicating with God," while only 20 percent referred to "the need to receive the Sacrament of Holy Communion," and only 6 percent said "the Church requires that I attend."[106] In 1955, only 4 percent of Americans did not belong to the religion of their childhood. By the mid-1980s, one in three Americans had switched from the faith in which they had been brought up.[107] All American religions, Alan Wolfe observes, are becoming more personalistic and individualized.[108]

In short, there continues to be broad agreement on the importance of religion. But the common denominator that constitutes religion no longer refers to the assent to a shared set of theological propositions. The 1950s idea of Judeo-Christian America is untenable for the same reason that the idea of Protestant America became untenable over a century ago. Demographics have changed. The remainder is too large.

Scalia's Atavistic Synthesis

The obsolescence of the 1950s settlement has been shown, inadvertently, by Justice Scalia, who has sought to rely on it as a guide to the interpretation of the religion clauses. He offers his approach as a solution to the free exercise/establishment dilemma: "We have not yet come close to reconciling [the requirement that government not advance religion] and our Free Exercise cases, and typically we do not really try."[109] The solution he, Justice Thomas, and the late Chief Justice William Rehnquist have proposed would impose dramatic limits upon the Establishment Clause. They would read the Clause only to prohibit favoritism among monotheistic sects, while permitting states to favor monotheistic religion over its rivals, religious and nonreligious.

Of this group, Scalia has offered the clearest formulation of the alternative rule: government should be barred from "specifying details upon which men and women who believe in a benevolent, omnipotent Creator and Ruler of the world are known to differ (for example, the divinity of Christ.)"[110] The Ten Commandments, for example, "are assuredly a religious symbol, but they are not so closely associated with a single religious belief that their display can reasonably be understood as preferring one religious sect over another. The Ten Commandments are recognized by Judaism, Christianity, and Islam alike as divinely given."[111] Justice John Paul Stevens objected that "[t]here are many distinctive versions of the Decalogue, ascribed to by different religions and even different denominations within a particular faith; to a pious and learned observer, these differences may be of enormous religious significance."[112] Scalia (here joined by Rehnquist, Thomas, and Kennedy) retorted that "[t]he sectarian dispute regarding text, if serious, is not widely known. I doubt that most religious adherents are even aware that there are competing versions with doctrinal consequences (I certainly was not)."[113]

Justice Scalia thus envisions a role for the Court in which it decides which articles of faith are sufficiently widely shared to be eligible for state endorsement (and in which determinedly uneducable judicial ignorance is a source of law). Evidently, the state may endorse any religious proposition so long as that proposition is (or is believed by a judge unacquainted with doctrinal niceties to be) a matter of agreement between Judaism, Christianity, and Islam. It would, for instance, be permissible for the state to declare that Gabriel is one of the most important archangels. The interpretation of the Establishment Clause would then depend on the further development of the Muslim idea of the People of the Book—those who have received a revelation that is deemed (formerly by the Koran, now by the Supreme Court) to be reliably from God.

Scalia's solution has a fatal flaw. It discriminates among religions. Chief Justice Rehnquist thought that the Establishment Clause forbids "asserting a preference for one religious denomination or sect over others."[114] Scalia once agreed: "I have always believed, and all my opinions are consistent with the view, that the Establishment Clause prohibits the favoring of one religion over others."[115] As we have already noted, not all religions involve a belief in "a benevolent, omnipotent Creator and Ruler of the world." Christians, Jews, and Muslims are in; Hindus, Buddhists, and atheists are out. And the outs are a lot of people.

Justice Scalia acknowledges that the size of the remainder matters, but he has been unwilling to acknowledge the magnitude of his own. He claims that the monotheistic religions "combined account for 97.7 percent of all believers."[116] But his numbers are wrong: In calculating the level of exclusion here, nonbelievers are doubly excluded, since they are not even entitled to be part of the denominator. If one adds the nonbelievers, as enumerated in the 2004 Statistical Abstract of the United States which Scalia cites, the excluded adult population is 33 million out of 207 million, or 16 percent.[117]

These people have no interest in being part of the official theism that Scalia wants to license. Steven Gey observes that, in order to calculate the number of people excluded from Scalia's formula, one ought also to include the large number of theists who reject state sponsorship of religion, including "[t]raditional Roger Williams-style Baptists, Seventh-day Adventists, Jehovah's Witnesses, most Jews, many Presbyterians, and other modern nonfundamentalist Protestants."[118] Scalia does not explain his indifference to these people while he conspicuously includes Jews (who, as Gey notes, tend to be unenthusiastic about their inclusion) and Muslims, who together comprise fewer than four million Americans.

Scalia's position is essentially that the state may take one side in modern religious controversies, in favor of traditionalists and against modernists. This kind of religious division, with the imprimatur of the state as the prize for which the religious factions struggle, is one of the central evils that the religion clauses have from the beginning sought to prevent. One may also wonder why he thinks that the state's competence extends to this particular religious question, when he concedes its incompetence with respect to so many others.

Scalia's central concern, as we saw in the Introduction, is to promote a certain kind of civic unity which recognition of the common elements of religion—which he takes to mean, the propositions of fact upon which religions converge—makes possible. The problem with his prescription of official monotheism is that Baptists and Catholics and Jews can indeed be part of the overlapping consensus he contemplates, but we live in a society that also includes millions who either aren't monotheists or don't want official endorsement of their monotheism. In contemporary America, theism is no better as a basis for social unity than generalized Protestantism. If the aim is shared agreement, then it is counterproductive to propose unifying principles that large numbers of citizens will never agree to.

Scalia is right about the importance of shared norms. A sense of solidarity is indispensable to democracy: if majorities are to rule legitimately, then the losers need to feel that they have some stake in the system.

As the common ground shrinks, however, its basis must become more abstract and vague. Christianity will no longer do the job given America's increasingly diverse demographics. Neither will monotheism. But the idea that religion is something of value, and that that value is jeopardized when religious questions are adjudicated by the state, may continue to provide the common ground that is needed.

The Meaning of Religion-in-General

The most important recent innovation in the law of religious liberty is the Religious Freedom Restoration Act of 1993 and its cognates, at the federal and state level. The RFRA laws pervasively single out religion for special treatment in the law. They require courts to consider religious (and only religious) accommodation claims, and to grant them unless there is some very strong state interest to the contrary. The federal RFRA was invalidated by the Supreme Court as applied to state and local government (on states' rights grounds that had nothing to do with the Establishment Clause),[119] but continues to apply to federal action.[120] The Religious Land Use and Institutionalized Persons Act of 2000 protects religion (and only religion) from land use and prison regulations. Similar protections against state law are given by many state constitutions and state Religious Freedom Restoration Acts. There are thousands of exemptions in specific statutory schemes, and the Supreme Court has held that these are permissible even when they are not constitutionally required.[121]

The sentiment in favor of such accommodations is nearly universal in the United States. When Congress enacted the RFRA, the bill passed unanimously in the House and drew only three opposing votes in the Senate.[122]

Yet the vagueness of the legal understanding of "religion" is troubling. It is surprisingly uncertain what is the object of all this protection. The closest the Court has come to addressing the question of how to define religion is a pair of draft exemption cases during the Vietnam War. Both involved claimants who conscientiously objected to war, but who would not avow belief in God. The Court responded with a functional definition of religion, holding that the question a court must answer is "whether a given belief that is sincere and meaningful occupies a place in the life of its possessor parallel to that filled by the orthodox belief in God of one who clearly qualifies for the exemption."[123] It explained that the pertinent objection "cannot be based on a 'merely personal' moral code," but it gave no example of the line that it was drawing. These were statutory interpretation cases, only tangentially related to the constitutional issue: two concurring opinions declared that if the statute were read less broadly, it would violate the Establishment Clause.[124] Since then the Court has offered no further clarification of what it means by "religion." Nor has Congress done any better. None of its religious liberty statutes offer a definition of religion. So what does American law mean by religion? If neutrality is in fact being specified here, what is the specification?

Few modern readers would endorse the position of Henry Fielding's Mr. Thwackum, who denounced the "absurd errors and damnable deceptions" of "all the enemies to the true Church" and declared, "[N]or is religion manifold, because there are various sects and heresies in the world. When I mention religion I mean the Christian religion; and not only the Christian religion, but the Protestant religion; and not only the Protestant religion, but the Church of England."[125] Mr. Thwackum's definition of religion is not abstract enough. Yet how abstract should the definition be?

The Supreme Court's early definitions of religion take for granted that religion is theistic. In 1890, the Court declared that religion consisted in "one's views of his relations to his Creator, and to the obligations they impose of reverence for his being and character, and of obedience to his will."[126] In a 1931 dissent, Chief Justice Charles Evans Hughes referred to "belief in a relation to God involving duties superior to those arising from any human relation."[127] The Court has abandoned these, because they exclude nontheistic religions such as Buddhism.

At the same time that we try to avoid an overly narrow formulation, it is equally important to avoid overbreadth. If religion is defined too abstractly, then everything is religion.

The best modern treatments of the definition problem have concluded that no dictionary definition of religion will do, because no single feature unites all the things that are indisputably religions. Religions just have a "family resemblance" to one another. In doubtful cases, one can only ask how close the analogy is between a putative instance of religion and the indisputable instances.[128]

This process need not yield indeterminacy. The concept of "family resemblance" is drawn from the philosophy of Ludwig Wittgenstein, who famously argued that "the meaning of a word is its use in the language." Thus, for example, there is no single thing common to "games" which makes them all games, but "similarities, relationships, and a whole series of them at that." The use of the word "game" is thus not circumscribed by any clear rule. But that does not mean that it is not circumscribed at all. "[N]o more are there any rules for how high one throws the ball in tennis, or how hard; yet tennis is a game for all of that and has rules too."[129]

Explaining Wittgenstein's idea here, Charles Taylor observes that, with respect to a great many rule-guided social practices,

> the "rule" lies essentially in the practice. The rule is what is animating the practice at any given time, and not some formulation behind it, inscribed in our thoughts or our brains or our genes, or whatever. That's why the rule is, at any time, what the practice has made it.[130]

The rules of appropriate comportment when riding on a bus, for instance, are not codified anywhere. But natives of the culture may understand quite well what they are, and there may be no doubt at all as to how they apply in particular cases, even if they have not been codified and could not be codified.[131]

Anthropologists disagree about whether there is any identifiable essence to "religion." Jonathan Z. Smith and Talal Asad each claim that the term "religion" denotes an anthropological category, arising out of a particular Western practice of encountering and accounting for foreign belief systems associated with geopolitical entities with which the West was forced to deal.[132] William Cavanaugh argues that the distinction between religion, understood as a distinctively unstable and dangerous set of beliefs, and patriotism, imagined as a stabilizing and valid reason to kill and die, is part of the legitimizing mythology of the modern state.[133] Arising thus out of a specific historical situation, and evolving in unpredictable ways thereafter, "religion" would be surprising if it had any essential denotation. Martin Riesebrodt, on the contrary, argues that all religions serve common functions: they promise to avert misfortune, help their followers manage crises, and bring both temporary blessings and eternal salvation.[134] For legal purposes, it does not matter who is correct. Even if theorists could converge upon a single definition, American law will not have relied upon that definition, and the definition may not be well suited to the law's purposes.

In American law, there is no set of necessary and sufficient conditions that will make something a "religion." But, as noted in the Introduction, it is remarkable how few cases have arisen in which courts have had real difficulty in determining whether something is a religion or not.[135]

American law has abandoned the idea that there is a common denominator of religious propositions upon which all religions converge.[136] But it persists in treating religion as such as a good. The precise character of the good being promoted is deliberately left vague, because the broad consensus on freedom of religion would surely collapse if we had to state it with specificity. The state is agnostic about religion, but it is an interested and sympathetic agnosticism. The state does not say "I don't know and you don't either." Rather it declares the value of religion in a carefully noncommittal way: "It would be good to find out. And we encourage your efforts to do that."

— 2 —

Corruption of Religion and the Establishment Clause

Has American neutrality any deeper point than political compromise and accommodation? Do the state's efforts to minimize religious remainders, to avoid taking sides on any live theological controversy, show any aspiration that is not hostage to shifting patterns of political power?

This chapter will show that there is such an aspiration—one that antedates the founding, that animated the framers of the First Amendment, and that has had a powerful influence on the Supreme Court when it laid the foundations of contemporary doctrine. This is the idea that religion can be corrupted and degraded by state control. It entails that even overwhelmingly large religious majorities should not attempt to have the state endorse their views.

Two accounts of the purposes of the Establishment Clause dominate contemporary theory. One of these, whose leading proponent was Chief Justice Warren Burger, focuses on political division. The other, principally articulated by Justice O'Connor, focuses on alienation. Doubtless these concerns are among those that underlie the religion clauses; those clauses have multiple purposes.[1] But it is a fatal mistake to place either at the center.

Burger argued that a state program could be unconstitutional because of its "divisive political potential." This mattered because "political division along religious lines was one of the principal evils against which the First Amendment was intended to protect." Such division constituted a "threat to the normal political process" and could "divert attention from the myriad issues and problems that confront every level of government."[2] The argument has often been invoked in Supreme Court opinions, though it is unclear that it has done any analytical work in deciding cases.[3]

The most fundamental defect with this argument, as a basis for any constitutional rule, is that political division is an unavoidable part of life in a democracy.[4] It is not clear why division along religious lines is worse than division along lines of race, gender, age, ethnicity, or economic class. As a standard for constitutionality, the division criterion is not administrable: it is impossible for a court to predict which measures will produce it.[5] Moreover, the Supreme Court's Establishment Clause decisions themselves have been causes of political division; its decisions to invalidate prayer and Bible reading in the public schools have been very unpopular. If this is the aim, the law has been counterproductive.[6]

O'Connor thought that the Establishment Clause "prohibits government from making adherence to a religion relevant in any way to a person's standing in the political community." One way that government may run afoul of that prohibition is by endorsement or disapproval of religion. "Endorsement sends a message to nonadherents that they are outsiders, not full members of the political community, and an accompanying message to adherents that they are insiders, favored members of the political community. Disapproval sends the opposite message."[7] This criterion, O'Connor argues, is better able than any rival conception to "adequately protect the religious liberty [and] respect the religious diversity of the members of our pluralistic political community."[8]

It is not clear, however, how endorsement either threatens religious liberty or fails to respect diversity. Alienation is as inescapable a part of political life as division. In a democracy, somebody loses any vote and therefore feels like an outsider. Here, too, judicial intervention may simply make things worse.[9] The focus on alienation distorts the Establishment Clause, transforming it from a prescription about institutional arrangements into a kind of individual right, a right not to feel like an "outsider."[10] The inevitability of alienation led O'Connor to shift her focus from the perceptions of actual people to those of a fictitious objective observer, so that her decisions often turned on facts that had nothing to do with the message that was actually received by anyone.[11] The "objective observer" was untroubled by messages that caused intense alienation in actual people. Assuming that Supreme Court opinions are reported by newspapers and read by the public, O'Connor's approach exacerbates the very alienation that it ostensibly seeks to combat. Jews may be offended by a state-sponsored nativity display, but at least the display does not lecture to them, as some of O'Connor's opinions do, that they are unreasonable to feel offended!

IN SHORT, both the division theory and the alienation theory suffer from the same defect. The pathology each seeks to prevent is not preventable. Division and alienation will happen no matter what courts do, and it is not even clear that courts help. Nor is it apparent why these effects, however regrettable they may be, are always worse when they are connected with religion. (Another problem with these theories is that, because they treat religion as a divisive, disruptive force in political life, they reinforce the notion that First Amendment law is somehow hostile to religion.)

It is, however, possible to disable the government from adjudicating live religious questions. This is a curiously neglected theme in the law of the religion clauses. The neglect is apparent, for example, in Frederick Gedicks's otherwise acute analysis of the Supreme Court's treatment of religion. Gedicks thinks that the Court is nominally committed to principles of secular individualism, which are suspicious of and hostile toward religion, while much of the country is devoted to a very different ethic, "religious communitarianism," which permits the community to define itself and its goals in expressly religious terms, and which exerts a gravitational pressure of its own on constitutional interpretation. Contemporary doctrine, Gedicks thinks, is an incoherent congeries of these incompatible elements.[12] His work articulates widely shared assumptions about the character of contemporary controversies.[13] However, he omits an important middle view, one that is friendly to religion but, precisely for that reason, is determined to keep the state away from religion. It is associated with the most prominent early proponents of toleration and disestablishment, including Milton, Roger Williams, Locke, Pufendorf, Elisha Williams, Backus, Jefferson, Paine, Leland, and Madison.[14] The omission of this view makes the controversy over the meaning of the Establishment Clause more polarizing than it needs to be.

If any interpretive question simply turns on a choice between secular individualism and religious communitarianism, then in any Establishment Clause controversy, the state is taking sides in the bitterest theological issues that divide American religion. The corruption argument offers a way to reframe the rhetoric of the Establishment Clause in a way that could moderate these tensions and make it possible to find common ground.

"Corruption" and the Free Exercise/Establishment Dilemma

The corruption argument rests on the core assumptions that religion is valuable and that neutrality exists in order to protect it. This is apparent in the Court's most extensive statement of the corruption argument. In its 1962 decision invalidating a state's imposition of a nonsectarian, state-composed prayer to be read in public schools, the Court explained:

> [The] first and most immediate purpose [of the Establishment Clause] rested on the belief that a union of government and religion tends to destroy government and to degrade religion. The history of governmentally established religion, both in England and in this country, showed that whenever government had allied itself with one particular form of religion, the inevitable result had been that it had incurred the hatred, disrespect and even contempt of those who held contrary beliefs. That same history showed that many people had lost their respect for any religion that had relied upon the support of government to spread its faith. The Establishment Clause thus stands as an expression of principle on the part of the Founders of our Constitution that religion is too personal, too sacred, too holy, to permit its "unhallowed perversion" by a civil magistrate.[15]

The Court makes two arguments here. The first is a contingent sociological claim that establishment tends to produce negative attitudes toward the "particular form" of religion that is established. The second runs much deeper. In the final sentence, the Court claims that there is something fundamentally impious about establishment. It breaches the "sacred" and the "holy." It is remarkable to find such prophetic language in the U.S. Reports, but it has appeared there repeatedly.[16]

Any notion of "corruption" or "perversion" implies a norm or ideal state from which the corruption or perversion is a falling off. A claim that "we ought not to do A, because that is bad for B," implies (1) that B is a good thing, and (2) that we can tell what is good and what is bad for B. Thus the Court's claim presents, in a different form than accommodation, the free exercise/establishment dilemma: it presupposes that religion is a good thing, and that we can tell what is good and what is bad for religion.

These ideas made perfect sense at the time of the founding. They played a large role in the movement toward disestablishment. But they depend on contestable theological claims. In order to for them to be usable today, they must be formulated in terms sufficiently abstract for a society as diverse as ours.

Protestant Origins

The corruption argument's basis is at least as ancient as Jesus Christ's insistence on distinguishing the things that are Caesar's from the things that are God's.[17] But that argument did not prevent the church from enlisting the coercive power of the secular state when that seemed convenient. The corruption argument was born with the Protestant Reformation, and its earliest formulations are shot through with Protestant assumptions. I will show this by focusing on two leading seventeenth-century proponents, John Milton and Roger Williams.

John Milton

Milton wrote against establishment in its classic form. The central elements of the English religious establishment were government control over the doctrines, structure, and liturgy of the state church; mandatory attendance at the religious worship services of the state church; public financial support of the state church; prohibition of religious worship in other denominations; the use of the state church for civil functions; and the limitation of political participation to members of the state church.[18] There was also a restriction of the dissemination of heretical doctrines by means, inter alia, of licensing of the press: it was illegal to publish anything without prior permission of the Crown.[19]

Milton was opposed to all of these. He attacked different strands of establishment in different writings.

In *Areopagitica*, Milton argued for the abandonment of licensing. This, he admitted, would allow the proliferation of heretical religious doctrines, and so undermine the established church's monopoly over religious opinion. But Milton insisted that even correct religious doctrine would not bring about salvation if it was the consequence of blind conformity rather than active engagement with religious questions. "A man may be a heretic in the truth; and if he believe things only because his pastor says so, or the Assembly so determines, without knowing other reason, though his belief be true, yet the very truth he holds becomes his heresy."

Religious salvation was to be achieved only by struggle against temptation: "Assuredly we bring not innocence into the world, we bring impurity much rather: that which purifies us is trial, and trial is by what is contrary." It follows that "all opinions, yea errors, known, read, and collated, are of main service and assistance toward the speedy attainment of what is truest."[20] Here we already see a version of the argument from futility (which I described in Chapter 1). Religious behavior without sincerity, Milton claims, is devoid of religious value. What matters is not outward conformity, but adherence to the inner light. All that coercion can produce is "the forced and outward union of cold and neutral and inwardly divided minds." Even if errors can be prevented that way, "God sure esteems the growth and completing of one virtuous person more than the restraint of ten vicious."[21]

We already saw in Chapter 1 that Milton makes an argument from character, which is closely related to his argument from futility because a certain kind of Christian character is precisely the goal that he aims at. He also develops arguments from moral pluralism and from state incompetence. The diversity that toleration would produce is not a bad thing; "those neighboring differences, or rather indifferences, . . . whether in some point of doctrine or of discipline, . . . though they be many, need not interrupt 'the unity of spirit,' if we could but find among us the 'bond of peace.'" Moreover, "if it come to prohibiting, there is not aught more likely to be prohibited than truth itself; whose first appearance to our eyes bleared and dimmed with prejudice and custom, is more unsightly and unplausible than many errors."[22]

These arguments depend on radical theological innovations. Christopher Hill observes that Milton's theology rests on a radical Arminianism, in which salvation is available to all men who believe, and is in no way dependent on the formal ceremonies of Catholicism or the Anglican Church.[23] In sacraments as Milton understands them, "it is the attitude of the recipient that matters, not the ceremony."[24] This extreme individualism was connected with a range of heretical religious views, many of them idiosyncratic to Milton.[25] Prominent among these was the priesthood of all believers: anyone with a gift for making the Word of God known should be free to disseminate it.[26] These views were strange at the time, but their premises are widely shared today. Most importantly, the idea that there is something futile and repugnant about coercing religious behavior is now shared across denominations, an assumption so pervasive in American religious culture that it rarely even needs to be articulated.

Given Milton's individualism, there was little of value left for a state-sponsored church to do. Here we find a different form of the argument from futility: state support produces contempt for religion.

Thus, Milton opposed any state funding for the support of ministers. State-mandated tithes for the established clergy "give men just cause to suspect that they came neither called nor sent from above to preach the word, but from below, by the instinct of their own hunger, to feed upon the church." The clergy's claim to a share of each person's earnings, Milton observed, had led to "their seizing of pots and pans from the poor, who have as good right to tithes as they; from some, the very beds," from which "it may be feared that many will as much abhor the gospel."[27]

Another form of the argument from futility is the claim that the church's dependence on the state elevates the civil power over God, subjecting the church to the "political drifts or conceived opinions" of the civil ruler, and thus "upon her whose only head is in heaven, yea, upon him who is her only head, sets another in effect, and, which is most monstrous, a human on a heavenly, a carnal on a spiritual, a political head on an ecclesiastical body."[28]

Some authorities have suggested that state support of religion should not be deemed to violate the Establishment Clause unless someone is coerced to support a religion with which they disagree.[29] Certain versions of the corruption argument, we shall see, condemn only coercive establishments, whereas others reach any state support for religion. Milton falls into the latter category. He never seems to have considered the possibility of a noncoercive establishment, but the argument just quoted reaches such an establishment as well. Any state influence over religion is a usurpation.

So we already see, in the mid-1600s, the claims at the core of the modern corruption argument. Religious behavior is valuable only if it is sincere. Doctrinal divisions are not important. The state is an unreliable source of religious authority, and dependence on the state thereby makes religious teaching less reliable and tends to produce contempt toward religion. The state has no legitimate authority over religious questions. In Milton, these arguments are tightly intertwined with his idiosyncratic Protestantism, but they have the potential to stand on their own, and eventually they do.

Roger Williams

In the Americas, the germinal formulation of the corruption argument is that of Milton's friend Roger Williams, who invented the modern, religiously tolerant state when he founded Rhode Island in 1635. Williams also was one of the first to use the metaphor of the "wall of separation" between church and state; his overriding concern was that, absent such a wall, the church would be corrupted by the world.

Williams's religious views are deeply alien to modern sensibilities, perhaps even more so than Milton's. He was no secular individualist. Timothy Hall observes that Williams was "a religious fanatic" who "did not champion a proto-ecumenism and was not the sort of person likely to attend an interfaith community worship service."[30] Williams's weirdness shows the breadth of the range of views that can join in an overlapping consensus.[31] Common ground can be found even between modern liberals and the likes of Williams.

Williams's political views grew out of his religious ideas.[32] Williams was a part of the Separatist movement, which held that only those who had personally received God's grace could partake in the sacrament of communion. The Puritans who believed this eventually concluded that they had to leave the Church of England, which ministered to saints and sinners alike, and form new, separate churches. Williams accepted this argument, and eventually radicalized it by holding that the Separatist churches of New England were unregenerate as long as they did not publicly repent for ever having had anything to do with the Anglican church. Even regenerate persons, such as Martin Luther or the martyrs burned by Queen Mary, were unqualified for church membership until they repented their past associations with corrupted churches, whether Catholic or Anglican. Similar logic led him to hold that a man should not pray with his wife unless both were regenerate.[33]

The Puritans departed from English establishment by separating religious from political authority. No clergyman held any public office in early Massachusetts. The state was responsible, however, for the spiritual welfare of its citizens, and heresy was a punishable offense; Williams himself was exiled for his heretical views. Ministers were supported by taxes, and voting and public office were restricted to church members.[34]

Williams condemned all this. Religious activity, Williams thought, was worthless unless it was sincere: "[W]hat ever Worship, Ministry, Ministration, the best and purest are practiced without *faith* and true perswasion that they are the true institutions of God, they are sin." Authenticity of belief was, on the contrary, the central requirement for salvation.[35]

State coercion to participate in religious services was sinful for everyone present; it corrupted the service by introducing the presence of sinners, and it lulled the sinners into a false sense of security, hiding from them their awful condition. Moreover, no human being had the power to start churches—that right was reserved to God—and so the people could not delegate to the state an authority (control over religion) that they did not themselves possess.[36] To subject religion to temporal power was thus "to pull *God* and *Christ*, and *Spirit* out of *Heaven*, and subject them unto *naturall*, sinfull, inconstant men, and so consequently to *Sathan* himselfe, by whom all *peoples* naturally are guided."[37]

Williams's defense of freedom of conscience was crucially dependent on his ideas about the incompetence of government in religious matters. He did not value freedom for its own sake. For Williams, Perry Miller observes, "freedom was something negative, which protects men from worldly compulsions in a world where any compulsion, most of all one to virtue, increases the quantity of sin."[38] Conscience should be respected, not because it was less likely to err in religious matters, but rather because the conscientious search for religious truth was the only possible path to salvation.[39] Although only a few people could be saved, conscience alone could bring even this small number to God.

A consequence of disestablishment that troubled most of Williams's contemporaries was that voluntary contributions might not be enough to support churches. This did not bother Williams because he thought that only false churches existed in the world, and, therefore, the world would be no worse if they all disappeared.[40] It followed from Williams's radical individualism that any religious institution at all was a corruption of Christianity. The worthlessness of any state-sponsored church was a corollary.

If you do not accept the theological premises of Separatism, then Williams's arguments about corruption will not move you at all. But it was by way of his Separatism that he arrived at a view of the proper role of government that bracketed religious controversy from public life.

Because Williams's theological views are so pessimistic and intolerant, he is a wonderful counterexample to Jean-Jacques Rousseau's dictum that "[i]t is impossible to live in peace with people whom one believes are damned."[41] It is hard to find another American thinker who was as convinced as Williams that his neighbors were headed for the inferno.[42]

Other Early Protestants

In reviewing the precursors of the American founding, we may pass briefly over John Locke, whose arguments for disestablishment were discussed in Chapter 1 as illustrations of the futility of neutrality. Locke loathes insincere religiosity as much as Milton or Roger Williams: "[N]o Man can, if he would, conform his Faith to the Dictates of another,"[43] so coerced worship would be "Hipocrisie, and Contempt of his Divine Majesty."[44] Locke's argument is, of course, loaded with religious premises: that conscience is valuable because it is a way of discovering God's will; that it is sinful to act against conscience; that the rights of conscience are inalienable; and that no one can legitimately grant to another the right to make one's religious decisions.[45] But skeptical modern commentators need to keep reminding us that this is so, because the arguments seem so natural and familiar.

The sincerity requirement is also central in the German philosopher Samuel Pufendorf's *Of the Nature and Qualification of Religion in Reference to Civil Society*, written in 1687, two years before Locke's *Letter*, in reaction to the revocation of the Edict of Nantes by King Louis XIV. Pufendorf is not a direct source for American constitutional thought, but he was widely read and influential. He declared that "every body is obliged to worship God in his own Person, Religious Duty being not to be performed by a Deputy, but by himself, in Person, who expects to reap the Benefit of religious Worship, promised by God Almighty." The state could have nothing to do with this: "It was not God Almighty's pleasure to pull People head-long into Heaven."[46]

Another precursor of the founding is the Congregationalist minister, and Rector of Yale College, Elisha Williams. His pamphlet, *The Essential Rights and Liberties of Protestants*, denounced a 1742 Connecticut law prohibiting ministers from preaching outside their own parishes. "Every one is under an indispensable obligation to search the scripture for himself . . . and to make the best use of it he can for his own information in the will of GOD, the nature and duties of Christianity." Any "faith and practice which depends on the judgment and choice of any other person, and not on the person's own understanding judgment and choice, may pass for religion in the synagogue of Satan, whose tenet is that ignorance is the mother of devotion; but with no understanding Protestant will it pass for any religion at all." The principle of establishment, Williams argued, "has proved the grand engine of oppressing truth, Christianity, and murdering the best men the world has had in it; promoting and securing heresy, superstition and idolatry; and ought to be abhorred by all Christians."[47]

Williams did not, however, object to noncoercive endorsement of religion: "[I]f by the word *establish* be meant only an approbation of certain articles of faith and modes of worship, of government, or recommendation of them to their subjects; I am not arguing against it."[48] Thomas Curry observes a deep tension within Williams's views on this point. He and other Congregationalist writers "assumed that there existed a fundamental Christianity that every reasonable Christian could advocate and, consequently, that the State could promote without violating anyone's conscience." This "usually took the form believed in by themselves."[49] But they would become uncomfortable as soon as the state began to promote positions with which they disagreed.

The Founding Generation

The corruption argument was pervasive during the period of the founding, appearing in much popular rhetoric of the time.[50] Its proponents consisted of two very different religious factions. By far, the more numerous were the Baptists, led by Isaac Backus and John Leland. But the principal spokespersons for the argument were Enlightenment Deists such as Jefferson, Paine, and Madison. Madison, the principal author of the First Amendment, brilliantly mediated between both.

The Baptists

ISAAC BACKUS

The minister Isaac Backus wrote "the most complete and well-rounded exposition of the Baptist principles of church and state in the eighteenth century."[51] Backus declared that "bringing in an earthly power between Christ and his people has been the grand source of anti-Christian abominations."[52] His specific target was the levying of religious taxes upon those who did not subscribe to the established religion and the jailing of unlicensed preachers, both of which were persistent grievances of the Baptists.[53]

Backus, too, relied on religious voluntarism: "[N]othing can be true religion but a voluntary obedience unto [God's] revealed will, of which each rational soul has an equal right to judge for itself."[54] After some agonizing on the issue, he rejected infant baptism.[55] He thought preachers should be those who feel God's call. External qualifications, such as a college education or ordination, hindered God's work.[56]

Christian establishment did not lead to pure religion. Rather, "tyranny, simony, and robbery came to be introduced and to be practiced so long, under the Christian name."[57] Ministers who sought state support were unchristian. Religious duties could not be delegated. The state was also an unreliable source of religious guidance. "[T]he same sword that Constantine drew against heretics, Julian turned against the orthodox."[58]

Backus was, however, a less strong separationist than his ally Jefferson. He did not oppose official proclamation of fast days and days of prayer. He supported a law confining public office holding to Christians. He endorsed a petition requesting Congress to create a bureau to license the publication of Bibles, lest there be erroneous or heretical translations.[59] He did not object to laws requiring attendance at church.[60] In one tract, he opposed paying Episcopalian chaplains for Congress, but, McLoughlin observes, "that was because they were Episcopalians."[61] Backus's views on church and state, McLoughlin concludes, were "far less logical and consistent" than those of his better-known contemporaries Madison, Jefferson, or even Leland.[62] Rather, his view resembled that of the proponents of noncoercive establishment, such as John Adams, who regarded the rights of conscience as "indisputable, unalienable, indefeasible, [and] divine," yet who nonetheless favored state-supported establishments.[63]

JOHN LELAND

Like Backus, Leland was primarily concerned with systems of taxation and licensing that burdened nonconforming religions.[64] Far more consistent than Backus, he strongly opposed any involvement of the state in religious matters.[65] He was an important source of the pressure to promise an amendment banning establishment in exchange for the ratification of the Constitution.[66] There are even unconfirmable stories indicating that, had Madison not promised Leland to work for such an amendment, Leland would have derailed the Constitution by blocking ratification in Virginia.[67]

Leland took religious voluntarism as a basic premise. "If government can answer for individuals at the day of judgment, let men be controled by it in religious matters; otherwise let men be free."[68] The argument from state incompetence also played a role in his argument:

> It is error, and error alone, that needs human support; and whenever men fly to the law or sword to protect their system of religion, and force it upon others, it is evident that they have something in their system that will not bear the light, and stand upon the basis of truth.[69]

Establishments foster contempt for religion; they "metamorphose the church into a creature, and religion into a principle of state; which has a natural tendency to make men conclude that bible religion is nothing but a trick of state." Even if nonconformity were tolerated, but certain beliefs favored, "the minds of men are biassed to embrace that religion which is favored and pampered by law (and thereby hypocrisy is nourished) while those who cannot stretch their consciences to believe any thing and every thing in the established creed are treated with contempt and opprobrious names."[70] The state should not have any power to provide for ministers, enact Sabbath laws, pay military chaplains, or have any religious qualifications for office.[71] He opposed a proposal to end delivery of the mail on Sundays.[72]

Leland was as suspicious of dead religious forms as Milton. He opposed Sunday schools, theological seminaries, and missionary societies because their "natural tendency" was "to reduce the gospel to school divinity, and represent the work of the Holy Unction in the heart, to be no more than what men can perform for themselves and for others; and also to fill the ministerial ranks with pharisaical hypocrites."[73] Even communion was of doubtful value because after "more than thirty years experiment, I have had no evidence that the bread and wine ever assisted my faith to discern the Lord's body. I have never felt guilty for not communing, but often for doing it."[74]

Thomas Sanders observes that Leland brought the individualism of the Enlightenment into religion by abandoning the Puritan conception of a community governed collectively by God's law. "The form, nature, and significance of the church receded behind a preoccupation with the conversion of single souls, and the church represented no more than a voluntary compact of individuals."[75] This assumption was pervasive at the time of the founding. In the late eighteenth century, Mark Noll observes, most Americans were "united in the conviction that people had to think for themselves in order to know science, morality, economics, politics, and especially theology."[76] A state-sponsored orthodoxy was as counterproductive in theology as it would be in any of these other fields. Salvation was a matter for the individual. "My best judgment tells me that my neighbor does wrong," Leland wrote, "but guilt is not transferable. Every one must give an account of himself."[77]

Leland was one of the most loyal allies of the Deist Thomas Jefferson,[78] yet he was no rationalist. He preached "the great doctrines of universal depravity, redemption by the blood of Christ, regeneration, faith, repentance, and self-denial."[79] He once heard the voice of God speaking to him. One night, some devilish ghost approached his bed, groaning so horribly that Leland hid under the bedclothes and prayed to God for help. He said, "I know myself to be a feeble, sinful worm."[80] Yet, he was indifferent to most theological controversies.[81] Feeling mattered to him more than doctrine.[82] He made Jeffersonian political philosophy appealing to his poor, ignorant, and enthusiastic followers, and thus "succeeded in linking the political philosophy of the American enlightenment with the camp-meeting spirit."[83]

The Deists

THOMAS PAINE

Not all proponents of the corruption argument shared the severe Protestantism of Backus and Leland. Some were Enlightenment Deists who rejected all traditional religious dogmas. Of these the most forthright was Thomas Paine, the author of the most widely read pamphlet of the Revolutionary era, *Common Sense*. His strident antidogmatism places him well outside the mainstream of contemporary American religion, though the ideals he articulates were pervasive among the educated elite.[84] He trumpeted ideas that other framers, such as George Washington and Benjamin Franklin, privately believed but thought it prudent to keep to themselves.[85]

Paine believed in God, but rejected all of the specific doctrines of Christianity, which he regarded as a collection of unbelievable superstitions. He thought that "religious duties consist in doing justice, loving mercy, and endeavouring to make our fellow-creatures happy."[86] This, he thought, was the true teaching of Jesus Christ, but institutionalized Christianity "has set up a religion of pomp and of revenue, in pretended imitation of a person whose life was humility and poverty."[87] Establishment corrupted religion precisely insofar as state support tended to perpetuate "wild and whimsical systems of faith and of religion."[88]

> The adulterous connection of church and state, wherever it has taken place, whether Jewish, Christian or Turkish, has so effectually prohibited by pains and penalties every discussion upon established creeds, and upon first principles of religion, that until the system of government should be changed, those subjects could not be brought fairly and openly before the world; but that whenever this should be done, a revolution in the system of religion would follow. Human inventions and priestcraft would be detected; and man would return to the pure, unmixed and unadulterated belief of one God, and no more.[89]

Paine confirmed the worst fears of proponents of establishment by holding that without state support, the central dogmas of Christianity would wither away. Paine, however, regarded this as cause for celebration.

THOMAS JEFFERSON

Jefferson's religious views, and his idea of corruption, were much like Paine's. He, too, was a Deist who regarded any religious mystery as a foolish superstition. He was an admirer of Joseph Priestley's *A History of the Corruptions of Christianity*,[90] which denounced such core Christian doctrines as the resurrection and the Trinity.[91] While he was president, he prepared a new, corrected version of the Bible, using scissors and paste to excise from the New Testament any claim of the divinity of Jesus.[92] The corruption of Christianity consisted precisely in its capture by institutions that sought state largesse:

My opinion is that there would never have been an infidel, if there had never been a priest. The artificial structure they have built on the purest of all moral systems, for the purpose of deriving from it pence and power, revolt those who think for themselves, and who read in that system only what is really there.[93]

Jefferson became an ally of Baptist proponents of disestablishment, notably Leland, but this alliance depended on a delicate silence about their dramatically different views of religious truth and therefore of what counted as corruption.[94]

Jefferson did, however, share the Baptists' religious voluntarism, and so could sincerely present religious arguments designed to appeal to them. In his 1777 *Bill for Establishing Religious Freedom*,[95] he proposed to do away with all religious coercion and all taxation to support churches: "[N]o man shall be compelled to frequent or support any religious worship place, or ministry whatsoever, nor shall be enforced, restrained, molested, or burthened in his body or goods, nor shall otherwise suffer, on account of his religious opinions or belief."[96]

The law's justification relied on theological premises. "Almighty God hath created the mind free," and it followed that

all attempts to influence it by temporal punishments, or burthens, or by civil incapacitations, tend only to beget habits of hypocrisy and meanness, and are a departure from the plan of the holy author of our religion, who being lord both of body and mind, yet chose not to propagate it by coercions on either, as was in his Almighty power to do.

This argument from futility was accompanied by an argument from state incompetence:

[T]he impious presumption of legislators and rulers, civil as well as ecclesiastical, who, being themselves but fallible and uninspired men, have assumed dominion over the faith of others, setting up their own opinions and modes of thinking as the only true and infallible, and as such endeavoring to impose them on others, hath established and maintained false religions over the greatest part of the world and through all time.

Establishment, he argued, "tends also to corrupt the principles of that very religion it is meant to encourage, by bribing, with a monopoly of worldly honours and emoluments, those who will externally profess and conform to it."[97] And all this was unnecessary, because "truth is great and will prevail if left to herself."[98]

He repeated these arguments a few years later in his *Notes on the State of Virginia*. He explained that religious dissent in Virginia had been fostered by establishment: "[T]he great care of the government to support their own church, having begotten an equal degree of indolence in its clergy, two-thirds of the people had become dissenters at the commencement of the present revolution." Establishment was a violation of natural right. "[O]ur rulers can have authority over such natural rights only as we have submitted to them. The rights of conscience we never submitted, we could not submit. We are answerable for them to our God." The effect of religious coercion has been "[t]o make one half the world fools, and the other half hypocrites." But Jefferson's argument, too, goes beyond coercion to imply a more general state neutrality toward religion. "Difference of opinion is advantageous in religion. The several sects perform the office of a Censor morum over each other."[99]

Thus, Jefferson famously advocated a "wall of separation between church and State."[100] He eliminated the chairs of Divinity at the College of William and Mary and prevented such chairs from being established at the University of Virginia, which did not even have a chaplain while he was its rector.[101]

JAMES MADISON

The radical Protestantism of Backus and Leland and the Deism of Paine and Jefferson were brilliantly synthesized in Madison's *Memorial and Remonstrance against Religious Assessments*, the classic description of the pathologies that the founding generation associated with establishment. Madison, of course, led the movement for disestablishment, first in Virginia, then as principal author of the First Amendment.

Madison's argument reaches well beyond coercion because it was offered against a bill that attempted to provide nonpreferential aid to religion. The bill in question would have allowed all Christian churches to receive tax money, and would have permitted each taxpayer to designate the church to receive his tax. If the taxpayer refused to designate a church, the funds would go to schools.[102] Even this nonpreferential aid, Madison thought, tended to corrupt religion.

Madison was a rationalist Deist. He deplored the fact that "accidental differences in political, religious, and other opinions" were the cause of factional disputes.[103] The coalition he led, however, consisted predominantly of Baptists and Presbyterians. All supported freedom of conscience, thought that religion was essentially voluntary, and regarded man's allegiance to God as prior to state authority. But the rationalists "emphasized natural rights" and "the use of reason in the pursuit of [religious] truth," whereas the religious dissenters wanted to free man "to respond to God's call" and "the scriptural . . . teachings of Christ." Each side drew on the other's rhetoric, but they had fundamentally different goals.[104] Madison's task was to bring them together into a political coalition that could disestablish Anglicanism in Virginia.

The *Memorial and Remonstrance* begins with a theological claim, offering an understanding of religious duty that at this point will be familiar: "It is the duty of every man to render to the Creator such homage, and such only, as he believes to be acceptable to him. This duty is precedent both in order of time and degree of obligation, to the claims of Civil Society." Madison further argued that the idea "that the Civil Magistrate is a competent Judge of Religious truth . . . is an arrogant pretension falsified by the contradictory opinions of Rulers in all ages." The idea that religion should be promoted because it is conducive to good citizenship, an idea that we often hear even today, Madison denounced as an attempt to "employ Religion as an engine of Civil policy," which he thought "an unhallowed perversion of the means of salvation." Moreover,

> experience witnesseth that ecclesiastical establishments, instead of maintaining the purity and efficacy of Religion, have had a contrary operation. During almost fifteen centuries, has the legal establishment of Christianity been on trial. What have been its fruits? More or less in all places, pride and indolence in the Clergy; ignorance and servility in the laity; in both, superstition, bigotry and persecution.[105]

Madison was reticent about his own religious beliefs, which were probably some variant of Deism,[106] but the *Memorial and Remonstrance* is nonetheless the most useful source of antiestablishment thinking. It was a public document, not a private statement of Madison's views. It presented a synthesis of the antiestablishment views that prevailed in his time, combining religious arguments designed to appeal to Evangelical Christians and secular arguments designed to appeal to Enlightenment Lockeans.[107] It is unlikely that these groups agreed on anything more than the propositions stated by Madison himself. But they did agree on *them*.[108]

What Madison achieved in Virginia is a fine early example of the kind of overlapping consensus to which Rawls later aspired: a collection of different comprehensive views of the purpose of human life converges on a set of political principles. The *Memorial and Remonstrance* states a set of pathologies that are to be avoided, which can be regarded as pathologies from a variety of different points of view. Different members of his coalition had different ideas about why these were pathologies. They had fundamentally different ideas of what a noncorrupted religion would look like. Madison was carefully noncommittal about which of them was right. The coalition did not last long; it shortly fragmented over support for the French Revolution.[109] But by that time, the Establishment Clause had been adopted, and it remains in the Constitution.

Later, as president, Madison vetoed a congressional act incorporating an Episcopal congregation in the District of Columbia, and at first refused to issue proclamations of days of thanksgiving and prayer. He later did issue such proclamations, but still later, said that this was a mistake. In an unpublished memorandum written late in his life and found after his death, he opposed the creation of congressional and military chaplains.[110]

Contemporary Significance

The corruption argument has remained a powerful force in the interpretation of the religion clauses. It certainly was part of the legal culture at the time of the framing of the Fourteenth Amendment, and there is powerful evidence that the framers of that amendment intended the disestablishment norm to apply to the states. Freedom from established religion was understood to be an aspect of freedom of conscience.[111]

Corruption was a familiar part of this discourse. It was invoked in 1872 by the Supreme Court of Ohio, upholding a prohibition on religious instruction in public schools, in one of the first cases to cite the federal Establishment Clause as a constraint on the states.

> Let the state not only keep its own hands off, but let it also see to it that religious sects keep their hands off each other. Let religious doctrines

have a fair field, and a free, intellectual, moral, and spiritual conflict. The weakest—that is, the intellectually, morally, and spiritually weakest—will go to the wall, and the best will triumph in the end.[112]

This idea of spiritual laissez-faire is an increasingly powerful aspect of the corruption argument. To close this survey, consider some versions of the argument that are influential today. These focus exclusively on the secular benefits of religion when it is not controlled by the state.

Here as elsewhere, the principal laissez-faire theorist is Adam Smith. Smith did not participate in the framing. He never traveled to the United States, spending most of his life in his native Scotland. But he was widely read in America. *The Wealth of Nations* was found in 28 percent of American libraries in the period from 1777 to 1790, exceeding the holdings of Locke's *Treatises* and any book by Rousseau except *Emile*.[113] Smith had a substantial impact on the thinking of the framers of the Constitution, and particularly on Madison's views about religious liberty.[114]

Smith focused not on coercion, but on state financial support for an established church. He thought that if clergy were given dependable incomes from the state, "[t]heir exertion, their zeal and industry,"[115] were likely to be much diminished. Absent establishment, on the other hand, there would be "a great multitude of religious sects."[116] This multitude would have a salutary effect on each sect's doctrines.

> The teachers of each little sect, finding themselves almost alone, would be obliged to respect those of almost every other sect, and the concessions which they would mutually find it both convenient and agreeable to make to one another, might in time probably reduce the doctrine of the greater part of them to that pure and rational religion, free from every mixture of absurdity, imposture, or fanaticism.[117]

Smith also thought that small religious sects were much more likely than large churches to police the conduct of their members and keep them away from the dangers of profligacy and vice that were particularly ubiquitous in large cities.[118] It is unlikely that Madison had read *The Wealth of Nations* at the time he wrote the *Memorial and Remonstrance*, but his arguments against establishment just cited may have influenced Madison's famous argument in *Federalist 10*[119] that political factions could more easily be controlled in a large republic.[120]

One aspect of the corruption argument holds that establishment can generate only the kind of religion that people are likely to hold in low regard. Recall the Court's declaration in *Engel* that, at the time of the framing, "many people had lost their respect for any religion that had relied upon the support of government to spread its faith." A similar argument was pressed during the election of 1800 by followers of Jefferson, who wanted to discourage Federalist clergy from opposing Jefferson for his Deism.[121]

Here, the baseline against which corruption is measured is not the Protestant one of personal communion with God, but simply sincere religiosity, whatever its content. People are less likely to feel such religiosity if they associate it with political views they reject. The argument thus is less pervasively Protestant. But it continues to presume that religion is a good thing, and that this good thing can be corrupted by state sponsorship.

Alexis de Tocqueville is the classic proponent of this argument. Writing at about the time that the last establishment in America was being abandoned, he thought that in the new egalitarian regime of the United States, the old feudal morality had disappeared, and a pressing question was what kinds of morality would take its place. The answer was that people would be motivated by "self-interest properly understood." They could be made to understand that it was in their self-interest to do good and serve their fellow creatures. The rational pursuit of self-interest would not produce heroes, but it would shape "a lot of orderly, temperate, moderate, careful, and self-controlled citizens."[122]

Religion played a crucial role in bringing about this understanding. "The main business of religions is to purify, control, and restrain that excessive and exclusive taste for well-being which men acquire in times of equality." Tocqueville was silent on the theological issues, but he thought religious belief important to the well-being of democracy. "How could society escape destruction if, when political ties are relaxed, moral ties are not tightened? And what can be done with a people master of itself if it is not subject to God?"[123]

The American experience had taught that the best way to promote religion was to keep the state away from it. Man is naturally religious. Because "the incomplete joys of this world will never satisfy his heart," he is naturally driven, by "an invincible inclination,"[124] toward contemplation of another world.

The "intellectual aberration" of unbelief had arisen in Europe, Tocqueville thought, only because of establishment. Because religion had become identified with a conservative politics, it aroused the opposition of anyone who opposed the conservative party. "[R]eligion cannot share the material strength of the rulers without being burdened with some of the animosity roused against them." All the clergy with whom Tocqueville spoke during his visit to America agreed that "the main reason for the quiet sway of religion over their country was the complete separation of church and state."[125]

Tocqueville was surely too sanguine in his suggestion that "even . . . the most false and dangerous religions"[126] could produce these valuable results. Marvin Zetterbaum observes that Tocqueville's solution to the problem of how to make self-centered people virtuous "lies in a simple extension of the principle of self-interest to include the rewards of a future life."[127] But it matters what those rewards are supposed to be rewards for. One must look beyond narrow self-interest in order to be willing to fly an airplane into a building.[128] Steven Smith has observed that "we cannot sensibly talk about the effects of 'religion' on character because different forms of religion attempt to inculcate very different character traits." Whether religion is conducive to virtue "also depends on the kind of virtues that a particular society chooses to foster."[129] But historical experience has vindicated Tocqueville's hypothesis within the borders of the United States.

Hugo Black

The architect of modern Establishment Clause law is Justice Hugo Black, who wrote the most important early opinions interpreting the Clause.[130] Decisions authored by him declared that the Establishment Clause was applicable to the states,[131] that a "released time" program in which religious instruction was offered in the public schools was unconstitutional,[132] that state officeholders could not be required to profess a belief in God,[133] and that state-authored school prayers violated the Constitution.[134]

What is remarkable about Black is that, despite his modern provenance, he does not rely on arguments like Smith's or Tocqueville's about the secular benefits of disestablished religion. Rather, he echoes Baptist dissenters such as Backus and Leland when he declares that "religion is too personal, too sacred, too holy, to permit its 'unhallowed perversion' by a civil magistrate."[135] According to one account, when Black delivered the judgment of the Court, "his voice trembled with emotion . . . as he paused over 'too personal, too sacred, too holy' . . . [a]nd he added extemporaneously, 'The prayer of each man from his soul must be his and his alone.'"[136] Three days after the decision was announced, in a letter explaining his decision to a niece, Black dismissed the idea that "prayer must be recited parrot-like in public places in order to be effective," citing the passage of the Sermon on the Mount that emphasizes the value of praying privately.[137]

Similarly strong language appears in his dissent in *Zorach v. Clauson*:

> Under our system of religious freedom, people have gone to their religious sanctuaries not because they feared the law but because they loved their God. The choice of all has been as free as the choice of those who answered the call to worship moved only by the music of the old Sunday morning church bells. The spiritual mind of man has thus been free to believe, disbelieve, or doubt, without repression, great or small, by the heavy hand of government.[138]

The language of the holy and the sacred appears once again: "State help to religion injects political and party prejudices into a holy field. . . . Government should not be allowed, under cover of the soft euphemism of 'co-operation,' to steal into the sacred area of religious choice."[139]

Similar themes can be found in almost all of his Establishment Clause opinions.[140] He quoted with approval the religious antiestablishment arguments of Roger Williams, Jefferson, and Madison.[141] On this basis he laid down the most fundamental Establishment Clause restrictions, most of which remain unquestioned to this day:

> The "establishment of religion" clause of the First Amendment means at least this: Neither a state nor the Federal Government can set up a church. Neither can pass laws which aid one religion, aid all religions, or prefer one religion over another. Neither can force nor influence a person to go to or to remain away from church against his will or force him to profess a belief or disbelief in any religion. No person can be punished for entertaining or professing religious beliefs or disbeliefs, for church attendance or non-attendance. No tax in any amount, large or small, can be levied to support any religious activities or institutions, whatever they

may be called, or whatever form they may adopt to teach or practice religion. Neither a state nor the Federal Government can, openly or secretly, participate in the affairs of any religious organizations or groups and vice versa. In the words of Jefferson, the clause against establishment of religion by law was intended to erect "a wall of separation between Church and State."[142]

Repudiating the claim that his decisions manifested hostility to religion, he wrote that "the First Amendment rests upon the premise that both religion and government can best work to achieve their lofty aims if each is left free from the other within its respective sphere."[143] He rejected a requirement that a notary public profess a belief in God, because "[t]he power and authority of the State of Maryland thus is put on the side of one particular sort of believers—those who are willing to say they believe in 'the existence of God.'" He then quoted an earlier opinion: "'[W]e have staked the very existence of our country on the faith that complete separation between the state and religion is best for the state and best for religion.'" He cited the old theme that establishment breeds hypocrisy, arguing that the rule followed "the historically and constitutionally discredited policy of probing religious beliefs by test oaths or limiting public offices to persons who have, or perhaps more properly profess to have, a belief in some particular kind of religious concept."[144] The school prayer decision declared that

> the constitutional prohibition against laws respecting an establishment of religion must at least mean that in this country it is no part of the business of government to compose official prayers for any group of the American people to recite as a part of a religious program carried on by government.[145]

Disestablishment meant that "the people's religions must not be subjected to the pressures of government for change each time a new political administration is elected to office."[146] The Establishment Clause, Black claimed,

> was written to quiet well-justified fears which nearly all of them felt arising out of an awareness that governments of the past had shackled men's tongues to make them speak only the religious thoughts that government wanted them to speak and to pray only to the God that government wanted them to pray to.[147]

Recent scholarship has emphasized Black's suspicion of the Catholic church and his early involvement in the Ku Klux Klan as evidence that modern Establishment Clause doctrine is contaminated with bias.[148] Yet, the more important factor in explaining his approach to the Establishment Clause is that he was raised a Baptist. By the time he wrote *Engel*, he was no longer formally affiliated with any church.[149] He told his son, "I cannot believe. But I can't not believe either."[150] However, he continued to hold a typically Baptist view of the corrupting effects of establishment.[151] The corruption claim, as he states it in the passages just quoted, could have been written by Backus or Leland.

A shrewder critique of Black was offered immediately after *Everson* and *McCollum* by the Catholic theologian John Courtney Murray. Murray argued that the idea of separation that underlay these decisions depended on "a particular sectarian concept of 'religion.'" The idea that religion is a fundamentally private and individual matter, one that can never be expressed in communal ritual, depends, Murray argued, on "a deistic version of fundamentalist Protestantism." The idea of an absolute ban on assistance to religion "even in the demonstrable absence of any coercion of conscience, any inhibition of full religious liberty, any violation of civil equality, any disruption of social harmony"[152] cannot be sustained without this religious premise, he thought. Responding to Justice Wiley Rutledge's claim that separation "is best for the state and best for religion,"[153] he asked: "[B]y what constitutional authority is the Supreme Court empowered to legislate as to what is 'best for religion'? I thought church and state were separated here."[154]

The problem about the religious roots of the corruption argument is nonetheless a pressing one, and for just the reason that Murray notes. A rule against establishment of religion ought not itself to establish a religion. The point is a powerful one, and it is remarkable that so little has been made of it since Murray wrote.

The corruption rationale cannot be imported without modification into modern jurisprudence. Any invocation of the corruption rationale presupposes that religion is a good thing and that we can tell what is good and what is bad for religion. The framers' understanding of the corruption rationale relied on Protestant or Deist understandings of what uncorrupted religion consisted in. No court today could embrace those understandings without engaging in precisely the kind of intervention in live theological controversy that the Clause was intended to forestall. This difficulty has received almost no attention,[155] but it poses a fundamental challenge to the coherence of Establishment Clause jurisprudence, because that jurisprudence, we just saw, owes so much to the corruption argument.

The answer is the one that Madison adopted: to be determinedly vague about the specifics of uncorrupted religion. The framers' specific idea of the "religion" that must be protected from corruption has been supplanted, in modern American law, by a different idea of religion, one which resists definition yet is quite clear in application. There is, in contemporary American culture, a proliferation of different understandings of the good of religion. Yet, as we have seen, courts generally know religion when they see it. Many people who are divided on religious questions nonetheless agree that the object of their contestation will be damaged and degraded by state interference with it. The basic elements are the ones we traced back to Milton and Roger Williams: the idea that insincere religious behavior lacks religious value, that a variety of religious positions are somehow valuable, that the state is an unreliable source of religious authority, that religious teachings are likely to be altered in a pernicious way if the teachers are agents of the state. Establishment tends to produce undeserved contempt for religion. The legitimate authority of the state does not extend to religious questions. There are many theological paths to these propositions, and the state takes no position on which of them is correct.

The Limits of the Corruption Argument

Murray's concern highlights a limitation of the corruption argument. This may be the most paradoxical aspect of all: the argument, even if it plays a powerful role in Establishment Clause theory, cannot be directly relied upon to decide cases. If a court tries to decide whether corruption has occurred in any particular case, it must first decide what a noncorrupted religion looks like. And that would itself violate the Establishment Clause.

Justice David Souter, the principal modern proponent of the corruption rationale,[156] fell squarely into this trap.[157] Dissenting in *Zelman v. Simmons-Harris*, in which the Court upheld a program that allowed parents to pay religious school tuition with state-funded vouchers, he cited the risk of corruption described by Madison. Then he declared: "The risk is already being realized." He noted the decisions of many religious schools to comply with the Ohio program's requirements that schools not discriminate on the basis of religion, nor "teach hatred of any person or group on the basis of . . . religion."[158]

Kevin Pybas observes that Souter's argument amounts to "an accusation that the religious have been unfaithful to their God and to what their God requires of them." Pybas is correct to belabor Souter with the familiar concern about the limits of state competence:

> [H]ow does Justice Souter know when a particular religious community has compromised its principles? Is he or the Court generally so well-versed in the theologies of the various religious traditions in this country that he or it is in a position to say to a religious community that it has violated its own principles?[159]

Souter's error shows that, even if the corruption rationale is accepted, it cannot be operationalized as a requirement that courts look for corruption in particular cases. It is rather a reason for the state to avoid making any religious determinations at all. The corruption concern cannot support a rule that bans state action that corrupts religion. It should rather be understood as a rule-generating device, "a set of factors that courts [or other rule makers] should consider in defining the more precise rules."[160]

Souter offers a more telling objection to the voucher program's restrictions when he observes that the ban on teaching "hatred" itself raises religious questions. This condition, he notes, "could be understood (or subsequently broadened) to prohibit religions from teaching traditionally legitimate articles of faith as to the error, sinfulness, or ignorance of others."[161] Any such understanding would violate the rule against deciding religious questions, for the same reason that it was violated by the charge of fraud against Edna and Donald Ballard for claiming that St. Germain had given them extraordinary healing powers.[162] Claiming that the Christian religion is the only path to salvation and that all non-Christians are damned may or may not constitute "hatred." It is not clear how a state can decide that without getting into forbidden questions of theology. For example, a religious group might argue that its claims about the damnation of nonbelievers reflects loving concern rather than hatred. How could a state respond to that?

This objection is not fatal to the program, however, because the "hatred" proviso does not unambiguously require this result. A familiar canon of statutory construction holds that ambiguous laws are not to be read in a way that renders them unconstitutional.[163] Federal courts are also not to adjudicate the constitutionality of ambiguous state laws before the state courts have the opportunity to interpret them.[164] For the same reason that a court cannot decide whether the Ballards' religious claim is fraudulent, it cannot decide whether such a claim is hateful. If Ohio were to read its hatred proviso in the way Souter suggests, then that would raise constitutional difficulties. It has not happened yet, however, so it cannot be an argument against the law's constitutionality.

Back to Ceremonial Deism

What about ceremonial Deism? Questions of religious doctrine are in fact directly addressed by the placement of "In God We Trust" on currency, or "under God" in the Pledge of Allegiance. The Supreme Court has sometimes claimed that these practices are not really religious. Please. They are overtly and conspicuously religious.[165] There is even a residue of specifically Christian public ceremony, most notably the holiday of Christmas, which almost no one thinks to question. (Crèche displays, we will see, are a more complicated matter.)

Only recently has anyone on the Court articulated a principle that purports to distinguish permissible from impermissible Deism. The general rule now seems to be that old forms of Deism are grandfathered, but newer ones are unconstitutional.[166] Thus, the Court recently held that an official Ten Commandments display is unconstitutional if it was erected recently, but not if it has been around for decades.[167] Justice O'Connor, in her concurrence in a decision concerning the inclusion of the words "under God" in the Pledge of Allegiance, explicitly made the age of a ceremonial acknowledgment relevant to its constitutionality. She thought that constitutionality was supported by the absence of worship or prayer, the absence of reference to a particular religion, and minimal religious content. But the first of her factors was "history and ubiquity." "The constitutional value of ceremonial deism turns on a shared understanding of its legitimate nonreligious purposes," O'Connor wrote. "That sort of understanding can exist only when a given practice has been in place for a significant portion of the Nation's history, and when it is observed by enough persons that it can fairly be called ubiquitous."[168] The consequence is to make old and familiar forms of ceremonial Deism constitutional, but to discourage innovation.

This casual identification of God with the nation is hard to defend, and I am not eager to defend it. On the other hand, it is clearly not going away, so we ought to consider what can be said in favor of drawing the line here. Two considerations are especially salient.

The first is that ceremonial Deism represented a common-ground strategy—an effort, in its own time, to understand "religion" in an ecumenical and nonsectarian way. At the time that these elements of civil religion were put in place, we saw in Chapter 1, the existence of God appeared to be the one aspect of religion that was common to the various religious factions then dominant in American life. The continuation of this old settlement is not an effort by an incumbent administration to manipulate religion or a triumphalist effort to exclude outsiders. It simply perpetuates the background that is in place. It recognizes that people are invested in the status quo.[169]

The second is that new manifestations are not at all ecumenical. Today, the invocation of theism, and specifically the erection of a Ten Commandments display, is an intervention in the bitterest religious controversies that now divide us. Douglas Laycock thinks that a lesson of O'Connor's opinion is that "separationist groups should sue immediately when they encounter any religious practice newly sponsored by the government."[170] That is precisely the right lesson for them to take. New sponsorship of religious practices is far more likely to represent a contemporaneous effort to intervene in a live religious controversy than the perpetuation of old forms.[171] An alternative proposed by some critics—of construing "traditional acknowledgment" broadly enough to include anything the state wants to do—would read the Establishment Clause out of the Constitution.

Of course, ceremonial Deism has an effect on religion. It produces a culture in which many people feel that their religious beliefs are somehow associated with patriotism. This has the salutary effect of fostering civic unity and common moral ideals and tempering religious fanaticism. It also has the less attractive effect of encouraging self-righteous nationalism and the idea that whatever the United States does, however repugnant, is somehow divinely sanctioned.[172] However, neither of these effects is specifically aimed at by government when it perpetuates these rituals. Political manipulation, in that sense, is not occurring. Some writers have argued that government should aim to minimize its effect on religion, but that goal is not a coherent one: any government actions at all will cause religion to be different from what it otherwise would have been.[173]

Hardest of all are the Christmas display cases, which lie precisely on the line between permitted ceremonial Deism and forbidden state endorsement of religion. They have been around for a long time, and the Court cannot bring itself to enjoin them, so instead it demands that their religious content be watered down. The Court's decisions in this area are opaque. In *Lynch v. Donnelly*,[174] a majority of the Court permitted a nativity scene that was surrounded by a Santa Claus house, reindeer, candy-striped poles, a Christmas tree, carolers, figures of a clown, an elephant, a teddy bear, hundreds of colored lights, a banner stating "Seasons Greetings," and a "talking" wishing well. But in *County of Allegheny v. American Civil Liberties Union*,[175] the Court declared unconstitutional a nativity scene standing alone, but upheld a menorah accompanied by a Christmas tree and a sign saluting liberty. Michael McConnell observes that the court has in effect declared a "three-plastic animals rule": religious displays are permissible only if they are surrounded by dreadful holiday kitsch.[176] What lower courts end up doing is trying to determine, on the basis of their own interpretation of the social meaning of the display, whether that social meaning is too sectarian.

It is a mess, but it is probably not possible to do better. McConnell has argued that the public cultural sphere should mirror not secularism, but "the state of public culture in the non-government-controlled sector."[177] If many different cultural symbols are sponsored throughout the year, then each of them will merely signify pluralism. In many parts of the United States, however, government speech that mirrors "the state of public culture in the non-government-controlled sector" will be overwhelmingly Christian. Whatever the weaknesses of the prevailing approach, it has the virtue of ruling this out.

Absent the special case of Christmas, some old accommodations are too sectarian to be grandfathered. One example is the Latin cross atop Sunrise Rock in the Mojave National Preserve.[178] The cross was erected in 1934 as a memorial to the American soldiers who died in World War I. Litigation challenging its constitutionality was filed in 2001. Congress responded by selling the land on which the cross stood to the Veterans of Foreign Wars. When the Supreme Court vacated an injunction against the sale (on technical grounds not pertinent here), several of the justices commented on the underlying merits. The dissenters thought that the sale had an impermissible religious purpose, but Justice Anthony Kennedy, writing for a plurality, thought it important that the placement of the cross "was not an attempt to set the *imprimatur* of the state on a particular creed" or "promote a Christian message."[179] The sale of the land, he thought, was a sensible response to the difficulty that the government "could not remove the cross without conveying disrespect for those the cross was seen as honoring."[180] What is lost amid this argument is the shared assumption that the cross, which was not likely to have been challenged when it was first erected, could no longer stand on government land. The narrow question was how to make the transition to a regime in which there were no more such displays. With that as the broader context, it is hard to justify indignation about the way in which the government manages the moment of transition.

One aspect of ceremonial Deism has turned out to be unsalvageable. In its 1983 decision *Marsh v. Chambers*,[181] the Court upheld legislative prayers, citing a long history of such prayers. Doubtless the Court thought that, by upholding the prayers, it was avoiding a divisive controversy. Yet this relaxation of the neutrality requirement is different from other forms of ceremonial Deism, such as "In God We Trust" on the currency, in a crucial respect: as Christopher Lund observes, it requires "a continual set of discretionary religious choices." The prayer issue now divides municipalities all across the country, in a zero-sum battle in which the state is required to decide disputed points of theology. In the years following *Marsh*, some jurisdictions have rejected proposed prayers precisely on the basis of their nonmajoritarian religious content: one clerk systematically eliminated Muslims, Jehovah's Witnesses, Jews, and Mormons from the list of invited participants, while another rejected Wicca as "neo-pagan." Elections have sometimes been fought over whether official prayers should be overtly Christian. Members of the clergy have tailored their prayers to make them more likely to be acceptable to authorities.[182] There is no way to have legislative prayers without inviting these results. *Marsh* should be overruled.

The corruption concern has not been completely answered. H. Jefferson Powell thinks that these professions "ought to provoke Christian outrage," because the "equation of the United States and the biblical city on the hill" is "an attempt to manipulate public sentiment that is as cynical as it is essentially blasphemous."[183] I cannot say that Powell is wrong. This aspect of the present disestablishment regime is hardest to defend.

A God without Predicates

So the contemporary religion clause is layered. An old abstract conception of religion, which in light of growing plurality is not nearly as abstract and uncontroversial as it used to be, is allowed to persist, but not to grow. By grandfathering the old 1950s civil religion, and saying that it could proceed as far as it has and no further, the Supreme Court has essentially declared it immune from further tinkering. Ceremonial Deism is secure, but it dwells in a walled city, safe but trapped. The new civil religion, on the other hand, is the primary generator of the law of religion in the United States today.

Religion is a topic that incumbent administrations must now remain silent about. Its object is a negative God, a God without predicates.[184]

—3—

Religion Clause Doctrine Explained

Is the corruption argument an appropriate basis for legal doctrine? It may be that Americans had good reasons for conceptualizing religious liberty in the way that they did. But courts are supposed to make their decisions on the basis of the law, not the full range of reasons that any human being might have for acting. Why is it legitimate for courts to try to minimize the remainder of religious outliers and avoid the corruption of religion?

The religion clauses do not state a rule. Neither "establishment of religion" nor "free exercise" is self-defining. Many constitutional rules are like this. The task of the courts is to take vague provisions and construct administrable rules that implement the pertinent provision's underlying purposes.[1]

In crafting such rules, they legitimately rely on multiple sources of law. American constitutional argument draws upon text, original purpose or meaning, precedent, inferences from the overall structure of the government that has been established, prudence, and the court's sense of the national ethos. Constitutional arguments aim to draw all of these together into coherent accounts of constitutional meaning.[2]

Original Meaning and Legitimacy

In the interpretation of the religion clauses, perhaps more than in any other field of constitutional law, both the Court and commentators feel impelled to make originalist arguments.[3] The corruption claim is one such argument, focusing on an aspect of establishment that was of particular concern to the founding generation. It is a central basis for the rule that government may not declare religious truth—a rule, we shall now see, at the center of the doctrine. So consider the role of original intent or meaning in constitutional interpretation.[4]

The "originalist" movement has had a huge impact in constitutional theory, but that impact has been blunted by fragmentation. Originalism's core claim is that the appropriate way to read the Constitution is to give original intent or meaning absolute and dispositive weight.[5] Doing so supposedly will reduce or eliminate judicial discretion. Yet originalists are now divided on multiple methodological questions. Is the object of inquiry the original intentions of the drafters of the Constitution, the original semantic meaning of the language, or its original public meaning? Is the meaning that matters the meaning that is subjectively held at the time of enactment or the objective meaning of the language? Is it the actual understanding of those who lived at the time, or that of a hypothetical reasonable interpreter? Can original meaning include standards and general principles, which may be understood at a high level of generality? Is the law appropriately based upon the entire set of original expectations about the application of constitutional principles, or some original meaning more narrowly construed? Is construction, the practice by which the interpreter exercises discretion to create specific applications of broad and vague terms, legitimate? Originalists are on all sides of these debates.[6] As a consequence, originalism has fragmented into an enormous number of different theories.

In scholarship, fragmentation is not normally a problem at all. Most scholarly fields are fragmented. But the stated purpose of originalism is to produce unique and indisputable answers to legal questions in order to eliminate the possibility of judicial discretion.[7] The proliferation of originalisms, and the certainty that none of them will vanquish its rivals, together with the concession in many of the sophisticated variants that interpretive discretion is unavoidable, make this enterprise a forlorn one. Multiple originalisms are problematic for the same reason that multiple popes are problematic. Some writers have concluded that there is no longer any practical difference between originalism and nonoriginalism.[8]

Yet the appeal to originalism has continuing power. The proliferation of originalisms is testimony to that power: everyone wants to get into the act.

The explanation is local. Originalism is a manifestation of American exceptionalism. In Canada and Australia, whose legal systems in many ways resemble that of the United States, originalism has had no rhetorical or legal traction: almost no one makes such arguments. Jamal Greene offers several possible explanations for this distinctive national tendency: America's tendency to lionize its founders, our Constitution's revolutionary origins, the originalists' desire to constrain the Warren Court, the public nature of Supreme Court confirmations, assimilationist tendencies in American identity, and the fundamentalist elements of American religion.[9] Jed Rubenfeld observes that some degree of identification with the past is an indispensable part of national identity.[10]

It is the identification, and not any promise of judicial constraint, that is really doing the work in originalism. That is why the debate among originalisms can never end. There are many different ways of identifying with the past, because there are so many different aspects of the past with which one can identify. Original intention (to the extent that it can persuasively be shown), original public contextual meaning, and original semantic meaning each have a plausible claim to constitute a link to the revered framers, and so each has a plausible claim upon our attention. Similar points could be made about each of the other factional divisions within originalism. Each of these approaches therefore can do useful rhetorical work, and will be conscripted when that is likely to help with a constitutional argument. There is no way to stop constitutional interpreters from using all the tools they find in the kit, and so none of these can be permanently elevated to exclusive authority.[11] Originalism is fundamentally about a narrative of rhetorical self-identification with the achievements of a founding historical moment. That is the real basis of its power. An originalist argument will succeed to the extent that it can persuade its audience that it can keep faith with that identification.

I am not being pejorative when I say that originalist argument is a kind of constitutional rhetoric, connecting us with the past, constructing a narrative of national identity. Persuasive advocacy is an honorable undertaking. It can never be illegitimate to call your audience's attention to something that they care about, or ought to care about, such as "your father would have been appalled by what you are proposing to do."

Originalist argument can be an argument from authority, citing texts that state legal rules or from which such rules can be inferred, or it can describe commitments, laid down at the time of the framing and still attractive today. If the latter, then originalist argument must offer a story about the pertinent commitment. Where the commitment is a decision to *break* with the past in some way, then a story must be told about what was wrong with that past. Then the argument must contend that the same kind of wrong is present in the instant case.

One may object that this understanding of originalism as a rhetorical strategy misrepresents originalism, which is in fact a distinctive set of theoretical claims, entirely unrelated to rhetorical considerations. But the question of definition is connected to the question of function. When I speak of a "chair," you may think of an assembly of arms and legs, but a chair can also be defined functionally, as an artifact designed for a person to sit on it. That is why a beanbag chair is a chair. Originalist argument is an artifact designed to recall the Constitution's origin and connect what we are doing now with that origin.

One mode of originalism is inference from paradigmatic cases that are objects of constitutional aversion. The role of paradigm cases in constitutional law has been emphasized by Jed Rubenfeld. He observes that such cases frequently anchor constitutional argumentation, sometimes in a way that is only distantly related to the semantic meaning of the pertinent constitutional provision. For example, the language of the Fourteenth Amendment is broad and vague. The amendment was enacted with the specific purpose of invalidating the Black Codes. Enacted by white-controlled legislatures after the Civil War, the Codes imposed specific legal disabilities on blacks, such as requiring them to be gainfully employed under contracts of long duration, excluding them from occupations other than manual labor, and disabling them from testifying against whites in court.[12] The language of the Fourteenth Amendment's text, however, standing alone, could support a judicial opinion upholding, say, a statute requiring all and only blacks to be employed as servants or laborers, by applying rationality review. That would obviously be an interpretive travesty. The unconstitutionality of the Black Codes is so much a part of the amendment's meaning that to say that this is a settled interpretation is a misleading understatement. Rather, "[t]his piece of the Fourteenth Amendment's meaning *precedes* interpretation."[13] Any interpretation of the amendment must be a chain of inferences from the core commitment represented by this paradigm case. A constitutional provision must be understood to address the very problem that it was designed to address.

In the case of the religion clauses, the paradigm case is clear: the Church of England, together with the restrictions on the free exercise of religion that accompanied that establishment. The Court's job is to decide what was bad about that paradigmatic case and craft rules that will prevent the recurrence of that evil.

In deciding that, the framers' own understanding of the evil they sought to prevent is, at a minimum, a useful source of guidance as to the meaning of the pertinent provision. If they aimed to keep the state away from contested religious questions, that is relevant. If they thought that state attempts to address such questions were likely to have a corrupting effect on religion, that is relevant.

The approach to original meaning that I have suggested here leaves considerable room for interpretive discretion. The predominant approach, among liberals and conservatives alike, has been to attempt to deduce specific rules of law from these abstract provisions. No such rules can be deduced, and the attempt to do so is likely to produce mischief.

The Establishment Clause is a particularly apt candidate for paradigm case interpretation because the core historical wrong that was intended to be barred—here, an establishment of religion of the kind that existed in England—is specifically named in the text.[14] But that specificity does not yield a rule. When the authors of the First Amendment condemned establishment, Thomas Curry notes, "they had in their minds an image of tyranny, not a definition of a system."[15] To make the problem more complicated, the survey in Chapter 2 shows that the framers did not all have the same understanding of what one of establishment's principal evils consisted in. There is no unitary intention of the framers for contemporary interpreters to follow.[16]

Such a unitary intention has been asserted in Donald Drakeman's admirably careful book, *Church, State, and Original Intent*. Drakeman shows that when the Supreme Court laid down the fundamentals of modern religion clause doctrine, it was trying to be faithful to the original meaning and was relying on the best historians of its time. Yet he goes on to argue that the Court's understanding of that original meaning was radically flawed. The paucity of discussion when the First Amendment was enacted suggests that the framers did not think they were doing anything especially important: at best, they were barring the creation of a national church, which was never a real political danger. He concludes that the religion clauses today should be understood to leave religious questions entirely to the political process—in other words, that the past half century of religion clause jurisprudence should be entirely discarded on the basis of new historical research.

Drakeman's work shows that his method, of trying to determine the specific intentions of the framing generation, would randomly produce massive changes in the law whenever new research, or (as in Drakeman's own case) a reinterpretation of already existing data, changes our interpretation of the history.[17] (Nor is Drakeman's latest conclusion more than an intriguing hypothesis: he might be right, but it is hard to be confident.) Such unpredictable upheavals are routine in scholarship, but it is irresponsible to build them into a legal regime. He thus inadvertently casts doubt on the method of deriving specific results—not just broad principles, but specific rules—from originalist research and discarding all other modalities of constitutional law. And Drakeman is a conscientious scholar who is manifestly willing to follow the argument wherever it leads. The self-styled "originalists" on the Court are more manipulative when they take up those materials.[18]

Even if Drakeman is right that the framers' only specific intention was to ban a national church, it is a large leap to the conclusion that the language they drafted accomplished nothing more. The framers of the Fourteenth Amendment clearly banned the Black Codes, but, although they did not understand the amendment to bar segregated schools, they did not commit themselves to permitting segregation. The framers of the Establishment Clause committed themselves to banning a national church. They did not commit themselves to permitting other manifestations of official religion.

In Establishment Clause cases, to the extent that one wants to rely on original meaning, one should ask: (1) why did the framing generation (or generations, since the clause is applicable to the states via the Fourteenth Amendment) think establishment of religion is a bad thing, and (2) is the same bad thing brought about by the challenged action in this case? William Brennan, who never called himself an originalist, wrote in 1963 that the Court should ask whether challenged practices "threaten those consequences which the Framers deeply feared; whether, in short, they tend to promote that type of interdependence between religion and state which the First Amendment was designed to prevent." The question is what are "those substantive evils the fear of which called for the Establishment Clause of the First Amendment"?[19]

With respect to the first question, why the framers thought establishment was a bad thing, the corruption argument is indisputably relevant. It was only one of the reasons why establishment was thought bad, but it was a consideration that played an important role, and so the Clause should be read in light of it (more so because, as we have already seen, it is a more appropriate basis for the law than political division or alienation). That, I will now argue, is what the Court has done.

The Secular Purpose Problem

To show how the Court has implemented the underlying concerns of the Establishment Clause, I will begin with an extended exploration of one central problem of religion clause doctrine. The solution to that problem will provide the key for making sense of the rest of the law.

Does the Establishment Clause bar the government from enacting laws whose only justification is based on the tenets of some religion? For decades the Supreme Court has thought so, holding that, to be constitutional, a law must have a secular legislative purpose. But that may soon change. A growing faction of the Court may be ready to scrap the secular purpose requirement.

The doctrine cannot be discarded, however, without effectively reading the Establishment Clause out of the Constitution altogether. What the doctrine needs is clarification, and this can be provided by the argument that has been developed here. What the state may not do— what the doctrine properly forbids it to do—is declare any particular religious doctrine to be the true one, or enact laws that clearly imply such a declaration of religious truth.

The secular purpose doctrine is part of the Supreme Court's test for violations of the Establishment Clause of the First Amendment. In the case in which the test was announced, *Lemon v. Kurtzman*, the Court held that in order to withstand an Establishment Clause challenge, "[f]irst, the statute must have a secular legislative purpose; second, its principal or primary effect must be one that neither advances nor inhibits religion; finally, the statute must not foster an excessive governmental entanglement with religion."[20] Here I will defend only the first prong of the test, the secular purpose prong.[21]

The Supreme Court has relied on the secular purpose prong six times to invalidate a state statute.[22] *Epperson v. Arkansas* struck down an Arkansas statute that prohibited the teaching of evolution in public schools and universities. The record contained "no suggestion . . . that Arkansas' law [could] be justified by considerations of state policy other than [a desire to support] the religious views of some of its citizens." The absence of a secular purpose was fatal to the law:

> The overriding fact is that Arkansas' law selects from the body of knowledge a particular segment which it proscribes for the sole reason that it is deemed to conflict with a particular religious doctrine; that is, with a particular interpretation of the Book of Genesis by a particular religious group.[23]

Stone v. Graham invalidated a Kentucky statute that required public schools to post in each classroom a copy of the Ten Commandments, paid for by private contributions. The Court found that the Commandments were a sacred text that included unquestionably religious edicts (for example, avoiding idolatry).[24]

Wallace v. Jaffree declared unconstitutional an Alabama law which mandated a period of silence in public schools "for meditation or voluntary prayer." The Court held that the law "was not motivated by any clearly secular purpose—indeed, the statute had *no* secular purpose." The statute's principal sponsor had said that the bill's only purpose was religious, and no evidence to the contrary had been offered by the state. Moreover, Alabama law already mandated a moment of silence for "meditation." The only conceivable purpose of the new law, therefore, was to endorse religion.[25]

Edwards v. Aguillard invalidated a Louisiana statute that mandated equal treatment for evolution and "creation science" in public schools. The Court noted the "historic and contemporaneous link between the teachings of certain religious denominations and the teaching of evolution." The legislative history revealed a purpose "to change the science curriculum of public schools in order to provide persuasive advantage to a particular religious doctrine that rejects the factual basis of evolution in its entirety."[26] *Santa Fe Independent School Dist. v. Doe* involved a policy that allowed student-led prayer before football games. The policy, while nominally allowing private speech, in fact "invites and encourages religious messages,"[27] the Court held. The purpose of the law, enacted in the face of challenges to the practice of official prayer before athletic events, was to maintain state-sponsored religious practice. In *McCreary v. ACLU*,[28] the Court barred the posting of Ten Commandments displays in two Kentucky courthouses.

These six cases are far from typical. The cases in which the challenged statute survives the prong vastly outnumber those in which the Court invalidates the statute. Two examples show how deferential the Court has sometimes been to the state's recitation of a secular purpose. When Sunday closing laws were challenged in *McGowan v. Maryland*, the Court acknowledged that these laws originally had a religious purpose, but held that "[t]he present purpose and effect of most of [these laws] is to provide a uniform day of rest for all citizens."[29] In *Lynch v. Donnelly*, the Court rejected an Establishment Clause challenge to a municipality's inclusion of a traditional nativity scene as part of a larger display depicting various observances of the Christmas holiday. The Court held that "[t]he evident purpose of including the crèche in the larger display was not promotion of the religious content of the crèche but celebration of the public holiday through its traditional symbols."[30] In both cases, the state's justification for its law was a thin secular rationalization for an obviously sectarian action, but the rationalization was enough to satisfy the Court.

Four Objections

The *Lemon* test has been criticized by many commentators, several sitting Supreme Court Justices have called for it to be overruled, and with recent changes in the Court's composition, there may be five votes to discard it. Some of this dissatisfaction focuses on the other prongs of the test, but the secular purpose requirement is a prime target. Critics of the doctrine raise four objections.

The rubber stamp objection claims that, as Justice Rehnquist put it, "the prong will condemn nothing so long as the legislature utters a secular purpose and says nothing about aiding religion."[31]

Justice Scalia has been the most forceful advocate of *the evanescence objection*. He argues that the legislative purpose upon which the prong depends either does not exist or is not knowable by judges, because "discerning the subjective motivation of those enacting the statute is, to be honest, almost always an impossible task."[32] Since the text of the Establishment Clause does not demand that judges undertake this task, Scalia argues, they should discard at least this much of the *Lemon* test.

The participation objection argues that a law may lack a secular purpose, yet still be the legitimate product of a democratic process. The secular purpose prong, it argues, denies religious people their right to participate in politics. If religious motives are impermissible, then the support of religious voters will be assigned *negative* weight, contaminating and invalidating otherwise acceptable legislation.

The callous indifference objection is the deepest of the four, going to the foundations of Establishment Clause theory.[33] This objection holds that there is nothing wrong with laws that favor religion as such. While the participation objection focuses on the prong's tendency to police the political process and argues the innocence of the types of process that the requirement would condemn, the callous indifference objection focuses instead on the outcome of lawmaking and claims that laws that explicitly single out religion for advantage are nonetheless permissible.

The callous indifference objection claims that the secular purpose prong, if taken seriously, would invalidate the specific religious accommodations that the Court has held permissible, and has sometimes even required, under the Free Exercise Clause. Thus Scalia notes that "our cases indicate that even certain kinds of governmental actions undertaken with the specific intention of improving the position of religion do not 'advance religion' as that term is used in *Lemon*." Rather, the Court has held that government *must* act to advance religion when it discovers that its employees are inhibiting religion or that there is a valid free exercise claim, and that government *may* do so when it permissibly accommodates religion.[34] These cases reveal a deep incoherence at the heart of the Court's religion jurisprudence, since the *Lemon* test seems to forbid what the free exercise cases require.

Justice O'Connor's Defense of the Doctrine

Justice O'Connor is the only member of the Court who has responded to these criticisms. She has attempted to defend the prong by relying on her "endorsement" test, described in Chapter 2. "Under this view, *Lemon's* inquiry as to the purpose and effect of a statute requires courts to examine whether government's purpose is to endorse religion and whether the statute actually conveys a message of endorsement."[35] Her approach has been influential. The Court relied on it in *Aguillard* and *Santa Fe*.[36]

In *Wallace*, O'Connor concurred in the judgment, which invalidated a state "moment of silence" statute, and found that "[t]he relevant issue [was] whether an objective observer, acquainted with the text, legislative history, and implementation of the statute, would perceive it as a state endorsement of prayer in public schools." This interpretation of the prong answers the rubber stamp objection, O'Connor argues, because courts are not as easily gulled as the objection assumes. Sometimes, it will be clear that a statute's recitation of a secular purpose is a sham. O'Connor's approach also answers the evanescence objection, because, rather than inviting courts "to psychoanalyze the legislators,"[37] it looks to the objective meaning of the statute. The prong does not improperly police the legislative process, as the participation objection alleges, because it looks to outcome rather than process.

O'Connor struggles, however, with the callous indifference objection. She acknowledges that accommodations of religion do not have a secular purpose: "[A] rigid application of the *Lemon* test would invalidate legislation exempting religious observers from generally applicable government obligations. By definition, such legislation has a religious purpose and effect in promoting the free exercise of religion." The formula of state neutrality toward religion is unhelpful here: "It is difficult to square any notion of 'complete neutrality' with the mandate of the Free Exercise Clause that government must sometimes exempt a religious observer from an otherwise generally applicable obligation. A government that confers a benefit on an explicitly religious basis is not neutral toward religion."[38] The secular purpose prong thus seems to contradict a practice of religious accommodation that is harmonious with, and perhaps even required by,[39] the First Amendment.

O'Connor chalks this up to a tension within the First Amendment itself—a tension that had been acknowledged in earlier decisions of the Court. As she observed in *Wallace*: "It is obvious that either of the two Religion Clauses, 'if expanded to a logical extreme, would tend to clash with the other.'" The solution that she proposes is simply to make an exception to the Establishment Clause in cases in which government creates exemptions, because "one can plausibly assert that government pursues Free Exercise Clause values when it lifts a government-imposed burden on the free exercise of religion."[40]

How O'Connor's Defense Fails

O'Connor's defense of the secular purpose prong is a failure. Steven Smith argues that the endorsement test as O'Connor has formulated it is incoherent, because the cultural meaning of arguably religious messages is likely to be ambiguous and contested. Any particular governmental action—the granting of conscientious objector status, for example—will or will not be thought to constitute illegitimate endorsement, depending on one's view of whether it is appropriate for government to take that substantive action. Different people in society will have different views about the substantive issues, and their opinions about whether endorsement has occurred will follow from those substantive views. The endorsement test thus is parasitic on some substantive vision of what government actions are appropriate, and the test, therefore, cannot be a substitute for that substantive vision.[41]

If Smith is correct, then O'Connor's defense of the secular purpose prong is defective at the core. If endorsement has no objective status—if one's perception of endorsement or nonendorsement merely reflects one's culturally subjective position—then the prong has no referent. Smith's objection to the endorsement test is analogous to Justice Scalia's objection to the search for subjective legislative intent: the thing sought either does not exist or is not knowable.

Smith's critique resuscitates all four of the objections to the prong. The rubber stamp objection regains its vitality, because so long as *some* observer might think that a law has a secular purpose, this observer can claim to offer the objective perspective that O'Connor seeks, and so to validate the challenged law. The evanescence and participation objections similarly survive so long as some people think that a law enacted by those with religious motives endorses its enactors' religion. As for the callous indifference objection, O'Connor does not explain why an objective observer would not perceive endorsement of religion when religion receives special advantages that are not themselves required by the Free Exercise Clause.

O'Connor argues that the requirements of the Establishment Clause should be relaxed when government grants religious exemptions, but she has elsewhere suggested that the lifting of certain government-imposed burdens, such as a hypothetical exemption of profit-making religious organizations from the Civil Rights Act of 1964, might violate the endorsement test.[42] O'Connor's answer to the callous indifference objection thus seems ad hoc and unprincipled. She admits that religious exemptions have no secular purpose, but arbitrarily carves out an exception (of unspecified scope) to the secular purpose prong in order to prevent the prong's operation from becoming too destructive.

McConnell objects that this attempt to reconcile accommodation and endorsement "is circular. If our reasonable observers know the 'values' underlying the Religion Clauses, and if those values are something other than endorsement and disapproval, what need have we of the endorsement test?"[43] Likewise, Smith argues that an attempt to modify the endorsement test in this way, by creating an exception for accommodations but forbidding all other forms of endorsement, is incoherent because "[f]ar from being mutually exclusive, 'accommodation' and 'endorsement' of religion are much more likely to coincide."[44]

The exception seems to permit legislators to act out of concern for the religious convictions of their constituents, but not because the legislators believe that religion is true or beneficial. This distinction immediately revives the difficulties of ascertaining legislative intent, already noted by the evanescence objection. It is also untenable on a theoretical level, because in a democracy, it is entirely legitimate for legislators to share their constituents' beliefs and values. And if they are allowed to act because they agree with a religion's beliefs, then we return to the rubber stamp objection: government will have "a broad license to support religion under the guise of 'accommodation.'" But if such legislators' intent invalidates an accommodation that would have been permissible if enacted by agnostics, then the participation and callous indifference objections arise once more.[45]

If O'Connor's defense of the secular purpose requirement is to be salvaged, it must be reformulated.

Why There Must Be a Secular Purpose Requirement

Why should there be a secular purpose requirement at all? I argued in Chapter 2 that a major purpose of the Establishment Clause is to prevent the corruption of religion by government manipulation. This means, at a minimum, that the state is forbidden from declaring religious truth. This is the key to the requirement's meaning and purpose.

The classic formulation is that of *Epperson v. Arkansas*: "Government in our democracy, state and national, must be neutral in matters of religious theory, doctrine, and practice."[46] So the First Amendment's prohibition of "establishment of religion" is, among other things, a restriction on government speech. It means that the state may not declare articles of faith. The state may not express an opinion about religious matters. It may not encourage citizens to hold certain religious beliefs.

The axiom that government may not declare religious truth entails restrictions on government conduct. It is a familiar point in free speech law that conduct which is not itself speech may nonetheless communicate a message and so be appropriately treated as speech.[47] This means that the Establishment Clause's restriction on government speech is also a restriction on symbolic conduct. If government cannot declare religious truth, then it cannot engage in conduct the meaning of which is a declaration of religious truth. It would be illegitimate for a state to carve, over the entrance of the capitol, an inscription reading "JESUS IS LORD" or "THE POPE IS THE ANTICHRIST." A crucifix would be illegitimate for the same reason. The state simply is not permitted to take an official position on matters of religion.

Government, however, does more than just erect symbols. The most obvious way in which the government expresses an opinion is through the passage of legislation. In this arena, the government has available to it a particularly powerful type of symbolic conduct that is unavailable to other actors. Through legislation, the government can, and often does, express a point of view.

Suppose a statute is passed that makes it a crime for anyone to break the commandment to obey the Sabbath, as that commandment is understood by Orthodox Jews. That is, the law makes it a felony to operate machinery on the Sabbath, to drive a car, to turn on an electric appliance, or to make a telephone call, and the law applies to private as well as public conduct, so that one can violate it by turning on the television while one is alone at home.[48] There is no substantive constitutional right to do any of these things. The problem with this law lies in its message. It asserts, as plainly as if it were declared in so many words, the correctness of the commandment to keep the Sabbath holy and of the Orthodox rabbis' interpretation of that sentence. It declares religious truth. Thus, the secular purpose requirement works as a corollary to the axiom with which I began. If government cannot declare religious truth, then it cannot use its coercive powers to enforce religious truth.

Steven D. Smith objects that "virtually every action taken by government at least tacitly teaches, if not the truth, then the falsity of some religious beliefs."[49] Thus, for example, teaching Darwin in the public schools implicitly contradicts the views of biblical literalists and six-day creationists. Laws against murder contradict the religious beliefs of the Aztecs. A stop sign on a corner implicitly declares that it is not contrary to God's will for the state to erect stop signs.

To see why Smith's objection is not fatal, consider Robert Audi's observation that the justification for some laws "evidentially depend[s] on the existence of God (or on denying it) or on theological considerations, or on the pronouncements of a person or institution *qua* religious authority."[50] Not all laws depend on theological considerations in this way. The law mandating the stop sign has no such evidential dependence. Nor the homicide law. Nor the inclusion of Darwin in the curriculum.

The ban on government declaring religious truth would, however, be violated if a science teacher were to say, at the end of the lesson, that "Darwin proves that God doesn't exist." The question of any lesson's religious implications is one that the schools are not authorized to address.

There are, of course, nice questions on the margin. Laws prohibiting the teaching of evolution, or requiring the posting of the Ten Commandments in every classroom in a state, are so obviously theologically loaded that the Court rightly judges that they go too far. But in the evolution case, unless the science teacher starts denying God's existence, the state is taking no particular religious line. A wide range of religious views are consistent with Darwin's theory.

Of course, government should give reasons for what it does, but it can easily do that without embedding its actions in any particular religious narrative. It is easy to defend the law against murder without saying anything at all about Aztec theology. Perhaps some religious orthodoxy is in some sense implicit in the stop sign at an intersection; at a minimum, it excludes the proposition that God wants you to speed through the intersection without slowing down. But there are many different theologies that can and do coincide in rejecting this proposition. People with radically differing theological views can have adequate reasons for obeying both laws. The question is whether any given law is capable of justification without directly relying on theological considerations or religious authority. The statute authorizing the stop sign is an example of such a law.[51]

The argument that I have just set forth is obviously a close cousin of O'Connor's endorsement test. Its focus, however, is different. The question is not how outsiders feel about what the government is doing, but what government is saying.

Recall that Smith's core objection to the endorsement test is that O'Connor's test is implicitly parasitic on some unspecified theory of what government can and cannot do. I have specified the theory upon which my modification of the endorsement test is parasitic. The secular purpose requirement, as I understand it, follows from the axiom that government may not declare religious truth. Forbidden endorsement, endorsement that violates the secular purpose requirement, is government action that declares religious truth.

Answering the Objections

If the secular purpose requirement logically follows from the requirement that government not formulate official answers to religious questions, then it is appropriately interpreted in terms of, and its application is appropriately guided by, that requirement. I will elaborate upon the operation of the test as I have reformulated it in the course of addressing the four objections to the requirement.

The answer to the rubber stamp and evanescence objections is that what government says is sometimes obvious on the face of the statute. The question of secular purpose, the Court has explained, is "to be answered on the basis of judicial interpretation of social facts."[52]

Questions at the margin of obviousness will turn on the range of meanings that natives of the culture can reasonably ascribe to the government action in question.[53] The Sabbath-keeping statute declares the authority of the Ten Commandments, and the theological correctness of the Orthodox Jewish interpretation of those Commandments, as clearly as if the government were to declare Orthodox Judaism the official religion. The question of explicit endorsement will turn on what native speakers of English think that, for example, "Jesus is Lord" means. There will be doubtful cases, and in such cases it makes sense to give the legislature the benefit of the doubt.[54] But the set of cases invalidated by such a test is not an empty set. Some laws will have *no* plausible secular purpose.

The evanescence objection fails because the secular purpose requirement does not inquire into subjective legislative intent. Justice Souter observed in *McCreary v. ACLU* that the inquiry into purpose "is a staple of statutory interpretation that makes up the daily fare of every appellate court in the country." Often, "an understanding of official objective emerges from readily discoverable fact, without any judicial psychoanalysis of a drafter's heart of hearts." If the religious motive of a law is not apparent, "then without something more the government does not make a divisive announcement that in itself amounts to taking sides. A secret motive stirs up no strife and does nothing to make outsiders of nonadherents."[55] Justice Scalia, who has insisted that "discerning the subjective motivation of those enacting the statute is, to be honest, almost always an impossible task," concedes that "it is possible to discern the objective 'purpose' of a statute (i.e., the public good at which its provisions appear to be directed)."[56] In part because of the difficulties that Scalia catalogues, even in the discriminatory purpose cases, the Court tends to rely on objective rather than subjective legislative purpose.[57]

The answer to the participation objection is that the secular purpose prong looks at legislative outcomes rather than legislative inputs. In the discriminatory purpose cases, subjective intent is necessarily the very thing that the Court is searching for, because the whole point of the judicial inquiry is to police the legislative process for contamination by prejudice.[58] When the Court relies on objective purpose, it is using it as a proxy for the subjective legislative intent that is so hard to discern. But there is nothing wrong with a legislative process that is influenced by religious people, who, after all, are not second-class citizens. The basic premises of democracy condemn a political process in which the decision makers are racist, but not a political process in which some of the decision makers have religious views and allow those views to influence their political positions.[59]

Of course, the participation objection remains accurate insofar as the secular purpose requirement does prevent some religious people from getting what they want from the legislative process. But so does any other reading of the Establishment Clause. In fact, any constitutional provision that limits the range of permissible political outcomes prevents some people from getting what they want in the legislative process.

The participation objection, when directed against the secular purpose requirement as I have formulated it, is thus tantamount to a quarrel with constitutionalism in general, not with any particular version of it. Under even a modest view of the Establishment Clause, a petition to make Anglicanism the established church of the United States, or to make felonious the celebration of the Catholic Mass, will not be addressable by the legislature. This prohibition may restrict the ability of some citizens to get what they want in the political process.

What about the callous indifference objection? This is the deepest objection, because it makes religion jurisprudence seem contradictory at its core. But the answer to the objection should by now be clear. This is just the free exercise/establishment dilemma in a different form. And the answer is the same: government can treat religion-in-general as a good thing (and thus rebut the objection) without deciding any issue of religious truth.

The Court declared in *Epperson* that the Establishment Clause requires "government neutrality between religion and religion, and between religion and nonreligion."[60] This language is ambiguous. Does it mean (1) that government can never take any action favoring religion as such, or (2) that government cannot endorse religious beliefs, such as the belief that God exists, or repudiate a view that denies those beliefs, such as atheism? It is commonly assumed that these are the same thing. They are not. It is possible for the state to favor religion-in-general as such, in all the ways that free exercise requires and that the Court has traditionally permitted, without declaring religious truth and so without violating the secular purpose prong.

In Chapter 1, we explored the definition of "religion." We have not yet analyzed its opposite, "nonreligion." McConnell observes that "there is no identifiable entity that goes by the name of 'nonreligion.' Rather, there are an infinite number of ideas, highly disparate among themselves, that are not religious." Thus he concludes that "a rigid insistence that religion be treated the same as 'nonreligion,' or the same as a secular analog, is pointless and incoherent. There is no single entity that meets the description of 'nonreligion' and there will always be more than one secular analog."[61] In practice, however, the doctrine regards "nonreligion" more narrowly and coherently, as the repudiation of conventional religious doctrines such as theism. As already noted, government is barred from endorsing nonreligion in that sense. So understood, what I propose is consistent with the doctrine, and it avoids McConnell's otherwise sound charge of incoherence.

What If There Were No Secular Purpose Requirement?

Finally, the secular purpose requirement protects the integrity of every area of constitutional law, because the law would be radically transformed if overtly religious considerations were a permissible basis for state decision making. Much that is now unconstitutional would become permissible if religious justifications could be offered. In particular, there would be little left of the Fourteenth Amendment, since most forms of discrimination that the amendment forbids have at one time or another been sincerely defended on religious grounds.

Romer v. Evans did not rely on the secular purpose prong of *Lemon* or even mention the Establishment Clause, but it is nevertheless pertinent. *Romer* struck down an amendment to the Colorado Constitution which barred any antidiscrimination protection for gay people. The amendment, the Court observed, "has the peculiar property of imposing a broad and undifferentiated disability on a single named group." This broad disability "raise[d] the inevitable inference that the disadvantage imposed is born of animosity toward the class of persons affected."[62]

Daniel Crane observes that the motivation for Amendment 2 was largely religious. Yet the Court refused to recognize this biblical view as a legitimate reason for a law, instead equating it with bare hostility. Crane argues that this was a major and indefensible shift in equal protection jurisprudence. The earlier "bare animosity" cases that the Court cited in *Romer* involved laws whose purposes—"[a]n unthinking, knee-jerk dislike of hippies, the children of illegal aliens, and the mentally retarded"—were very different from the religious motivations of Amendment 2's supporters. Those earlier classifications "were irrational in the sense that they lacked any mooring in a comprehensive view of the public good." Amendment 2, on the other hand, reflected a coherent, religiously based view of morality. The bare animosity principle of *Romer* "insists that the religious translate their views into non-religious terms when presenting public policy justifications for classifications disadvantaging groups of individuals," he observes. Even then, the Court may not be persuaded by the translation and may invalidate the law because of its religious purpose. The result, Crane asserts, is to disenfranchise the religious.[63]

Crane's objection fails, but it sheds valuable light on the secular purpose requirement. It fails because the right to participation cannot be as absolute as Crane would make it. As I have already explained, any constitutional restriction is a constraint on participation, since any such restriction entails that citizens may not work together to pass the laws it forbids. Crane is correct that, if religious claims are excluded from constitutional argument, this exclusion may affect the outcome even in cases that do not mention the secular purpose requirement. Were his objection accepted, it would certainly have been easy for the Court to uphold Amendment 2. The opinion could have been very short: "The Amendment is legitimate because it reflects the electorate's rational view that homosexual conduct is an abomination before God. See Leviticus 18:22; Leviticus 20:13; Romans 1:26–27." But an opinion of that sort is unimaginable, and for good reason.[64]

If the state were no longer limited to secular purposes, the effects would be so far reaching that constitutional law would be unimaginably different from what it is now. Consider *Loving v. Virginia*, in which the Court invalidated the prohibition of interracial marriages. The trial judge had upheld the law on frankly religious grounds:

> Almighty God created the races white, black, yellow, malay and red, and he placed them on separate continents. And but for the interference with his arrangement there would be no cause for such marriages. The fact that he separated the races shows that he did not intend for the races to mix.[65]

Religious arguments had often been made on behalf of these laws, and indeed on behalf of the subordination of blacks generally.[66] The Supreme Court did not even pause to consider whether the trial court had correctly understood God's intentions. Instead, it invalidated the law because it was "designed to maintain White Supremacy," and because the purpose of the statute thus "violate[d] the central meaning of the Equal Protection Clause."[67] Without the secular purpose requirement, the Court could not have delivered the opinion it did.

What then would the Court's options have been? There are only two, neither of them attractive. On the one hand, the Court could defer to the state's determination of what divine law required. Even if the state were required to show a compelling state interest, compliance with God's ordinances would appear to be as compelling an interest as one could imagine. In that case, the statute would have been upheld, as would every other racially discriminatory statute that might come before the Court.

On the other hand, the Court could have undertaken its own theological inquiry (or remanded the question for trial), perhaps relying on the expert opinions of philosophy professors to decide whether God exists, on theologians to determine whether Christianity is the true religion, on biblical scholars to determine whether racist interpretations of biblical sources are sound, and so forth. The Court could then have invalidated the statute if and only if it concluded that the state had committed theological error.[68] Courts would face similar problems any time an invasion of constitutional rights is given a religious justification. Reference to divine law is, of course, a classic justification for sex discrimination.[69] Biblical justifications might be offered for whipping convicts. And so forth.

The secular purpose requirement insulates the Court from such dilemmas. If government may not declare religious truth, then the Supreme Court may not declare religious truth. When the Court attempts to discern a rational basis for a law, it may not cite revelation as the basis that it is seeking. It must look elsewhere. And if it cannot find a rational basis elsewhere, then it must invalidate the law. This procedure does ignore religious arguments, but the price of taking those arguments into account would be exceedingly high.

A last consideration supporting the reading of the secular purpose requirement offered here is that it fits the case law well.

The Boundaries of Accommodation:
The Case of Tax Exemptions

The understanding of the secular purpose requirement that I have offered here can address some perennial theoretical conundrums in the law of accommodation. Consider the puzzle of tax exemptions for churches. William Marshall observes that "despite the Court's protestations on this point, tax exemptions constitute state sponsorship of religion."[70] Such exemptions are often justified in light of the community service that some churches sometimes perform,[71] but the Court did not rely on this rationale in *Walz v. Tax Commission*, which upheld an exemption statute that had no community service requirement.

Walz involved a provision in the New York Constitution that provided a tax exemption for "real or personal property used exclusively for religious, educational or charitable purposes." The Court upheld the law because of the breadth of the exemption, which included "a broad class of property owned by nonprofit, quasi-public corporations which include hospitals, libraries, playgrounds, scientific, professional, historical, and patriotic groups."[72] *Walz* thus suggests that religious exemptions are permissible if the exemptions are part of a broader class.[73] I will refer to this rule as the "breadth principle."

What is the basis of the breadth principle, and just what does it require? There are two possible interpretations of the principle. Neither of them means that government cannot favor religion as such, nor that the New York law was not favoring religion as such.

On the first interpretation, benefits to religion are an incidental effect of a policy that makes no reference whatsoever to religion. The classic example is police and fire protection for churches. Such protection certainly benefits the churches, and may even benefit core religious activities, as when it is given to religious articles that have only religious uses. This interpretation does not, however, describe the law challenged in *Walz*, which benefited religion specifically *as* religion. Some, but not all, property held by religious entities is used for charitable or educational purposes. The New York law exempted from taxation even religious property that served no charitable or educational purpose.[74]

The second interpretation of the principle holds that it is permissible to specifically benefit religion, so long as the benefit to religion is one item on a list that includes nonreligious elements. Justice Rehnquist embraced that reading in *Mueller v. Allen*, in which the Court upheld a tax deduction for parents of parochial school children. The deduction "is only one among many deductions." He noted that deductions could also be taken for medical expenses and charitable contributions.[75]

This reading of the breadth principle makes the principle ridiculously easy to satisfy. Any deduction, no matter how sectarian, can easily be placed on a laundry list with a few others. A statute could exempt from taxation "alpaca farms, Andrew Koppelman's home, and Baptist churches" and satisfy Rehnquist's test. Here we are back to the rubber stamp objection. Why make the state go through this charade? Any test that is so easy to get around is not worth the bother of having in the first place.

On either reading, then, the breadth principle does not help us to understand why the New York law was permissible. Marshall is correct: "The organization in *Walz* received the tax benefit solely because it was a religious institution."[76]

The fact that religion as such had been singled out for benefit in *Walz* was indignantly emphasized by Justice Scalia's dissent in *Texas Monthly v. Bullock*, which invalidated a statute that provided a sales tax exemption only for religious publications. The challenge to the statute in *Walz*, Scalia claimed, "was in all relevant respects identical" to the one in *Texas Monthly*. He derided as "incomprehensibl[e]"[77] the rationale offered in the *Walz* concurrence by Justice Brennan, who also wrote the plurality opinion in *Texas Monthly*, that religious organizations were appropriately favored by the legislature for the secular reason that they "uniquely contribute to the pluralism of American society by their religious activities."[78] The claim was incomprehensible, Scalia argued, "because to favor religion for its 'unique contribution' is to favor religion as religion."[79]

The opinions that made up the majority in *Texas Monthly*, however, do not entail the impermissibility of favoring religion as such, if religion is understood as broadly as I have proposed. Both opinions—I quoted them in the Introduction—emphasized the fact that only theistic publications, but not atheistic or agnostic publications, would receive the benefit of the exemption. Texas's selective support for theism thus impermissibly took a position on a religious question.

The idea that government may favor religion-in-general invites the following objection. Would this not permit direct government subsidies for religious activities as such, so long as these subsidies are available to all religions? Yet it is settled in First Amendment law that such subsidies are impermissible. The answer is that no subsidy could possibly achieve the requisite neutrality among religions. Were government to attempt to *fund* religion-as-such, it would have to pick and choose whom to fund, and this would inevitably lead to discrimination among religions. That is what has happened in regimes that have attempted "evenhanded" funding.[80] But this is not true of other benefits that go to religion, such as tax exemptions. Even with such exemptions in place, Brennan observed, "the church must raise privately every cent that it spends."[81] The state does not decide what proportion of funds will go to which religious groups.

The Boundaries of Establishment: Back to the Secular Purpose Cases

If we look again at the secular purpose cases in light of the endorsement test as I have reformulated it, we end up not far from the law as the Court has declared it.

The anti-Darwinism statute in *Epperson v. Arkansas* endorsed the Christian fundamentalist view that the book of Genesis is literally true. Justice Black, who would have invalidated the statute for vagueness, thought that the law might not be an endorsement of Christianity, but merely an effort to remove from the curriculum a subject "deemed too emotional and controversial for its public schools."[82] But if the secular purpose requirement can be satisfied by legislators' secular desire to mollify their constituents' religious sensibilities, then this exception would swallow the rule. Even a bill establishing a church might in some circumstances be enacted by agnostic legislators hoping to avoid being voted out of office. Once more, the question is not whether the legislators had secular motives, but whether the law itself endorses a religious proposition.

The secular purpose that Justice Rehnquist thought validated the law in *Stone v. Graham* was education: "[T]he Ten Commandments have had a significant impact on the development of secular legal codes of the Western World," and the state could legitimately decide that this "should be placed before its students, with an appropriate statement of the document's secular import."[83] The trouble with this argument is its understatement. The Ten Commandments were not merely "placed before" the students; they were posted in every classroom in every grade, from kindergarten through high school. Probably no other document was so ubiquitous. The document instructed students in "the religious duties of believers: worshipping the Lord God alone, avoiding idolatry, not using the Lord's name in vain, and observing the Sabbath Day."[84] The purpose of the law, plain on its face, was to proclaim a certain idea of religious truth. *Stone* is an easy case, and so is *McCreary v. ACLU*, which presented the Court with similarly incredible claims of secularity.

The plausibility of the state's proffered secular justification is context-dependent. The objective approach to legislative purpose does not confine the Court's attention to the four corners of the statute. The context in which the law was enacted is an objective fact about it, and one that the Court may properly take into account in discerning the law's purpose.[85] Gedicks observes that the states' actions in *Epperson* and *Stone* were so contextually strange that they cannot plausibly be justified in terms of ordinary curricular decision making.[86]

Similarly with the "private" prayer that began the high school football games in *Santa Fe*. The Court was right to "refuse to turn a blind eye to the context in which this policy arose," which "quells any doubt that this policy was implemented with the purpose of endorsing school prayer."[87]

Wallace v. Jaffree is the least defensible of the decisions. This is the secular purpose opinion that relied most heavily upon the legislative history of the law in question—prominently, the postenactment statements of a single legislator. It is never appropriate to rely on such history to find a lack of secular purpose. The Court also relied on objective evidence, such as the addition of the word "prayer" to the statute. There was, however, a persuasive secular reason for this addition: "clarifying that silent, voluntary prayer is not *forbidden* in the public school building."[88] There had been considerable confusion about the meaning of the Court's decisions with respect to school prayer, leading to horror stories that had become familiar by the time the law was enacted.[89]

The question about the role of religion in political decision making turns on a variant of the participation objection.[90] The debate pits the right of religious citizens to participate in politics against the right of religious minorities to be free from religious domination. Because the secular purpose requirement, properly understood, focuses on what government is saying, rather than the process by which decisions are arrived at, the doctrine allows religious participation to any degree, so long as that participation does not produce the forbidden result.

Edwards v. Aguillard is harder to decide than *Epperson* because a benign explanation is possible, though implausible. Any legal distinction will have hard cases at the boundaries, and the secular purpose prong is no exception. Justice Scalia thought that the legislature was entitled to regard creationism as "a collection of educationally valuable scientific data that has been censored from classrooms by an embarrassed scientific establishment," which supported on scientific grounds "the theory that the physical universe and life within it appeared suddenly and have not changed substantially since appearing." Justice Lewis F. Powell Jr. thought it impermissible for state officials "to pick and choose among [scientific theories] for the purpose of promoting a particular religious belief," but it was disputed in this case whether the legislature's purpose was to promote Christianity or to offer what it regarded as the most persuasive scientific information. This debate is not resolvable in abstraction from the facts. Since the purpose of the legislative regime is difficult to discern from the face of the statute, the Court should have allowed evidence to be taken on the secular plausibility of the statute, rather than allowing the matter to be disposed of by a motion for summary judgment before trial.[91]

In cases involving mandated teaching of "creation science" or "intelligent design," the real question before the Court is whether there is a secular purpose that is plausible. The only federal court that has squarely confronted that question is the district court in *Kitzmiller v. Dover Area School District*,[92] which found that "intelligent design" was not a plausible scientific theory, and was therefore a religious view in disguise.

If *Aguillard* was too skeptical of the proffered secular purpose, *McGowan v. Maryland* was too credulous of a secular purpose for Sunday closing laws. These have no plausible secular purpose.[93] These cases show how modest the doctrine really is.

The Rest of the Doctrine

The premise that government may not declare religious truth, the key to the secular purpose doctrine, can also help to resolve difficulties in the rest of religion clause doctrine.

The most important break in American law from earlier traditions of religious persecution is not the law specifically of religious liberty, but that of free speech. Speech, religious or otherwise, may not be restricted on the basis of its viewpoint.[94] Consequently, the state may not punish blasphemy or heresy. So the issues of religious toleration that were once the most urgent and bitter are settled before we even start talking about the religion clauses.

There are also, of course, religion-specific rules. "Neither a state nor the Federal Government can set up a church. Neither can pass laws which aid one religion, aid all religions, or prefer one religion over another."[95] There is today a hotly contested question on the margins, as to whether the state can fund religious activity, so long as the principle that determines who gets the funding is not itself religious.[96] But this marginal case should not make us forget the clear core rule, that government may not support religion qua religion.[97]

Government may not conduct religious exercises, such as official "nonsectarian" prayers and Bible readings, in the public schools.[98] Marginal questions remain here, too: When may student-organized religious groups meet in public schools?[99] Are student-initiated prayers at school events permissible in some circumstances?[100] The answers to these questions are highly context-dependent, so the law in specific circumstances tends to be somewhat unpredictable. But, once more, the rule at the core is clear.

Government—this term refers equally to the federal government, state government, and municipalities—may not burden people, with criminal penalties, taxes, or the loss of employment or licenses, for their religious beliefs.[101] Nor may it discriminate against religious conduct; it "cannot in a selective manner impose burdens only on conduct motivated by religious belief."[102] (There is, however, a controversial question, which I'll take up below, whether government may, or even is required to, exclude religion from certain funding programs.) The state may not engage in speech that endorses a particular religion, or religion generally.[103]

Government may not discriminate among religions.[104] It may not discriminate against nonreligious people, for example by requiring an officeholder to profess belief in God.[105] The Constitution bars such tests for federal offices,[106] and the prohibition has been extended to the states.

Government also may not decide whether any particular religious doctrine makes sense, is internally consistent, is true (e.g., in a fraud prosecution for making false statements in order to solicit money), is central to a particular religion, or is consistent with the tenets of a group's faith. The state may not attempt to determine the "truth or falsity" of religious claims;[107] courts may not try to resolve "controversies over religious doctrine and practice," may not undertake "interpretation of particular church doctrines and the importance of those doctrines to the religion,"[108] may make "no inquiry into religious doctrine,"[109] and may give "no consideration of doctrinal matters, whether the ritual and liturgy of worship or the tenets of faith."[110] The truth or falsity of religious doctrine is "a forbidden domain."[111]

Government may not delegate certain kinds of government power to religious institutions. For example, it may not give churches the right to veto certain land uses by neighbors, such as the sale of liquor.[112]

These rules of disestablishment follow easily from the premise of religion-friendly neutrality. If the state may not declare religious truth, or take sides in live theological controversies, then of course it cannot persecute blasphemy or heresy. Any kind of religious coercion is barred. Government may not discriminate among religions, or burden people for their religious beliefs, or delegate political decisions to religious institutions. All of these would involve the deployment of state power based on official answers to religious questions.

The Establishment Clause is also a restriction on government speech. School prayers are obviously impermissible. Either the state would have to decide which religion's prayers to use, or it would have to devise its own official religion by composing its own prayers.

Endorsement

It is because government speech endorsing religious propositions is barred that so much litigation turns on whether a given instance of religious speech is attributable to government or to private actors. Courts have held that when private actors exercise their free speech rights in a public forum such as a park, the Establishment Clause is not violated. But they have also asked, is the claim that the speech is "private" a sham? For example, "student-initiated" prayers at high school football games can turn out to be barely disguised official exercises.[113] Here as in many areas, the inquiry is fact-specific, but the inquiry is oriented by a coherent question: is the state taking an official line on a religious proposition?

The inevitableness of this inquiry becomes clear when we consider its principal rival, the "coercion" test proposed by Justice Kennedy.

Kennedy reads the establishment clause to mean that "a government may not coerce anyone to support or participate in religion or its exercise."[114] However, he has a remarkably broad understanding of what counts as coercion—encompassing, for example, "the permanent erection of a large Latin cross on the roof of city hall."[115] He later held that the psychological pressure on a student to attend high school graduation could count as coercion,[116] and suggested that symbols that "promote a Christian message" or "set the *imprimatur* of the state on a particular creed" are unconstitutional.[117] Evidently he is increasingly drawn to an inquiry into the social meaning of state action.[118]

Institutional Separation

The law also includes rules of church autonomy, which prevent the state from interfering with matters of internal church governance. For cases involving disputes within religious organizations, the Court has had to craft special rules, distinct from those governing other controversies. At English common law, if issues of religious doctrine arose in disputes over contract obligations, tort claims, criminal fraud charges, or the administration of a trust, the courts would resolve those issues. Most notably, property contributed to a religious body by a member would bear an implied trust in favor of the fundamental doctrines of that religious body, and in a dispute would be awarded to the group most faithful to those doctrines.[119] The Supreme Court has repudiated that approach. In this and other contexts, the Court gives more deference to the decisions of church tribunals than it would give to similarly situated secular bodies.[120] The Court has also held that employment legislation must have a "ministerial exception," protecting the right of religious groups to select their leaders without state interference.[121]

This doctrine has elicited the objection that it is incoherent as applied to actual practice, since government in fact constantly makes religious judgments, notably when deciding who is entitled to a religious accommodation, or who the relevant religious tribunal is.[122] The rule is even self-contradictory, because it requires courts to decide which controversies are religious and thus beyond the state's cognizance. Because the rule can't be applied consistently, it allegedly is applied inconsistently and arbitrarily.[123] The incoherence disappears if we understand that government is permitted to declare that religion is a good thing and to support it generically, but not to make any further religious determinations. In order to avoid corrupting religion, government must determine whether this or that is a specimen of what it is staying away from. But it must stop there and make no finer distinctions among religions.

Hard Cases: Accommodation and Funding

Two large questions about the religion clauses are central axes of controversy, in both the Court and the academy: (1) Does the state have a constitutional obligation to accommodate religious objections to generally applicable laws? (2) Can religion receive financial support from the state, so long as the criterion for allocating that support is itself religion-neutral? The analysis offered in this book will not resolve those divisions. What it can do is highlight the areas of agreement that are the background of these disputes. (It also makes clear the limits of religion neutrality as a basis for insulating programs from establishment clause challenge, as I shall shortly explain.) Those areas of agreement support the claim I have offered here, that American law presupposes the goodness of religion, understood very abstractly.

It should be clear, though it is not often noted, that common ground underlies the debate about religious accommodation. For several decades, the Court held that states had a constitutional obligation to accommodate conscientious objectors from generally applicable laws. Then it abandoned that view. But it continues to hold that such accommodations are permissible when they are made by legislatures. The division over whether accommodations are properly crafted by legislatures or by courts distracts attention from the consensus that it is appropriate for *someone* to do it. Given the Establishment Clause, however, how can there be religion-specific accommodation at all? The argument here offers an answer: such accommodation is a permissible way of recognizing the good of religion, so long as it does not discriminate among religions.

Our response also makes clear how there can be hard cases, and why the existence of hard cases doesn't show that the basic enterprise is mistaken. Once it is acknowledged that the law treats religion as a good thing, then we can see that the task of accommodation is essentially that of balancing the good of religion against other goods. Sometimes this will be difficult. *Wisconsin v. Yoder*[124] presented the question of whether the Old Order Amish could remove their children from high school. The answer turns on how important those years of high school are, and reasonable people disagree on that question. It is possible to compile horror stories in which far too much weight is given to the religious claim, and legitimate secular interests are unreasonably overridden. Church-run day care centers have been exempted from safety requirements.[125] But this shows only that the balance has been gotten wrong in particular cases.

The right to religious accommodation is a peculiar kind of right. It is sometimes suggested that it is in the nature of rights that they are trumps against the ordinary weighing of costs against benefits.[126] But a right to free exercise, if it includes any right to accommodation, can only be a right to a certain kind of weighing, in which religion is treated as a good that should be allowed to be pursued in specific cases unless the marginal cost is too high.[127] The right is a right to have that marginal cost considered in individual cases—a favor that is not done for most of those who object to obeying particular laws.

The argument for giving these judgments to the judiciary is that courts hear cases one at a time and so are confronted, as legislatures are not, with concrete situations. Courts are also committed to treat like cases alike. Legislatures often overlook the impact of rules on minority religious groups. If those groups are able to go to court, even with the support of a rule as vague as the so-called "compelling interest" test, they will often prevail.[128]

The regime we now have in most of the United States is one in which courts are instructed by legislatures to balance on a case-by-case basis, but the results that courts reach can be revisited and overridden by legislatures. Eugene Volokh has observed that this result plays to the strengths of both courts and legislatures. Courts get to decide, in the first instance, what to do in concrete instances of hardship. But the ultimate tough calls are governed by the political process. The result is not all that different from the common-law regimes that already govern issues of property, contract, and tort, where courts craft rules in response to specific disputes, but legislatures have the last word.[129] This is not a bad place to end up.[130]

Now consider the funding question. The Court for many years took the "no aid" position that any financial support for a religious institution—most often in litigation, a religious school—was unconstitutional. Such aid, the Court reasoned, will cause division among religious groups competing for limited public funds. It also reasoned that taxpayers' liberty is violated when they are compelled to support religions with which they disagree. More recent decisions have upheld such aid when it is part of a general program that is available to nonreligious recipients as well. The Court has specifically approved "private choice" programs, such as school vouchers, in which aid is given to individuals who can then choose the institution, secular or religious, where they will use it. Proponents of "private choice" argue that it is improperly discriminatory to deny support for services that have secular value just because they are also religious. Justices Thomas, Scalia, and Kennedy have argued that, so long as the criterion for funding is religion-neutral, a program should be immune from constitutional challenge. Justice O'Connor was not satisfied with this, and insisted that a program also provide genuine nonreligious options. She also thought that aid provided directly by government to religious entities may not be used for religious indoctrination, and that government must monitor the aid to make sure that it is not diverted to such uses. But she has retired from the Court.

The value of religion is common ground on both sides of this debate. So is the idea that some prophylactic constraints on funding are necessary: even the judges, such as Rehnquist and Scalia, who would permit support for religion-in-general (understood as meaning theism) think that funding for religious activity must be given under a description that is religiously neutral. Even if government may support religion in an evenhanded way, funding presents such a danger of discrimination among religions that additional safeguards are necessary. This judgment is eminently sensible: if the allocation of scarce resources is going to depend on a state determination that this or that claimant qualifies as a religion, then it is hard to see how such discrimination could be avoided.

The "no-aid" view, as we saw in the discussion of Justice Black in Chapter 2, is motivated by the concern that state support can corrupt religion. The "private choice" view is motivated by the idea that the "no-aid" view is unnecessarily restrictive; it claims that religion will not be corrupted by equal access to state support, and that vouchers are good for religious liberty because they maximize educational choice. The two views are divided by different accounts of the likely consequences of generally available support. They agree about which consequences matter.

It is perhaps because judgments about this question turn on contestable predictions of consequences that, although the Court has abandoned the "no aid" view as an Establishment Clause requirement, it continues to allow the states to adopt that requirement in interpreting their own bans on establishment.[131]

The weakness of the secular purpose requirement, which we have already examined, shows the inadequacy of Justice Thomas's view that formal neutrality toward religion insulates funding from challenge. That view has not yet prevailed, although it may be getting close. Recall that the rubber stamp objection *almost* succeeds. The secular purpose requirement is an exceedingly weak constraint, one that will hardly ever be violated. (Thomas has not explained how it can make sense both to scrap the secular purpose requirement and to make it a safe harbor for funding religious activity.) If formal neutrality becomes the sole requirement of the Establishment Clause, then that provision could be practically nullified, and state-authorized religious coercion could be the result.

The danger was made manifest in an Iowa "faith-based" prison program, described in detail in Winnifred Fallers Sullivan's book *Prison Religion*. The program, which was successfully challenged in federal court, egregiously violated the Establishment Clause. Prisoners were told that, if they professed Evangelical Christian beliefs and allowed their families to be proselytized, they would get better living conditions within prison. Many were also led to think they would have a greater likelihood of early release. Inmates unwilling to so profess stayed out of the program and so forfeited its benefits. Yet this result came about through a process in which the state made no religious decisions, acted on the basis of generally applicable laws that were facially religion-neutral, and pursued indisputably valid secular purposes at every stage of the process.

Iowa, like every other state, has in recent decades enormously increased its prison population, from 2,650 inmates in 1983 to more than 8,500 in 2006. (The United States incarcerates more than 3 percent of its population, the highest per capita rate in the world.) Ninety percent of Iowa prisoners have substance abuse problems, and 30 percent suffer from mental health problems. Drug abuse and mental health services in Iowa prisons are grossly understaffed and under-funded. The Newton facility, built in 1997, was "value-engineered"—a euphemism for lowering building standards—to hold down costs. One wing, Unit E, was built with wooden cell doors rather than metal ones, and common toilet facilities instead of in-cell ones. It was initially used as an honor dorm for prisoners with good disciplinary records. There was almost no space for programs.[132] This created a huge prob-lem for administrators. As Department of Corrections director Walter Kautzky testified in a deposition,

> We were, as a practical matter, looking for anybody that might help us put these offenders into some sort of productive activities. We were look-ing for a way, a very low-cost way, to utilize and put some activities in place within a very, very large, and very, very new prison where there were literally no activities. There was no space for education. There was a small library with a law library squashed into it, and there were a couple of very small rooms, and beyond that, there was almost nothing for these 750 folks to do.[133]

He was intrigued by what he had heard about an in-prison, faith-based program in Texas, which had improved inmates' behavior and reduced rates of recidivism.[134] One attraction of that program was that it was privately funded and staffed by volunteers. It was clear that no addi-tional funding would come from the state of Iowa. The state solicited proposals for an in-prison program. The solicitation did not require that the program be religious, but the only bidder that met the state's requirements was the InnerChange Freedom Initiative (IFI), which ran the Texas program.

The IFI program, known within the prison as "the God Pod," is an intensive Bible-based, Christ-centered communal living course that aims at personal transformation. It regimented prisoners' behavior every hour of the day. It required that prisoners "must volunteer for the program being fully aware of the . . . Christ-centered, biblically based curriculum." The contract with the state provided that IFI could unilaterally expel prisoners who, in its judgment, were not progressing satisfactorily.[135]

Participants received a number of secular benefits, including more frequent contact with the prisoner's family, support in dealing with the parole board (which, it was made clear to prisoners, looked favorably on participation), and assistance after release. It also offered immediate material rewards: it took over the desirable facilities of Unit E of the Newton prison (and expelled the prisoners who were already housed there, one of whom objected to participation in the program because he was Catholic). Only participants in the program would have the benefit of a music room and computers, and substance abuse and anger management classes. The program's location in Newton prison was also an attraction for many prisoners, since it was closer than other state prisons to Des Moines, where many prisoners' families lived. Another comparative advantage of the program was that funds for programs in other prisons, such as libraries and gyms, were cut and diverted to the IFI program.[136]

The program was explicitly religious. Prisoners were "immersed in a world of Bible verses and Bible stories." Inmates were tested on their knowledge of the Bible and personal responses to such questions as "What does Jesus mean to you?" and "What has changed now that you have become a Christian?" Many participants testified that they felt pressured to become Christians. Not attending worship services could be grounds for dismissal from the program. Prisoners were given family visits in addition to those normally allowed under prison policy; IFI used these visits to evangelize the prisoner's family. In short, the program empowered IFI "to rely on state structures of authority to enforce the discipline of their utopian Christian community."[137]

The Christianity being propounded was specifically that of evangelical Protestantism. Instructional literature for the IFI substance abuse program states that "only JC [Jesus Christ] is a cure for addiction," and it calls on participants to renounce false religions, including Christian Science, Mormonism, Unitarianism, Buddhism, Hinduism, and Islam. At trial, the judge found that, although the Iowa prison system has no policy position about homosexuality, the program "indoctrinates inmates in the belief that homosexuality is morally wrong and profoundly sinful." Sullivan concludes that the program is, "from an objective historical and social scientific perspective, the very model of evangelical Protestant proselytization because it teaches that sin is at the root of all problems and that healing comes through a relationship with Jesus Christ."[138]

The evangelical Protestant orientation of the program was a serious problem for prisoners who were Jewish, Catholic, Mormon, Muslim, Native American, or Lutheran.[139] A Jewish prisoner said that a Jewish version of the program would have been helpful to him, but that he was unwilling to participate because he could not pray to Jesus Christ. A participant's request to invite a Catholic priest to offer Mass was rebuffed on the ground that the intensive twenty-four-hour program could not spare the time. A Native American was told at his evaluation that the sweat lodge ritual "was basically a form of witchcraft" and that "I'm worshipping false idols out there." Even some Protestants had difficulties: one Lutheran prisoner was uncomfortable with the Pentecostal style of worship.[140]

The federal courts had no difficulty, under present doctrine, invalidating the program.[141] But suppose that the rule was simply that any state action is valid so long as it has a secular purpose and does not classify on the basis of religion. The IFI program satisfies both of these requirements, even though it has the power to impose severe sanctions on those who will not profess their agreement with its religious creed.

The benefits of the IFI program, Sullivan concludes, stem from characteristics that could be provided on secular terms: "selectivity in admissions, intense staff involvement with prisoners, residential community support, and close mentoring during and after the in-prison portion of the program."[142] In light of the Iowa legislature's unwillingness to fund those services, however, prison administrators acted quite reasonably in inviting IFI into the prison.

The IFI program's state-sponsored religious indoctrination shows the dangerous implications of the approach to religious liberty that the Supreme Court is moving toward. The program satisfies the requirements laid down by the four-judge plurality opinion of Justice Thomas in *Mitchell v. Helms*. The solicitation for bids offered funding "to a broad range of groups or persons without regard to their religion." The money was distributed "pursuant to neutral eligibility criteria": as it happened, only IFI's bid met the parameters set forth by the state. The state's program does not "define its recipients by reference to religion," and does not "create a financial incentive to undertake religious indoctrination." The *Mitchell* plurality claimed that if the aid itself lacks religious content, "and eligibility for aid is determined in a constitutionally permissible manner, any use of that aid to indoctrinate cannot be attributed to the government and is thus not of constitutional concern."[143]

The same logic would apply if the state were to delegate any of its other functions to private contractors, and those contractors were to impose religious requirements on the recipient of the services. Fire services could be delegated to a low-bidding Christian fire department that would provide services only to recipients who would acknowledge the divinity of Christ in the call for help. All this would follow from the abandonment of Justice O'Connor's insistence that any funding program create genuine nonreligious options and that direct funding be monitored to assure it is not used for religious indoctrination.

O'Connor's formulation contains a crucial ambiguity about its scope. Some activities in civil society will be available only in religious forms without raising any problem of religious imposition: we are not much troubled if the only bingo game in town is at the Methodist church. The IFI program, on the other hand, involves the most extreme site of state coercion, the prison. Schools are somewhere in the middle: going to school isn't optional, so if there are no nonreligious options, religious coercion would be inevitable. But O'Connor's logic rests on the assumption that education of children will continue to be mandatory and a baseline function of the state. Other forms of welfare provision are less secure. There is no guarantee that there will be any funding at all for drug treatment, assistance for the disabled and mentally ill, or medical care for the indigent. These services are unlike bingo in that, if they are made available, no one can reasonably be expected to refuse them if they are offered on almost any terms. If these functions are devolved to private actors, and these actors all turn out to be religious and to impose religious requirements on their beneficiaries, then religious coercion is, once more, inevitable. The question then will be whether this coercion is attributable to the state that brought it about by privatizing these services.

The tendency to privatize in-prison rehabilitation is in keeping with the growing vogue of libertarianism in American politics, a subject far beyond the scope of this book. Libertarianism aims to shrink the domain of state power, leaving citizens to make the best deals they can with one another, given the resources they happen to have. Samuel Freeman has observed that this vision of a just society is not liberalism, but rather resembles its ancient adversary feudalism, in which parties trade their allegiance for protection by the powerful.[144] In libertarianism, the idea of a common good, understood as the freedom of each individual to pursue his own freely adopted conception of the good so long as it is consistent with justice, disappears. The Iowa prison program shows that the delegation of state power to private entities, with no attention to whether nonreligious options exist, tends to abandon a regime of religious liberty in favor of something like the Peace of Augsburg of 1555: everyone is obligated to manifest adherence to the religious views of their own local lord or baron. Iowa abandoned its own responsibility to provide rehabilitative services to prisoners, then placed them in the hands of IFI, where they would have to live with whatever religious impositions the program saw fit to impose.

Was O'Connor right? If genuine nonreligious options matter, why do they matter?

The problem begins with the ambiguity of the religion clauses of the Constitution. It is impossible to read any clear rule out of "Congress shall make no law respecting an establishment of religion, or abridging the free exercise thereof." Most pertinently here, is the restriction on the state's power over religion there only to prevent deliberate state manipulation of religion, or does impact count? In particular, is a constitutional issue raised if government makes a facially neutral decision that has the consequence of bringing it about that some people are coerced to engage in religious rituals? That is what O'Connor's genuine nonreligious options requirement is concerned about. O'Connor fears that a voucher program might altogether displace public schools, so that parents would have no choice but to send their children to a school that teaches religious doctrines that they reject. Would that violate the Constitution, as O'Connor believes?

Thomas proposes a hybrid between the requirement that a law have a secular legislative purpose and the requirement that a law be religion-blind. The secular purpose requirement here amounts to something like what the Court imposed in *Griffin v. County School Board of Prince Edward County*,[145] a desegregation case which invalidated a county's decision to close all its public schools and provide vouchers to attend private schools. The consequence of that decision was that for years, white children attended private academies while black children got no education at all. The case did not hold that there was an obligation to provide public education. Rather, the closing was invalidated because of its impermissible, racially discriminatory purpose.

If this is the rule, then it would be violated only if a school district were to adopt vouchers and close its public schools solely for the purpose of forcing nonadherents to receive religious indoctrination. The state has no general obligation to provide public education, or to provide education at all beyond "basic minimal skills."[146] It is possible that a voucher program could be adopted for this purpose. O'Connor might even be proposing her test for prophylactic reasons, to prevent this from happening.

O'Connor's rule assumes the legitimacy of the status quo that existed before a voucher program was put in place. On day 1, there is no religious coercion; on day 2, the state changes its law; on day 3, there is religious coercion. A shift in the status quo that produces this state of affairs means that the state is at least causally responsible for that state of affairs. But why privilege the status quo in this way? As critics of the public/private distinction have emphasized for a long time, the state is in some sense causally responsible for anything that happens in its jurisdiction. That doesn't mean that everything that happens is state action, subject to constitutional constraints.

Some justifications for making impact relevant are familiar from the race context. One is that impact is sometimes a good proxy for bad intent. (That would be one reason to privilege the status quo ante.) Another is that selective sympathy and indifference are themselves a violation of the equal concern that government owes all its citizens. A third is that patterns of subordination perpetuate the underlying problem of pervasive prejudice that engenders both public and private discrimination.[147] All of these make a good deal of sense, but the Court has been reluctant to make any of them the basis of constitutional doctrine. As a general matter, disparate racial impact raises no constitutional issue.[148]

In the religion context, however, there is another consideration with no analogue to the race case: the idea that free exercise is inconsistent with practices that coerce people to follow specific favored religions. This burden is different in kind, and more objectionable, than ordinary burdens on free exercise, such as the ban on marijuana use for Rastafarians. Such prohibitions leave the person free to reconcile the law's demands with his religion on any terms he likes. Typically adherents have modified their interpretations of their own religion's commands: Mormons no longer regard polygamy as a religious obligation, but they were not required to abandon Mormonism for some other religion.

What worries O'Connor, on the other hand, is coercion toward, rather than away from, a specific religious viewpoint. Such coercion is perhaps the paradigmatic violation of religious liberty, at the heart of what the Free Exercise Clause prohibits. It may not be state-dictated religion, but shares its pernicious qualities. And, of course, the coercion in question will indeed be state-dictated religion if, as will sometimes be the case, a jurisdiction adopting vouchers intends this result (or makes clear that it anticipates it—for example, if its declared rationale for vouchers is that its public schools are no good).

A major obstacle to O'Connor's approach is the Court's reluctance, and not just in race cases, to make impact matter in adjudication, or to place affirmative, judicially enforceable obligations on the state. Only one provision in the Constitution, the Thirteenth Amendment's prohibition of slavery, prohibits a state of affairs from being permitted to exist in the United States. The Court has repeatedly held that there is no obligation to protect individuals, even from violence, if the harm comes from nonstate actors.[149]

In those cases, however, the Court was clearly influenced by institutional worries about the competence of the courts to address a problem that different states might legitimately want to address in different ways.[150] There is no reason to think that the states cannot be trusted to protect their own citizens from private violence, and some reason to doubt that judicial intervention will make anyone safer. Here, on the other hand, the problem is oppression of religious minorities, oppression that takes the form of religious coercion. The normal political process cannot be trusted to reach the right result in such cases.

The question comes down to the importance of religious liberty, and specifically of the liberty not to be coerced to engage in religious rituals in which one does not believe. Such coercion was regarded as a central evil that disestablishment aimed to prevent. Coerced religion is insincere religion, and insincere religion is corrupt religion. One question that the present doctrinal structure leaves open is whether a constitutional concern is raised if the state acts in a way that brings it about, even if it does so through a scheme that is religiously neutral. Another is whether impact can ever be probative of impermissible purpose. Thomas thinks it can in the context of racial impact.[151] He has not explained why it could never be so in the context of religious coercion.

A FINAL AREA in which our analysis has clear implications is the question of standing to litigate. Who can file suit to enforce the Establishment Clause if the state violates it?

The disestablishment of religion is a structural part of the regime, not a matter of individual rights. This has implications for the appropriate role of the judiciary. A guiding principle, in constitutional interpretation generally, is that the Constitution should not be construed in a way that defeats its basic purposes.[152] Unlike other structural aspects of constitutional law, such as federalism and separation of powers within the federal government, there is no reason to think that this structure will be self-maintaining without judicial involvement. In contests between the states and the federal government, or between Congress and the president, each of the institutional sides has plenty of ability and incentive to preserve its place in the constitutional scheme.[153] With disestablishment, on the other hand, if individuals are not empowered to file suits, there is likely to be no enforcement of the constitutional provisions at all.

So the rules of standing appropriately include "taxpayer standing" to challenge state expenditures for religious purposes. The Supreme Court restricted this rule, in a way that really does make it incoherent, in *Hein v. Freedom from Religion Foundation*[154] and *Arizona Christian School Tuition Organization v. Winn.*[155] In *Hein*, Justice Samuel Alito, for a three-judge plurality, held that taxpayers have no standing to challenge executive (as contrasted with legislative) action that violates the religion clauses. The other six judges rejected this distinction. Justices Scalia and Thomas wanted to abandon taxpayer standing altogether, while four dissenters thought that there should be taxpayer standing in all such cases.

The upshot of the rule proposed by the plurality in *Hein*, Ira Lupu and Robert Tuttle have observed, is a perverse "justiciability-driven incentive to legislative silence":[156] the legislature can insulate its support for religious activities from judicial challenge just by giving the executive broad discretion that can be used to violate the Establishment Clause.

In *Arizona Christian School Tuition Organization*, Justice Kennedy, writing for the majority, held that there is no standing to challenge a tax credit for contributions to religious schools. The basis of taxpayer standing, Kennedy thought, was the injury individuals suffer when their property is transferred to a sectarian entity. There is no such injury when other taxpayers are able to reallocate their own funds from their tax bill to such an entity. This is in keeping with Kennedy's deeply individualistic vision of disestablishment as centrally concerned with preventing coercion of individuals—understood broadly, as evidenced by his invalidation of a graduation prayer in *Lee v. Weisman*, but harm to individuals nonetheless. Unless a law "disadvantages a particular religious group or a particular nonreligious group,"[157] no violation of the Clause demands a judicial remedy.

Justice Elena Kagan observed that the tax credit is the functional equivalent of a subsidy, and that the Court's decision allows the state to allocate funds for specifically religious purposes—in this case, to schools that use religious tests for admissions and scholarships. The very subsidy that Madison attacked in the *Memorial and Remonstrance* would be immune to judicial challenge on the majority's theory.[158]

The majorities in these cases disagreed about some important matters, but what they had in common, evidently, was that they don't like the Establishment Clause and don't want to enforce it. This is a poor basis for constitutional adjudication. Whatever one might say on behalf of the revolution they propose, it would not make the law of religious freedom more coherent. It would just make it weaker and easier to violate.

— 4 —

Why Single Out Religion?

American law treats religion, specified very vaguely, as a good thing. Should it? Some argue, with Christopher Hitchens, that "religion poisons everything."[1] If this is right, then American law is perverse, treating as a good something that is malign.

Our question is not whether religion, generically, is good. That question is profoundly unanswerable. In societies in which religious understanding and practice are implicated in most if not all of social life, such as ancient Sumerians or modern Brooklyn Hasidim, there *is* no secular world that stands apart from the transcendent cosmic order.[2] For those who live in such a framework, life without religion is no more possible than life without carbon atoms. Their religion gives them a language and practices that make sense of their lives, but can also be a source of pain and confusion that make difficult lives worse; these effects cannot be disentangled.[3]

Our question is whether, in the United States, it is appropriate for the state to treat religion as if it is good. The basis for doing so is in part the peculiar nature of the religion-based claims that find their way to the courts *here*.

By the time any claim does that, it has passed through two filters that inevitably eliminate many religious forms. The first is that the most toxic kinds of religion cannot exist on American soil: because they cannot obey the basic rules of criminal law, they must change or die. The other (which is in part a consequence of the first) is that most manifestations of religion in the United States generate no legal or political claims.

Some religious beliefs are obviously bad, both in themselves and specifically for a free society. Early liberalism had to do a job on religion in order to make it into something that could exist in a liberal state. For instance, the now neglected second half of Hobbes's *Leviathan* tried to show that Christianity, properly understood, did not require religious wars and persecutions. Hobbes's project has been a huge success. The kind of destructive religion that he worried about is nearly extinct in the contemporary United States.[4] Any religious group that tried, for example, to violently crush nonadherents would itself quickly be crushed.[5]

And then there is the second filter. American law is concerned only with the goodness of that subset of religion that is protected from corruption by the Establishment Clause, or is the basis of valid free exercise claims. Religions that demand state enforcement are not treated as good by the American regime. Most religious activity violates no law and so receives no judicial attention, positive or negative. The law must decide only which (if any) state entanglements with religion ought to be avoided, and which (if any) religious claims the state should, can, or must accommodate. With respect to establishment, our question is whether religion is likely to be better if it is not (or, if you prefer, worse if it is) linked to the power of the state. With respect to free exercise, our question is whether the practice of accommodating religious claims is likely to make people's lives better.

So why should we think that religion (even thus filtered) deserves this kind of solicitude? Why think that it plays a good role in people's lives?

There are two kinds of answer. One assumes arguendo that the religious beliefs in question are mistaken, and then asks whether they nonetheless have value. The other makes no such assumption.

The basic social function of religion, Peter Berger observed long ago, is one of a distinctive kind of legitimation. It gives people's lives and social roles an ultimate ontological status, giving them a cosmic, sacred frame of reference that can be the source of "an ultimate sense of rightness, both cognitively and normatively."[6] This way of putting matters sounds conservative, but the point applies equally to the roles of social critic, reformer, and revolutionary.

One may object that this is epistemically culpable: There is no basis for any confidence that anything in the world ultimately is validated by a transcendent frame of reference. We just have to learn to live without any ultimate sense of rightness. But this is also a kind of faith: there is no basis for confidence in the *rejection* of a transcendent frame of reference, either. The old agnostic point, that a finite being cannot know an infinite one, cuts both ways. How can you *know* that there is no transcendent frame?[7] What epistemic warrant is there for that bold claim? It is likewise possible to be a strong religious adherent while fully acknowledging one's lack of epistemic certainty.[8]

What is really indispensable is hope.[9] There is no epistemic warrant to assert with confidence that the religious person's hope is groundless. If this is true—and the arguments for agnosticism are familiar—then the insistence upon the contrary is itself a culpably false belief. Hope, by definition, involves an absence of sufficient evidence. It is not necessarily connected to acceptance of propositions.

We know that religion is not indispensable to intelligibility: many individuals, and even a few national cultures, function perfectly well without it.[10] But the ability to do without religion is a late and peculiar historical formation. Modern humanism is itself shot through with quasi-religious longings and even rituals.[11] For many people, liberation from their religious beliefs would produce only anomie and despair. The avoidance of such states is an appropriate object of positive appraisal. So is the capacity to articulate at least some of the enormous range of elans and experiences that resist expression in secular discourse.[12]

For many people, hope takes a religious form, and it would be hard for them to imagine it in any other way. A crucial episode in the career of Martin Luther King Jr. offers an illustration. During the Montgomery Bus Boycott, a series of death threats had left him demoralized. "I was ready to give up," he recalled later. Sitting in the kitchen, unable to sleep after a threatening phone call, he began trying to think of how he could pass the leadership of the desegregation movement on to someone else.

> Now of course I was religious, I grew up in the church. I'm the son of a preacher . . . my grandfather was a preacher, my great-grandfather was a preacher, my only brother is a preacher, my daddy's brother is a preacher, so I didn't have much choice, I guess. But I had grown up in the church, and the church meant something very real to me, but it was a kind of inherited religion and I had never felt an experience with God in the way that you must, and have it, if you're going to walk the lonely paths of this life.

Thinking about the danger to his family, King found himself praying out loud: "Lord, I'm down here trying to do what is right. I think I'm right. I am here taking a stand for what I believe is right. But Lord, I must confess that I'm weak now, I'm faltering. I'm losing my courage." And, he recalled, "it seemed to me at that moment that I could hear an inner voice saying to me, 'Martin Luther, stand up for righteousness. Stand up for justice. Stand up for truth. And lo I will be with you, even until the end of the world.'" Almost immediately, "my fears began to go." The basis for this new courage was a direct, felt connection with Christ: "I heard the voice of Jesus saying still to fight on. He promised never to leave me, never to leave me alone. No never alone. No never alone. He promised never to leave me, never to leave me alone."[13]

King persisted in his civil rights advocacy. It made him into the closest thing to a secular saint that twentieth-century America produced.

Perhaps King could have arrived in the same place on the basis of purely nonreligious considerations. Some have. But to do that, he would have to change in so many ways that it is hard to imagine what he would then look like. Martin Luther Kings don't turn up that often, so I'm not inclined to tinker with the ones we have.[14]

Nor is King unique. Many of the most progressive movements in American government, from abolitionism through the civil rights movement, have been grounded in religious considerations. Today, religion is a powerful constraint on the tendencies toward economic and political inequality in contemporary America. Religious organizations tend to foster civic and political participation and skills, particularly among the less wealthy. Religious affiliation also correlates with voting rates. The effects are particularly striking among African Americans, whose churches are more effective than white churches in educating and mobilizing members. American churches also provide social services that mitigate material inequalities, such as soup kitchens, homeless shelters, shelters for victims of domestic violence, and medical and dental clinics and hospitals. The experience of volunteering for such institutions may itself have a politicizing effect.[15]

Surveys of religious individuals further document the secular benefits of religion. Religious people are more likely to do volunteer work; more likely to contribute their money to charity; more likely to be involved in their communities. They are also happier.[16]

Thus far we have considered only the secular benefits of religion—goods that are manifest even if one stipulates that there is no transcendent reality and that religion is bunk. King's hopes did a lot of secular good, but they also got him killed. Were his hopes deluded? Was he a fool or a sucker?

Paul Horwitz has argued that agnosticism, the suspension of onto-logical commitments, can provide "a sense of openness to other per-spectives," a view that is "pregnant with possibility: an open space from which he can attempt to occupy, as best he can, the perspectives of oth-ers on questions of religious truth." From this standpoint, cultivating "the imaginative, empathetic adoption of a dizzying array of *different* viewpoints,"[17] a multitude of transcendent goods appear as possibili-ties, and the pursuit of those goods appears as not only intelligible, but admirable. Openness to the possibility that these goods are real is yet another reason to think that the state is promoting its citizens' well-being when it treats religion as a good.

"Religion," then, denotes a cluster of goods, including salvation (if you think you need to be saved), harmony with the transcendent ori-gin of universal order (if it exists),[18] responding to the fundamentally imperfect character of human life (if it is imperfect),[19] courage in the face of the heartbreaking aspects of human existence (if that kind of encouragement helps),[20] a transcendent underpinning for the resolu-tion to act morally (if that kind of underpinning helps),[21] contact with that which is awesome and indescribable (if awe is something you feel),[22] and many others.

Objections

Objections to American law's singling out of religion come from two directions. One view is that the law is too secular. The state ought to be able to endorse religious ideas that many citizens share: there should be prayer in schools, official religious ceremonies, perhaps even more spe-cific endorsement of, say, Christianity. The entire book up to this point has addressed this claim. The idea that religion flourishes absent state support should by now be familiar. Those who are eager to live in a reli-gion-friendly nation should reflect on the evidence that the regime they are attacking already gives them what they want. If the claim is that the Establishment Clause should be interpreted in a way that allows more local control over religious matters, this is a judgment about the substantive scope of the clause that must be defended on its merits. The most prominent formulations of this claim have ignored the corruption concern.[23]

Most of the philosophical literature attacks the regime from a different direction: claiming that the separation of church and state in America is too *weak*, that the regime should not be treating religion as a good at all. (This may have something to do with the fact that academic philosophy departments are dominated by liberal secularists.) This would rule out any significance for the corruption argument, which presumes religion as a value that needs protection from state interference. There are four principal ways in which this claim has been made.

The first objection is that there is nothing valuable about religion as such: that religion fails to conform to rational standards of evidence, and that any value associated with it is not captured by the semantic category of "religion."

The second objection is that this value is appropriately redescribed in nonreligious terms. Of the substitute terms that have been offered, the most prominent is "conscience."

The third objection is that the goodness of religion is too controversial to be an appropriate basis of political (much less judicial) decision in a diverse society.

The fourth objection stipulates that religion is good, but claims that it is unfair to privilege it over other, equally valuable human concerns.

Is Religion Valuable?

The first objection, that religion per se is not valuable, has been formulated in different ways by Brian Leiter and Timothy Macklem.

Leiter

An objection to the goodness of religion much like Hitchens's has been made succinctly in two papers by Brian Leiter,[24] who argues that there is no good reason for law to single out religion for special treatment, and that religion is not an apt candidate for respect in the "thick" sense of being an object of favorable appraisal. Special treatment would be appropriate only if there were some "moral reason why states should carve out special protections that encourage individuals to structure their lives around categorical demands that are insulated from the standards of evidence and reasoning we everywhere else expect to constitute constraints on judgment and action."[25] Favorable appraisal would be called for "[o]nly if there were a *positive* correlation between beliefs that were *culpably without epistemic warrant* and valuable outcomes."[26]

Leiter's concern about beliefs that lack epistemic warrant is understandable. Sometimes[27] religion leads people to believe things that are manifestly wacky: the Creation Museum in Kentucky depicts a triceratops with a saddle.[28] Leiter thinks "religious belief is a *culpable* form of unwarranted belief" in light of the "ordinary epistemic standards" that are followed "in common sense and the sciences."[29] Those standards, "the standards of evidence that have been vindicated a posteriori since the scientific revolution,"[30] are standards that any belief must now live up to. Basing one's behavior on anything else is culpable.

This condemnation does not extend just to religious beliefs. It obviously would extend to nonreligious beliefs that are based on a failure to adhere to the same epistemic standards. Just how far does it extend?

Pretty far. Far enough, in fact, that it is not clear that a decision that one has an obligation to act morally is not culpable in just the same way. It is far from clear that the existence of any particular moral obligation can be demonstrated using the ordinary epistemic standards that are followed in common sense and the sciences. Leiter recognizes this problem when he defends his definition. "For is not morality characterized both by categoricity of its commands and its insulation from reasons and evidence (as reasons and evidence are understood, e.g., in the sciences)?"[31] He does not want to drift too far away from the ordinary semantic meaning of religion, so he must show that his definition does not encompass all of morality.

He responds that the two leading philosophical schools of thought about the nature of morality agree that morality is not insulated from evidence in the way that religion is. Cognitivist realists think that moral judgments can be justified in the same way as any other judgments. For noncognitivist antirealists, the mental states expressed by moral judgments are "not truth-apt, i.e., are by their nature *insulated* from reasons and evidence," and this distinguishes them from religious judgments, which "do express beliefs and so, *in principle*, could be answerable to reasons and evidence, but are held to be insulated from them."[32]

But this does not epistemically exculpate the moral behavior of most people, who are unfamiliar with this philosophical literature. They are not *relying* on the fact (if it is a fact) that the philosophers have established that moral judgments are ontologically and epistemologically distinguishable from religious judgments. The conclusions of contemporary philosophy are even more esoteric than those of contemporary science. If one is culpable for not being familiar with the former, than most of humanity is invincibly culpable, if that label is even coherent. On a practical and phenomenological level, the basis for moral judgments is often indistinguishable from the basis for religious judgments. In each case, people rely on some combination of testimony and intuition, and even moral heroes may be inarticulate. Faith about unspeakable ends is a common part of moral life.

Leiter shares, and seeks to clarify, Simon Blackburn's concern about "respect creep," an unfortunate cultural pathology in which the reasonable demand for minimal toleration gets transmuted into an unreasonable demand for deference and reverence. But Blackburn's discussion leaves open the question of when reverence is appropriate. Blackburn himself positively admires religious artists such as Donne, Milton, and Bach, who "try to give voice to the great events and emotions of human life" in religious terms. His essay is fascinating because it begins with a stance of suspicious hostility toward religion and slowly works its way toward a complex ambivalence, in which religion perhaps simply stands for "remembrances and pieties that it is human to have and that desperately need protection against the encroaching world of cost-benefit analysis and the surrendering of unbridled power to economic interest."[33] Leiter agrees with Blackburn that religion can produce good outcomes, but Leiter is more transparently instrumentalist: religion is valuable only insofar as some religious people are led by their faith to do good things. The "remembrances and pieties" don't seem to have any intrinsic value for him.

It is not possible to offer a unitary account of what religion is good for. Like a knife or a rock, it is something that people find already existing in the world, which they then put to a huge variety of uses.

Macklem

Timothy Macklem has offered a different argument against treating "religion" as a good. Macklem applies to questions of religious liberty the perfectionist liberalism of Joseph Raz. Unlike Rawls, Raz thinks that political philosophers should not be shy about discerning the contours

of the good life. Raz rejects Rawls's political liberalism and his arguments for neutrality toward conceptions of the good.[34] The best reason
for liberal toleration is not neutrality, but a recognition that there is a
plurality of good ways of life, and that the state has no good reason to
disfavor any of these.

Macklem accepts and elaborates on Raz's claim that there is a plurality of good ways of life. He aims to work out its implications for
religious toleration. The consequences are in some respects unhappily
intolerant. But, I will argue, this is not a necessary implication of Raz's
approach, which could be interpreted in a way that supports American
religious neutrality.

Recall that I argued in Chapter 1 that "religion" should be given its
conventional meaning, as denoting a set of activities united only by a
family resemblance, with no set of necessary or sufficient conditions
demarcating the boundaries of the set. Macklem objects that the question of what "religion" conventionally means is a semantic one, but the
question of what beliefs are entitled to special treatment is a moral one,
and it requires a moral rather than a semantic answer.[35]

Macklem thinks that religion can contribute to human flourishing,
in the following way. Sometimes, a complete set of reasons for action
is unavailable, but action would nonetheless facilitate our well-being.
In such a situation, where commitment is rationally underdetermined,
Macklem argues that "faith is valuable where the inability to make the
commitments that faith makes possible would have a negative impact
on well-being, both because the commitments in question are potentially valuable and because failure to make them would be harmful."[36]

Macklem nonetheless worries: "The difficulty with faith, secular or
religious, is that it often serves as a substitute for knowledge and reason
in settings where these are not only available but constitute a sounder
basis for action and belief."[37] When this happens (and creationist pif-
fle illustrates that it does sometimes happen), religion is not good for
human flourishing, and the state has no reason to treat it as valuable.

Macklem is correct that what interests us is not religion's semantic
meaning, but its moral significance. Is there any reason to assign moral
significance to the contents of the loose baggy sack of heterogeneous
phenomena that fit within the semantic meaning of "religion"?[38] Is there
any reason to treat the stuff in the sack as *good*? Macklem doubts it.
The Wittgensteinian mess means that religion as such can't have moral

significance. He proposes that courts undertake "a frank examination of the contribution that any doctrine held on the basis of faith, be it traditional or non-traditional, is capable of making to well-being."[39]

There are two decisive objections to Macklem's proposal, one political and one moral. The political objection is that, in a pluralistic society, there are obvious dangers in giving judges the power to assign legal consequences to different religious beliefs based on the judges' own conceptions of well-being. Macklem's own confident withholding of protection from "cults" is not reassuring.[40] The moral objection is that it is arrogant to assess the entirety of another's lifeworld and confidently conclude that, taken as a whole, it is so silly that the person would be better off with a radical conversion. Perhaps we're entitled to do this with respect to people whose lives are manifestly wretched, such as homeless drug addicts, but we don't know most of our fellow citizens well enough to make such judgments with any degree of confidence.

Doubts on this score are reinforced by Raz's observation that modern life tends to generate what he calls "competitive pluralism": a liberal society tends to generate "virtues which tend, given human nature, to encourage intolerance of other virtues," and the virtue of toleration is therefore necessary.[41] If this is correct, and if state actors are likely to be inappropriately intolerant in just this way, then there is reason to constrain those actors by rules that require them to be neutral with respect to some matters about which they are convinced that they have sound views. Religion is one of those matters.

There are enough good things in the sack that there are sufficient reasons (at least for the purposes of the religion clauses) to pronounce the sack as such a container of good things, and to respect the other fellow's sack despite—or, perhaps, because—we aren't sure just what is in it. Macklem thinks that Jesus-worshippers are coming to terms with death in an intelligible way, while Elvis-worship has no such function.[42] I agree that it is a delusion to think that Elvis still lives, but how can Macklem know that this is not a way of coming to terms with life's mysteries? I'd need to know a lot more about the role of Elvis in these people's lives before I could confidently conclude that nothing about their strange beliefs is worthy of respect. From the standpoint of science, the belief in the resurrection of Jesus is equally indefensible. So the decision to define religion vaguely, relying on the fuzzy semantic meaning, itself rests on moral grounds.

Beliefs serve two functions, which we may call epistemic and existential. They can provide maps of the world; they can also help to cope with life's mysteries. These functions sometimes come into tension with one another. It's nice to be able to do both, but evidently that is not so easy for everyone. The epistemic folly of "scientific creationists," for example, is silly, but it is not pointless, and its effectiveness at performing the existential function may be an appropriate object of respect and even admiration, in the same way I can admire your skill at opening a can with a screwdriver.

The value of religion will sometimes be a fit occasion for ambivalence, in the same way that one is reasonably ambivalent about any human good that is sometimes abused by its possessor. It is good for people to be clever and resourceful, but it would have been better if Hitler had been less clever and resourceful than he was. Similarly, as Leiter observes, the devoutly religious include, on the one hand, those who opposed Naziism in Germany and apartheid in South Africa and the United States, but on the other, those who bomb abortion clinics and fly airplanes into buildings.[43] It would be better if the latter's ultimate sense of rightness were replaced by vertiginous disorientation. But that does not mean that the sense of rightness is not a human good, a good for the person who possesses it.

So there is warrant for deeming the contents of the sack, the whole set of beliefs and practices that constitute "religion," to be worthy of positive appraisal. This, then, can justify the special treatment of religion by the law.

Life is in many ways perplexing and hard. Finding a language to describe our deepest commitments and hopes is especially hard. Philosophy may possibly have the resources to fill this need for a few people, but it's a specialized taste. Some people find a full and satisfying meaning of life in the goods of the immanent world,[44] but that is a specialized taste too.

So even when I find that religious people believe things that seem to me incredible, I remind myself that many of them are simply doing the best they can with the limited information that's available to all of us. The smug superiority of some atheists is hard to take.[45] Intelligibility, and the courage we need to act well, is indeed a precious thing, and the fact that it exists at all is more important than the strange variety of forms that it takes.

Conscience and Not Religion?

A second objection to religion's special treatment, one to which many distinguished legal theorists and philosophers have been drawn, is that the proper object of the law's solicitude is not religion, but something else. There are many candidates for the replacement position, including human flourishing (as we saw with Raz and Macklem), individual autonomy, sources of meaning epistemically inaccessible to other people, and psychologically urgent needs (treating religion as analogous to a disability that needs accommodation). Of these, the most prominent is conscience.[46] I will here focus on conscience, but my analysis will have implications for any possible substitute for "religion."

"Conscience" is not a good explanation for the core exemption cases. It is present in cases that almost no one would want to accommodate, and fails to justify exemption in many cases where the claim for exemption is strong. Nor can it explain the Establishment Clause. Moreover, there has been remarkably little explanation of why conscience should be deemed a legitimate basis for objecting to the application of a law. Any such claim must rely on assumptions about political theory, about morality, and perhaps even about theology, but these are rarely stated. "Conscience" has been something of a black box.

I follow Thomas Hill in regarding "conscience" as a general concept that is capable of being specified in various particular conceptions. The general concept, Hill observes, is "the idea of a capacity, commonly attributed to most human beings, to sense or immediately discern that what he or she has done, or is about to do (or not do) is wrong, bad, and worthy of disapproval."[47] Different conceptions have different entailments about political obligation and the basis of moral claims against the state. It is necessary to sort these out in order to figure out what force the claim of conscience should have.

Much of the attractiveness of conscience arises from its perceived capacity to resolve the free exercise/establishment dilemma. "Conscience" promises a way out of the dilemma by describing the basis of free exercise in a way that specifies only the internal psychology of the person exempted, without endorsing any claims about religious truth. Thus it is possible to give religion special treatment without favoring religion as such.

Seeger and Welsh

The free exercise/establishment dilemma was presented to the Supreme Court most strikingly in a pair of draft exemption cases during the Vietnam War, and those cases have provided powerful support for the view that conscience is the appropriate object of constitutional protection. (These cases were discussed briefly in Chapter 1.)

The first concerned Daniel Seeger, who claimed the conscientious objector exemption from the military draft, but who was uncertain of God's existence. In a statement he attached to the draft board's questionnaire, which had asked whether he believed in a Supreme Being, he wrote that "the existence of God cannot be proven or disproven, and the essence of His nature cannot be determined. I prefer to admit this, and leave the question open rather than answer 'yes' or 'no.'"[48] (He explained, years later, that "I didn't make any particular connection between my theological beliefs and my determination not to fight in the army."[49]) He was quite clear, however, in his views about war: "I cannot participate in actions which betray the cause of freedom and humanity."[50]

The Selective Service Act exempted from the draft anyone "who, by reason of religious training and belief, is conscientiously opposed to participation in war in any form." The act defined its terms in a problematic way: "Religious training and belief in this connection means an individual's belief in a relation to a Supreme Being involving duties superior to those arising from any human relation, but does not include essentially political, sociological, or philosophical views or a merely personal moral code."[51]

The court of appeals thought that the statute was unconstitutionally discriminatory: "[F]or many in today's 'skeptical generation,' just as for Daniel Seeger, the stern and moral voice of conscience occupies that hallowed place in the hearts and minds of men which was traditionally reserved for the commandments of God."[52] When the case was appealed to the U.S. Supreme Court, that court evaded the constitutional issue by construing "Supreme Being" very broadly, so that the test was "whether a given belief that is sincere and meaningful occupies a place in the life of its possessor parallel to that filled by the orthodox belief in God of one who clearly qualifies for the exemption." The Court concluded that Seeger was entitled to the exemption "[i]n light of his beliefs and the unquestioned sincerity with which he held them."[53]

A few years later, the Court revisited the exemption issue in the case of Elliott Ashton Welsh II, who also conscientiously objected to participation in any war, but who stated that he did not believe in God and that his beliefs were not religious. His conscientious objection extended to an unwillingness to lie about his beliefs. As he explained in a later interview: "It was made very clear at the hearing by the hearing officer: is there anything you can say that you believe is God? When I think about it from where I am now, I'm thinking, why didn't I just say yes? But it wasn't true and I just wasn't going to say it. That's all I can say."[54]

A four-judge plurality concluded that Welsh's beliefs were "religious" as that term was defined in the statute. The plurality concluded that the law "exempts from military service all those whose consciences, spurred by deeply held moral, ethical, or religious beliefs, would give them no rest or peace if they allowed themselves to become a part of an instrument of war."[55]

Justice John Marshall Harlan II, concurring in the result, thought that the Court's removal of the statute's theistic requirement was "a remarkable feat of judicial surgery" that was inconsistent with the clear intentions of Congress. But he joined the result, because he thought, as the Court of Appeals had thought in *Seeger*, that the law impermissibly discriminated on the basis of religion—that it drew "a distinction between theistic and nontheistic religions." If Congress was going to create exemptions, Harlan thought, it was constitutionally required to show "equal regard for men of nonreligious conscience." "The common denominator must be the intensity of moral conviction with which a belief is held."[56] A dissenting judge in the court of appeals below had come to the same conclusion, noting that Welsh was "willing to go to jail rather than do violence to his beliefs, which is more than can be said for many who profess a belief in a Supreme Being."[57]

What Conscience Can't Explain

So the reliance on conscience produced a result that the Court found satisfying in the draft cases. Students of the religion clauses have tended to seize on these well-known cases to resolve the problem of defining religion. If one surveys the broader range of exemption cases, however, it becomes clear that conscience cannot be a functional substitute for religion.

One problem is that conscience can generate exorbitant demands.[58] Sometimes people feel conscientiously impelled to do pretty nasty things. It is not obvious why such impulses are entitled to any respect at all.

A deeper objection is that conscience *excludes* some claims that are widely recognized as valid. Many religious claims that are uncontroversially weighty, and which nearly everyone would want to accommodate, are not conscientious. A paradigm case for religious exemption, for most proponents of such exemptions, is the ritual use of peyote by the Native American Church, which the Supreme Court declined to protect in *Employment Division v. Smith*,[59] but which received legislative accommodation shortly thereafter.[60] Yet neither of the claimants in *Smith* was motivated to use peyote by religious conscience. Al Smith was motivated primarily by interest in exploring his Native American racial identity, and Galen Black was merely curious about the Church.[61]

The emphasis on conscience focuses excessively on duty. Many and perhaps most people engage in religious practice out of habit, adherence to custom, a need to cope with misfortune, injustice, temptation, and guilt, curiosity about religious truth, a desire to feel connected to God, or happy religious enthusiasm, rather than a sense of duty prescribed by sacred texts or fear of divine punishment. Core religious practices often have nothing to do with conscience. As we saw in Chapter 1, this experience-based religiosity is increasingly common in the United States across all religious denominations. The most recent congressional pronouncement on religious liberty, the Religious Land Use and Institutionalized Persons Act of 2000, declares that "[t]he term 'religious exercise' includes any exercise of religion, whether or not compelled by, or central to, a system of religious belief."[62]

Conscience is also underinclusive because it focuses on those cases in which the agent feels impelled by a duty that she is capable of performing without depending on external contingencies. "Conscience" is a poor characterization of the desire of a church to expand its building to be able to hold its growing congregation, as in *City of Boerne v. Flores*.[63] Conscientious resistance to the law was not an option. The reconstruction could not be done without the help of architects and contractors, whom the city could prevent from doing the work merely by withholding the necessary permits. The problem is even more pronounced in *Lyng v. Northwest Indian Cemetery Protective Association*, a widely criticized decision in which Native Americans objected to a proposed logging road that would pass through an ancient worship site sacred to their tribe. The logging road, the Court conceded, would "virtually destroy" the ability of the Native Americans "to practice their religion." Nonetheless, the Court, evidently persuaded that exemptions had to be based on conscience, held that there was no constitutionally cognizable burden, because the logging road had "no tendency to coerce individuals into acting contrary to their religious beliefs."[64] Once more, this result was quickly reversed by Congress.[65]

So conscience cannot be the basis for accommodation. It fails to fit the cases in which most people want to accommodate religion. It is both overinclusive and underinclusive. Yet any account of religious exemptions will need to explain why the idea of "conscience" so dominates the discourse.

The Intensity Hypothesis

Recall that in *Welsh* the plurality and Justice Harlan agreed that the basis for exemption is conscience. There are, however, many foundational questions that these opinions left unaddressed. Why is conscience the appropriate object of protection? The plurality does not explain, while Harlan suggests a clear answer: conscientious objections are the ones that are felt most intensely. But this answer gives rise to questions of its own. Why should intensity matter so much?

Harlan's focus on intensity raises a problem analogous to that of the "welfare monster," who constitutes a classic objection to utilitarian ethics. The welfare monster is someone who happens to be so constituted that she gets more happiness per unit of resources consumed than anyone else does (with no diminishing marginal utility). If utilitarian principles are accepted, the monster gets an unfairly large share of resources; in the limit case, no one else will get anything.

Harlan's opinion implies a sort of modified utilitarianism, in which particularly intense preferences are understood to make a particularly strong claim. This is, however, not all that far from the original utilitarianism of Jeremy Bentham, which sought simply to maximize pleasure and minimize pain, and which has been rejected as excessively crude by most modern philosophers. Bentham did not think that pleasures and pains were identical in weight, but thought that they could be distinguished by their intensity, duration, certainty or uncertainty, propinquity or remoteness, and likelihood of being followed by sensations of a like or of an opposite kind.[66] Harlan ignores every dimension except intensity. This is even cruder than Bentham.

For our purposes, Harlan's formulation, like conscience, is both overinclusive and underinclusive. Galen Black's desire to participate in the peyote ceremony was not particularly intense, while some very intense desires have no legitimate claim to respect.

A variation on the intensity hypothesis is the claim that the law ought to defer to a believer's fear of extratemporal consequences. The burden of obeying a law, so the argument goes, is greater for a person who believes that doing so will put his soul in jeopardy for eternity. But (aside from the problem that this approach leaves out Seeger, Welsh, and adherents of religions that do not believe in an afterlife) any special dignity for conscience has disappeared. This argument recasts conscience as a kind of prudent response to duress, God as a big thug who will thwack anyone who disobeys him, and conscientious objection as a strategy to escape thwacking.[67] What's more, it's not clear why deference is called for. If, for whatever reason, you aren't deterred by official punishment, then you should be willing to accept that punishment. The state's nastiest thwack is gentler than God's.

The Varieties of Conscience

If not intensity, then what is special about conscience? Historically, "conscience" has been a protean notion, with different meanings for different people. So there have been different answers to this question. What follows is not an exhaustive catalogue, but rather a brief sketch of a few ideal types, to clarify the main options that are on offer.

AQUINAS-CONSCIENCE

The idea of conscience has ancient antecedents.[68] A prominent ancestor is the thought of the Stoics. The Latin word *conscientia* originally referred to some knowledge, especially some secret or private knowledge, shared with another. In Stoicism, *conscientia* refers to a person's awareness of the natural moral law and his own actions' correspondence or lack of correspondence with that law.[69] Early Christians such as Paul and Jerome used the same word to refer to the soul's faculty that made a person aware of his own sinfulness.[70]

Peter Abelard made conscience central to his conception of sin: Objectively, sin was contempt of God, but it consisted in consenting to that which, it is believed, ought not to be consented to. It followed from this that sin consisted only in acting against conscience. Ignorance of God's will excuses sin; it is not sinful to fail to possess moral knowledge. Thus, even the crucifiers of Christ were not guilty of sin, because they were ignorant of the divinity of Christ.[71]

The most influential early formulation of the authority of conscience was that of Aquinas, who regarded it as a judgment by the rational part of the soul about the goodness or badness of an action. For Aquinas, conscience was not a feeling, intense or otherwise, but an exercise of the reason. This act of judgment relied on a person's innate knowledge of natural law. The judgment of the practical intellect was morally binding, and moral wrong consisted of the will's refusal to consent to that judgment: "[E]very act of will against reason, whether in the right or in the wrong, is always bad."[72]

Aquinas acknowledged that conscience could err, either by misunderstanding the correct moral principles or by misapprehending the circumstances in which one was to act. Such error would be culpable either if it were directly voluntary (because the agent deliberately avoided uncomfortable information) or if the agent were negligent about knowing what he ought to know. If, however, a person's ignorance were inevitable, that person would be excused if he acted on his erroneous conscience. The basic idea of the supreme authority of conscience had already been endorsed, in stronger terms than ever appeared in Aquinas, by Pope Innocent III (1198–1216): "One ought to endure excommunication rather than sin . . . no one ought to act against his own conscience and he should follow his conscience rather than the judgment of the church when he is certain . . . one ought to suffer any evil rather than sin against conscience."[73]

Here one sees the beginnings of the idea that conscience can trump even the objective law. Noah Feldman observes that the idea of freedom of conscience is already being suggested here: "If it was sinful to act against conscience, then there might be reason to avoid requiring anyone to act against conscience."[74] Perhaps individuals should endure anything rather than sin against conscience, but the more you make them endure, the more likely it is that they *will* sin against conscience.

But here this idea is only inchoate. Aquinas did not suggest that conscience entailed religious toleration. On the contrary, he supported the persecution of heretics.[75] Even modern neo-Thomist defenses of religious toleration reject only religious coercion intended as such; they do not necessarily entail religious exemptions from religiously neutral laws.[76] In Aquinas, conscience trumps positive law only in the eyes of God, for whom even the person who has committed a serious moral wrong is redeemed if his ignorance of moral truth is not culpable. The autonomy of conscience from law is thus an entirely internal matter, or at least a matter that is between only the person and God. Call this *Aquinas-conscience.*

LOCKE-CONSCIENCE

The modern idea of freedom of conscience as a limit on the state's legitimate power received its most influential formulation in John Locke's *Letter Concerning Toleration*, which radicalizes Aquinas's argument that the individual has an obligation to obey his conscience. "No way whatsoever that I shall walk in, against the Dictates of my Conscience, will ever bring me to the Mansions of the Blessed."[77] In Locke, this becomes a constraint on state power. In keeping with seventeenth- and eighteenth-century usage, however, "conscience" refers only to religious matters.[78] These are not the state's concern, but there is no basis for exemption from otherwise legitimate laws. If they offend anyone's conscience, she is in the position of Innocent III's heretic.

MCCONNELL-CONSCIENCE

But if Locke's view does not justify religious exemptions, it bears the seeds of such a justification. James Madison's *Memorial and Remonstrance* asserts that "[i]t is the duty of every man to render to the Creator such homage, and such only, as he believes to be acceptable to him," and that "every man who becomes a member of any particular Civil Society [must] do it with a saving of his allegiance to the Universal Sovereign."[79] Michael McConnell has made this a premise for an argument (never stated by Madison) that religion ought to be a basis for exemptions because it involves a duty to God.[80] "If the scope of religious liberty is defined by religious duty (man must render to God 'such homage . . . as he believes to be acceptable to him'), and if the claims of civil society are subordinate to the claims of religious freedom, it would seem to follow that the dictates of religious faith must take precedence over the laws of the state, even if they are secular and generally applicable."[81] He claims that religion has a unique claim to accommodation, because "[n]o other freedom is a duty to a higher authority."[82] Even those who do not believe in God should understand the value of avoiding "conflicts with what are perceived (even if incorrectly) as divine commands."[83] Here we do have a justification for exemptions.[84] Call this *McConnell-conscience*.[85]

McConnell's understanding of conscience is both overinclusive and underinclusive, in ways that by now should be familiar. Conflict between law and conscience is not uniquely religious (consider Seeger and Welsh), and not all religious activities are divinely commanded, capable of being obeyed by unaided individuals, or matters of conscientious obligation.

McConnell-conscience does not avoid the free exercise/establishment dilemma so much as squarely run into it. Exemptions thus conceptualized could be available only to theistic religions, because only those religions can generate the unique source of moral authority that this theory demands. The divine-command rationale is thus an inappropriate basis for public policy.[86] The implied endorsement of theism violates the rule that government is not to endorse religious propositions.

In sum, neither Aquinas-conscience, nor Locke-conscience, nor McConnell-conscience can help us out of the dilemma. Aquinas-conscience is not a constraint on the state at all. Locke-conscience objects only to laws that specifically restrict religion, and is no basis for exemptions from generally applicable laws. McConnell-conscience violates the Establishment Clause. If conscience is to be the basis for exemptions, then we must seek other descriptions of its salient characteristic. What other descriptions are available?

SANDEL-CONSCIENCE

Michael Sandel offers a description of conscience that deftly avoids the difficulties of McConnell's specification. Sandel observes that a person in the grip of conscience has such a strong need to act in accordance with it that he really has no other option. The aim of accommodation is "to prevent persons bound by moral duties they cannot renounce from having to violate either those duties or the law." Such protection recognizes "the role that religion plays in the lives of those for whom the observance of religious duties is a constitutive end, essential to their good and indispensable to their identity."[87] This justifies the results in *Seeger* and *Welsh*.[88]

This conception of conscience—call it *Sandel-conscience*—avoids the difficulties of the accounts of conscience we have just considered. It is a basis for political claims, unlike Aquinas-conscience. It is a claim against even laws that are legitimately enacted, unlike Locke-conscience. It is not based on theological propositions, unlike McConnell-conscience. Indeed, it is not based on anything beyond the internal psychological makeup of the actor, which is tightly bound up with the action that the actor wishes to take. These advantages doubtless are why so many sophisticated philosophers are drawn to it.

Sandel-conscience, however, raises new and intractable difficulties. People may indeed be constrained in the inescapable way that Sandel describes. But morality is not the only source of such constraint. Harry Frankfurt observes that the demands of love, of what we happen to care about, can be just as forceful as the demands of moral obligation.[89] Sandel's explanation of the force of conscience is underinclusive in its own way: the exigency that it points to sometimes arises from moral duties, but it arises from other sources as well.

"Conscience" is an imprecise word for an internal compulsion to act that is specified only by the possessor's internal psychology. A better term is what Frankfurt calls "volitional necessity." "Someone who is bound by volitional necessity is unable to form a determined and effective intention—regardless of what motives or reasons he may have for doing so—to perform (or to refrain from performing) the action that is at issue."[90] Frankfurt's paradigmatic case of volitional necessity is the declaration attributed to Luther: "Here I stand; I can do no other."[91] What Luther could not muster, Frankfurt observes, "was not the *power* to forbear, but the *will*."[92] Unlike an addict's compulsion, Luther accedes to the constraining force "because he is *unwilling* to oppose it and because, furthermore, his unwillingness is *itself* something which he is unwilling to alter."[93] This double unwillingness is what defines volitional necessity.

The advantage, for our purposes, of focusing on volitional necessity is that it brings forth with clarity the implications of a view of internal compulsion that is entirely denuded of any external referent. Volitional necessity thus completes the work of abstraction that "conscience" promises.

Luther's case involves an end that receives his undivided endorsement, such that it is unthinkable to act otherwise. Luther embraces it wholeheartedly; his will is undivided with respect to it. Volitional necessity is the marker of a person's identity: "As the set of its essential characteristics specifies the limits of what a triangle can be, so does the set of actions that are unthinkable for a person specify the limits of what the person can will to do. It defines his essence as a volitional creature."[94] A person who will do anything if the price is right has only accidental characteristics; he has no stable identity at all.[95] Following volitional necessity is itself a highest-order interest: one's integrity is at stake.

But this is a poor basis for legal exemption, because it is potentially so idiosyncratic. People identify with a lot of things. The object of one's love can be deeply unworthy.[96] Gerhard Weinberg, explaining why Hitler was determined to initiate World War II, observes that "[w]ithout war, his whole program and his whole life made no sense to him."[97] Neither conscience (in any of its varieties surveyed above) nor volitional necessity necessarily points toward anything that other people have any obligation to respect. Both produce analogues of welfare monsters. Perhaps it is terribly hard for someone to resist the force of volitional necessity, and perhaps that counts as a (rebuttable!) reason not to ask them to do it. But in that case, the appropriate response is not respect. It is pity.

Respect for Moral Motivation as Such

In order for a claim to accommodation to be entitled to respect, it needs that link to objective value. But what objective value could it be? It had better not be specified in a theistic way, because that brings back the difficulties of McConnell-conscience.

One candidate, one that is theologically neutral, is the will to be moral. This looks back to Aquinas, but it goes beyond him. Aquinas did not think that conscience could be the basis of claims on other people, or on the state, and even his modern followers are able to conclude only that laws that aim to coerce *religious* conscience are per se wrong. But one could argue, following Aquinas, that the desire to do what is morally right is a good thing in itself, and respect for that desire is a part of respect for persons.[98] The desire to be moral is not, however, exempt from the possibility of error. Mark Twain's Huckleberry Finn regarded himself as culpably weak-willed because he disregarded his own specifically moral compunctions about helping a slave to escape. (If it is presumed that one should always obey one's conscience, he *was* culpably weak-willed.)[99] Even if the will to be moral should be given some weight, however, this still will not do as a substitute for religion. Conscience, as moral compulsion, is over- and underinclusive with respect to the claims that are accommodated. We have not even begun to resolve the free exercise/establishment dilemma, because "conscience" does not explain what free exercise is about.

Beyond Conscience

If conscience cannot explain America's practices of religious accommodation, then what would a satisfactory account of those practices look like?

Our exploration of conscience has provided us with some parameters that any possible answer must satisfy. Unlike Aquinas-conscience, it must be a basis for claims upon other people, not only upon oneself and God. Unlike Locke-conscience, it must be a basis for claims against properly motivated, legitimately enacted laws. Unlike McConnell-conscience, it must not rest on the truth of theism or any other theological proposition. Unlike Sandel-conscience, it must rest on something more than volitional necessity, the internal psychological makeup of the actor. It must, then, rest on some source of value external to the actor. The idea of moral obligation as such is one possible such source of value, but as we have seen, that source is over- and underinclusive of the accommodations we are trying to account for. These conditions must be satisfied by any satisfactory defense of religious accommodations.

The *Welsh* plurality's opinion, unlike the conscience-based justifications that have been offered for it, satisfies these parameters. Recall the test announced by the plurality: in order for an objection to a law to be entitled to accommodation, it was necessary "[1] that this opposition . . . stem from the [objector]'s moral, ethical, or religious beliefs about what is right and wrong and [2] that these beliefs be held with the strength of traditional religious convictions."[100] Only the second prong of the test looks to the strength of the objector's volitional necessity. Harlan, with his focus on intensity, might have stopped there, but the other judges wanted more than intensity.

This first prong of the *Welsh* test appears to be the more important of the two, since it can explain the accommodation of religious beliefs that are not held with any particular intensity. (*Pace* Harlan, who may have wanted to rely solely on the second prong, evidently that prong is not even a necessary condition of a successful demand for accommodation.)

In both of the selective draft cases, the Court placed great weight on the conscientious nature of the claims, but it also was drawn to a conception of religion that was not confined to theism. The Court quoted with approval David Saville Muzzey's definition of religion as "the devotion of man to the highest ideal that he can conceive," and Paul Tillich's description of God as "the depths of your life, of the source of your being, of your ultimate concern, of what you take seriously without any reservation."[101] The volitional necessities at issue in those cases appeared to plug into some source of value that transcended Welsh and Seeger's personal preferences, however strong these might be. Here it appears some work is being done by the inherent attractiveness of pacifism.[102] Conscientious objection to, say, serving food to black restaurant patrons would not have been likely to elicit comparable deference.[103]

We can take a general lesson from our exploration of "conscience" as an unsuccessful substitute for "religion." Even if we find a single morally attractive factor that justifies many religious liberty claims, that factor won't do as a general basis for all such claims.

No single factor justification for singling out religion can succeed. Any single factor justification will be overinclusive and underinclusive. Any invocation of any factor X as a justification will logically entail substituting X for religion as a basis for special treatment, making "religion" disappear as a category of analysis. This substitution will be unsatisfactory because underinclusive. There will be settled intuitions about establishment and accommodation that it will be unable to account for.

There are many different versions of X on offer. The same analytic point applies to all of them. Any X will be an imperfect substitute for religion, but a theory of religious freedom that focuses on that X will not be able to say why religion, rather than X, should be the object of solicitude.[104]

There are two ways around this difficulty. One is to say that these are not ends that the state can directly aim at, and that religion is a good proxy. This does justify some imprecision in the law. We want to give licenses to "safe drivers," but these are not directly detectible, so we use the somewhat overinclusive and underinclusive category of "those who have passed a driving test." But this doesn't work for at least some of the substitutes on offer. The state can aim directly at accommodating conscience, say, or autonomy.

The other way is to say that religion is an adequate (though somewhat overinclusive and underinclusive) proxy for multiple goods, some of which are not ones that can directly be aimed at. Each of those goods is, at least, more likely to be salient in religious than in nonreligious contexts. The fact that there is so much contestation among religions as to which of these goods is most salient is itself a reason for the state to remain vague about this question. Because "religion" captures multiple goods, aiming directly at any one of them will yield underinclusiveness. That is enough to justify singling out religion.

Rawlsian Objections

The third objection is that the idea that religion is good, whether or not it is true, is too controversial to be a basis for law. The move to conscience is motivated in part by the intuition that the value of conscience is somehow less contestable than that of religion. Now let us confront the reasons for avoiding such contestable claims.

A particularly influential objection to government favoring of religion-in-general is that it violates requirements of public reason—requirements that must be satisfied if there are to be respectful relations among citizens. The state, it is claimed, ought not to enact coercive laws for reasons that some citizens reasonably reject, and religious reasons are prominent among these.

I will consider two formulations of this objection. One is presented, albeit inconsistently, by Rawls, the most prominent proponent of the idea of public reason as a constraint on the use of political power. The other is the neo-Rawlsian argument of Martha Nussbaum, who has specifically objected to American religious neutrality as I have presented it. In both formulations, however, the Rawlsian position turns out to be at least consistent with the American kind of neutrality, and may indeed endorse it.

Rawls

A well-ordered society, for Rawls, "is a society all of whose members accept, and know that the others accept, the same principles (the same conception) of justice."[105] The aim is a stable basis for mutually respectful political life in a society that is profoundly divided about comprehensive moral doctrines. This aspiration is possible, Rawls argues, because people with different comprehensive conceptions can and should reach an "overlapping consensus" on the principles of political cooperation. In an overlapping consensus, they may disagree about the ultimate foundations of the political principles that govern them, but they agree upon the principles. They believe those principles are moral and affirm them on moral grounds.[106]

American religious neutrality can and does satisfy these constraints. Even the most contestable claim underlying American neutrality, the idea that religion is corrupted by state involvement, is not a mere modus vivendi contingent on shifting constellations of political power. It is a principled reason for a majority religion to refrain from enlisting the state to impose its view on minorities, even if it can do so with impunity. Rawls, however, goes on to offer more stringent requirements for just terms of cooperation, terms that American neutrality may not satisfy.

Rawls says little about the specific place of religion in the political order. He does argue that one of the fundamental principles of a just basic structure of society is "equal liberty of conscience."[107] But he does not define this, and the term as he uses it might be limited to freedom from deliberate religious persecution. It certainly is not violated by noncoercive establishments of religion. So it cannot be the basis for any objection to the treatment of religion as a good in American law.

A more potent difficulty comes from Rawls's conception of public reason. The requirement that all agree on a public conception of justice might imply constraints on the reasons that can be given in political discussion, even with respect to actions by the state that do not infringe

upon liberty of conscience. Our reasoning in the public forum, in which
we discuss political proposals, should rely on principles that we can reasonably expect all citizens to accept.[108]

There is an important ambiguity in what this means. Sometimes—
call this *the more stringent interpretation of public reason*—Rawls suggests that when we exercise political power over others, we should seek
"to be able to justify our actions to others on grounds they could not reasonably reject." In other places, however, he writes that in justifying the
use of political power we are "to appeal only to those presently accepted
general beliefs and forms of reasoning found in common sense, and
the methods and conclusions of science when these are not controversial."[109] These are not the same thing. The second description—call this
the less stringent interpretation of public reason—is far less demanding.
A belief could be presently accepted and widely uncontroversial without being of a character that could not reasonably be rejected.

Other passages in Rawls's work support the less stringent interpretation. The constraints of public reason do not necessarily apply to all
political deliberation. Although "it is usually highly desirable to settle
political questions by invoking the values of public reason," its moral
requirements strictly apply only to constitutional essentials and matters
of basic justice.[110] When enacting regulations that do not infringe on
basic liberties, it is permissible for a legislature to rely on its comprehensive conception. "Fundamental justice must be achieved first. After that
a democratic electorate may devote large resources to grand projects in
art and science if it so chooses."[111] Thus political liberalism "does not
rule out as a reason the beauty of nature as such or the good of wild-
life achieved by protecting its habitat."[112] As Samuel Freeman puts it,
"[I]t may well be that majority democratic decision by itself is sufficient
'public reason' for restricting conduct."[113]

If the less stringent interpretation is accepted, then there would be no
Rawlsian objection to the American regime if most citizens agree that
religion, defined at a high level of abstraction, is a good thing.[114] The
goodness of religion would stand on the same footing as the goodness
of art, science, or natural beauty. If these are legitimately the basis of
coercive laws, such as habitat protection, then religion could be as well.
So the argument would easily permit noncoercive establishments,[115] and
a fortiori the milder preference for religion, understood very abstractly,
in the American regime. So long as freedom of conscience, however

defined, is respected, there is no basis for complaining about the role of religion in decisions that do not themselves infringe on that freedom.

But Rawls does not unambiguously endorse the less stringent interpretation. As already noted, he declares that, when we exercise political power, we should aim "to be able to justify our actions to others on grounds they could not reasonably reject."[116] Democratic deliberation, on the more stringent interpretation, would not furnish such a ground. The substantive basis for such decisions, not merely their procedures, would have to be thus justifiable. This, if accepted, would be a powerful basis for objecting to the religion-friendly character of the American regime. Some citizens do not think that religion is at all good. They deplore it and think that we would be better off without it. That is one reasonable view among many.

Freeman, an exceptionally careful and reliable expositor of Rawls's philosophy, sometimes endorses the more stringent interpretation. He concludes that Rawlsian public reason excludes all comprehensive conceptions (including religious conceptions) from public and even private deliberations about coercive laws. This is why "[a]ppeals to Christian doctrine simply do not count as good public reasons in our political culture."[117] Those who wish to legislate on the basis of their religious views "are proposing that state power be exercised in ways that cannot be justified on the basis of reasons all democratic citizens can endorse."[118] Even widespread acceptance is not sufficient: "[S]imply because people in a society commonly accept and reason in terms of a common religion does not make that doctrine part of public reason." Thus, for example, "Saudi Arabia has no public reason in Rawls's sense, only shared comprehensive reasons which rule out the possibility of a public reason."[119]

The entity within the government that has the strongest obligation to respect the constraints of public reason, Rawls thinks, is the Supreme Court. That court, he writes, "is the branch of government that serves as the exemplar of public reason." The justices "cannot invoke their or other people's religious or philosophical views. . . . Rather, they must appeal to the political values they think belong to the most reasonable understanding of the public conception and its political values of justice and public reason."[120]

This constraint entails that the body of American law we have here been studying is deeply defective. Judicial reliance on the corruption argument necessarily depends on a contestable conception of the good—in my formulation, the value of religion, understood very abstractly—and so can have no persuasive power to those who do not see any value in the thing the corruption argument seeks to protect. American law requires religious neutrality, and thus may appear to instantiate this constraint. But its neutrality is embedded within, and entailed by, a comprehensive conception of the good.[121]

A regime constrained by the more stringent interpretation of public reason would have something like the American Establishment Clause, forbidding government from relying on religious premises in lawmaking, but it would not be religion-friendly in the way American law is. The free exercise/establishment dilemma would disappear, because there would be no Free Exercise Clause. There would be only the functional equivalent of a strict Establishment Clause, together with a general set of liberties that would certainly protect a great deal of religious liberty, perhaps under some description of "conscience," but would not give any special status to religious claims.

How could the American regime be defended against this objection? The regime clearly violates the most stringent formulation of Rawlsian public reason. Any defense must then persuade the reader to reject that formulation. In order to accomplish that, I would have to persuade you that the constraints of Rawlsian public reason, understood as the set of propositions that no one could reasonably reject, constrain too much.

One way of doing that is to note that Rawls himself chafes under his own constraints. A conception of public reason that rules out environmental protection, for example, is one that he rejects, perhaps even reasonably rejects. For any reader of Rawls, if the strains of commitment of the more stringent interpretation are too great because it filters out too much, then this is a reason to reject that interpretation. The good of religion obviously will do that job for some citizens. Other possible candidates include sexual pleasure: if it cannot be given weight, because some citizens don't see anything good about it, how can one make a case for gay rights, or even condemn more radical intrusions on sexual autonomy such as female genital mutilation?[122]

The same burdens of judgment that make the doctrine of reasonable pluralism plausible also suggest that we will not be able to devise a social contract that fixes the terms of cooperation in advance. Such a social contract would not be accepted by all reasonable persons.

Moreover, it is not the only possible basis of cooperation. Cooperation occurs whenever we exchange reasons with one another. This can be done without ever relying on universally acceptable premises. I can try to take seriously the point of view that each of my fellow citizens holds, addressing them one at a time. My discourse inevitably will often be secular, in that I will avoid reliance on religious premises that I know my interlocutors do not accept.[123] But this is a response to a rhetorical imperative, not a moral one.[124]

If in fact most citizens, like Rawls himself, cannot live with the more stringent interpretation, then the proponent of that position faces a dilemma. You can try to devise a social contract that all rational persons have conclusive reason to enter into. That social contract will not in fact command the assent of actual persons, but you can console yourself with the knowledge that your interlocutors are being unreasonable.[125] This is not a recipe for social unity. On the other hand, if you aim at unity with your actual neighbors, you won't be able to describe the terms of cooperation until you actually talk to them and find out what they want.

Rawls thinks that the diversity of comprehensive conceptions of the good means that none of them can be a basis for a shared conception of justice. There is, however, a revealing slippage in Rawls's definition of a comprehensive conception. A conception is comprehensive, Rawls explains, "when it includes conceptions of what is of value in human life, and ideals of personal character, as well as ideals of friendship and of familial and associational relationships, and much else that is to inform our conduct, and in the limit to our life as a whole." "A conception is fully comprehensive if it covers all recognized values and virtues within one rather precisely articulated system." There can be no social consensus around such fully comprehensive conceptions.[126]

However, Rawls also relies on the notion of a "partially comprehensive" conception, which comprises "a number of, but by no means all, nonpolitical values and virtues and is rather loosely articulated."[127] This locution is odd. It is like saying that a person with a speck of dirt on his shoulder is partially buried. Evidently "comprehensive" refers to any conception of the good not derivable from the more stringent understanding of public reason, even if it is itself not very comprehensive at all.

Are partially comprehensive conceptions impossible bases of social unity? Bruce Ackerman, who, like Rawls, wants to expel contestable conceptions of the good from political decision making, claims that humanists ought, for the sake of civil peace, to renounce public support for the arts.[128] Most theists and most atheists might, however, agree that the market should not be the sole arbiter of which cultural forms flourish. Justice is not the only possible object of overlapping consensus.

The vague good of religion, too, could be an object of such consensus. Rawls has offered no basis for ruling out this possibility, and his occasional concessions suggest that his philosophy is open to it.

A last word about the notion of public reason. It is no accident that a vogue of theorizing, trying to show that it was immoral and disrespectful to make religious arguments about political matters, immediately followed the presidential election of 1980, when the religious right first became a potent force in American politics.[129] These claims elicited a bitter response from religious thinkers, who argued that such a limitation on public discourse would deprive politics of important moral resources and deny them the right to state what they believe.[130] This response, which has made little impression on liberal theorists, gives rise to a puzzle: Why did the liberals converge on and keep producing new articulations of a proposal, in the name of social unity and comity, that was so widely received as an insult? How could so many brilliant people have been so rhetorically clumsy?

Norms of civility may, paradoxically, be the reason. It is impolite to challenge someone else's religious beliefs. Religion is private. Even if you think your neighbor believes really stupid stuff, it's not nice to say so. He can go to his church. You go to yours. Don't bother each other.

This formula works only so long as neither of you offers a religious argument that is supposed to govern something that will affect both of you. Suppose, for example, that you propose that homosexual sex be criminalized because it's an abomination before God. How am I to respond? If I disagree, my obvious answer is to say that your religious beliefs are wrong. By hypothesis, that is what I really think. But it's not nice to say that. So I have to twist around to find some way to say that your views ought not to govern political decisions, without having to say that they're false.

This strategy has been a disaster. A doctrine that purports to be grounded in universal respect has left a lot of actual citizens feeling profoundly insulted. This suggests that the social norm should be revisited. As soon as A invokes religious reasons for his political position, then it must be OK for B to challenge those reasons. It may be acrimonious, but at least we'll be talking about what really divides us (and we'll avoid the strange theoretical pathologies that have plagued modern liberal theory, though these are mainly confined to the academy). It's more respectful to just tell each other what we think and talk about it.

Open discussion also takes religious claims seriously, which American liberals urgently need to do. Alienation from religion has been a disaster for the American left. In the United States, progressive change—the enactment of the Establishment Clause, the abolition of slavery, the New Deal, and the Civil Rights Act of 1964—has been achieved only by an alliance of the secular and the religious. Those on the left who rail against religion are playing into the hands of their enemies.

Nussbaum

Martha Nussbaum has reformulated the Rawlsian objection. She dispenses with the heavy philosophical machinery of public reason, and instead argues that the idea of religion as a good is too specific to be a plausible basis of political cooperation. The idea that the search for meaning in life is good

> is just a bit too dogmatic. We live in a country in which many people are skeptics, doubting that there is such a thing as the ultimate meaning of life, and where many others have dogmatic anti-meaning views. For the government to declare what Koppelman declares goes just a bit too far for true fairness to such skeptical and/or anti-metaphysical views.[131]

A regime that treats religion as a good is illegitimate for the same reason that a regime that treats Christianity as a good is illegitimate. She argues that political respect should be given instead to "the faculty with which each person searches for the ultimate meaning of life," not its goal, and that we should "agree to respect the faculty without prejudging the question whether there is a meaning to be found, or what it might be like."[132]

Her point is part of her larger argument about distributive justice. Her central contribution is a list of capabilities that, she claims, should be available to everyone: the ability to live a life of normal duration, the ability to have good health, the ability to move about freely, freedom from violence, reproductive choice, the ability to imagine, think, and reason, the ability to laugh and play, political and property rights on an equal basis with others, and many others.[133]

In her earliest work that pursued this strategy, she sought to avoid unfairly preferential treatment of religion by treating religious freedom as a conclusion rather than a premise. The foundations of that freedom are capabilities that can be described without reference to religion.[134] Later, religious capabilities were enumerated among the important ones. "To be able to search for an understanding of the ultimate meaning of life in one's own way is among the most important aspects of a life that is truly human." But she was still unwilling to say that religion is a separate basic capability.[135]

Nussbaum proposes to address the problem of potential unfairness in the following way: "First, we confine the explicit area of potential exemptions to religion; but we allow religion to be somewhat broadly defined, including non-theistic belief systems. . . . It remains essential, however, to determine that the exercise of freedom of conscience is religion-like in having a systematic and non-arbitrary character."[136] Here religion is the paradigm case to which other belief systems must conform in order to qualify for special treatment. Why give it that privileged place if it is merely one of many equally valid ways of exercising the pertinent capabilities?

In *Liberty of Conscience*, her work on religion, addressing American law rather than pure political philosophy, she argues that the reasons for accommodation should be modified by institutional constraints, so that religion receives special treatment only because a broader accommodation would not be administrable. The object of protection should be "conscience," by which she means "the faculty in human beings with which they search for life's ultimate meaning." Conscience should be protected because it is valuable and vulnerable; it "needs a protected space around it within which people can pursue their search for life's meaning (or not pursue it, if they choose)."[137]

She acknowledges that, "fair or unfair," the text of the Free Exercise Clause does single out religion. But in her examination of American law, she concedes that this might be appropriate. The best reason for this singling out is that nonreligious reasons for seeking accommodation "are more likely to be personal and individualistic, thus far more difficult to assess for sincerity and significance." Nussbaum approves of the Court's extension of the definition of religion to include "forms of committed searching for meaning that had no group affiliation," but she acknowledges that this stretch perpetuates a different kind of unfairness, because it will "reward articulate people and penalize those, equally sincere, who cannot give a good account of themselves."[138]

Nussbaum thus resists a formulation in which the object of searching is given objective value. But absent some account of the value of the object of the search, it is not clear how Nussbaum can maintain the distinction between her position and a libertarian view in which any regulation of anyone's conduct is presumptively invalid. The focus on "committed searching" may capture less conduct than she wishes it to. Those with dogmatic views, religious or antireligious, can hardly be said to be searching for life's ultimate meaning. The boundaries of protection in Nussbaum are thus uncertain.

She wants something like the present regime of accommodation, but under some description less exclusive than "religion." Her concern is that it is unfair to privilege religion over other ends that are equally valuable. She has not developed this specific objection in any detail, but this has been done by Christopher Eisgruber and Lawrence Sager.

Privileging or Protection?

Our conclusion, that it is not unfair to treat religion as something valuable, does not settle the question of what kind of special treatment it is entitled to. Here we come to the fourth objection to religion's special treatment. One may concede its value while arguing that it is unfair to treat it more favorably than other, equally valuable human activities.

Eisgruber and Sager are the most prominent proponents of this view.[139] They do not always object to the legal singling out of religion. Rather, their central claim is that such singling out is justifiable only in order to protect religion from discrimination. Unlike Leiter or Hitchens, they do not dispute religion's value, but argue that it should not be privileged over other deep and valuable concerns.

Privileging and protection, however, are not analytically distinct, but rather are logically continuous with one another. The question is not whether, but rather what, to privilege. Once this is understood, it becomes clear that their principle is empty and unhelpful in resolving any actual legal question. It is not a principle at all, but a worry about unfairness that can at best play a useful role in influencing judgment about inescapably discretionary decisions.

The Case against Privileging Religion

Eisgruber and Sager argue that it is unfair and arbitrary to treat religion differently from other deep human commitments—to require that "religious projects and commitments must be deprived of aid that . . . other endeavors receive," or to give religious commitments special privilege by making them "exempt from the burdens of democratic membership that the rest of us routinely bear."[140] Instead of privilege, they propose a principle that they call equal liberty. Equal liberty has three components: (1) "[N]o members of our political community ought to be devalued on account of the spiritual foundations of their important commitments and projects";[141] (2) "aside from this deep and important concern with discrimination, we have no constitutional reason to treat religion as deserving special benefits or as subject to special disabilities"; (3) "citizens in general enjoy broad space within which to pursue and act upon their most valued commitments and projects, whether these be religious or not." This "broad understanding of constitutional liberty generally" will "allow religious practice to flourish."[142]

Eisgruber and Sager think that the free exercise/establishment dilemma creates a huge problem for religious accommodations. Government, they note, is specifically forbidden from subsidizing religious activity as such.[143] This is a problem for any religious exemption. "There is no sound reason to distinguish subsidies from exemptions that alleviate purely financial burdens (and thereby provide a financial benefit). If it is impermissible to prefer religion in one setting, it cannot be mandatory to prefer it in the other."[144] If we create "some distinct constitutional status for religion," self-contradiction will result: "[W]e will be obliged to fashion constitutional tests that require the state to say who or what is in the right way religious, and then attach distinct advantages or disadvantages to the resulting judgment."[145]

Sometimes, however, religion should get special treatment—not because it is especially valuable, but because it is vulnerable to discrimination. "The Constitution expresses special concern for religion because and to the extent that religious difference inspires inequality in stature and reward." The fundamental norm is that "minority religious practices, needs, and interests must be as well and as favorably accommodated by government as are more familiar and mainstream interests." Thus, for example, when the drug laws of some states refuse exemptions for the sacramental use of peyote by Native Americans, while more mainstream religions can use wine, and other states have found that such exemptions do not lead to any increase in drug abuse, this refusal could reasonably be found to be a violation of equal liberty.[146]

Eisgruber and Sager do not propose to revolutionize the law of religious liberty. As they present it, quite a lot of the law of religious accommodation can be justified as nondiscrimination. So can much of the law of disestablishment, which they take to likewise be concerned with equality: when government "affiliates itself with or endorses a particular theological perspective," it "implicitly disparages other ones." Their understanding of the Establishment Clause is entirely rooted in this concern about disparagement, which they think is always present, intentionally or not, when government endorses a religious view.[147]

Religion raises issues of equality because of its social meaning: religions constitute insiders and outsiders, and the stakes of being in or out are regarded as very high. Government endorsements of religion "assign powerful and pervasive judgments of identity and stature to the status of being in or out."[148] The major premise evidently is "that government not devalue people on grounds that are important constituents of how people view themselves and others, grounds that have historically been fault lines of hostility and neglect, grounds that give way in our time to exclusion and subordination."[149]

Statutes that give wholesale protection to religious liberty are suspect under this standard. The federal Religious Freedom Restoration Act, for example, is unconstitutional, because it goes beyond this guarantee of equality. Rather, it "relieved religious organizations and persons of burdens shared by others." RFRA is unconstitutional to the extent that it operates "to confer a benefit upon religion that other important human commitments did not enjoy." The Religious Land Use and Institutionalized Persons Act (RLUIPA) is justified in protecting prisoners, because there is ample evidence that states are hostile to their religious freedom claims. But there is no such record of hostility to justify special protection of religious land use claims, which are usually treated very sympathetically. State mini-RFRAs similarly "come drenched in the language of extraordinary special privilege, not in the language of equality."[150]

The Nondiscrimination Norm

Their understanding of nondiscrimination norms is fundamentally process based, turning on the motivations of the government decision maker.[151] "Equal regard is a public stance or posture, an attitude." When a minority religious concern is overridden, we must ultimately ask "the counterfactual question of whether more mainstream concerns would have been treated more favorably."[152] The ban on discrimination does not only bar hostility to minority religions. It also forbids "neglect," a term they use repeatedly to describe what religion needs protection from.[153] Sometimes, "a failure to accommodate bespeaks a failure of equal regard."[154]

The nondiscrimination norm, Paul Brest observes, is violated by "selective sympathy and indifference," meaning "the unconscious failure to extend to a minority the same recognition of humanity, and hence the same sympathy and care, given as a matter of course to one's own group."[155] It is this insight that animates Eisgruber and Sager's concern about neglect. But as Ronald Dworkin notes in a well-known defense of affirmative action, a nondiscrimination norm that requires equal concern for everyone does not necessarily entail equal treatment:

> If I have two children, and one is dying from a disease that is making the other uncomfortable, I do not show equal concern if I flip a coin to decide which should have the remaining dose of a drug. This example shows that the right to treatment as an equal is fundamental, and the right to equal treatment, derivative.[156]

What, then, does treatment as an equal entail?

The trouble with a balancing approach to religious liberty, Eisgruber and Sager argue, is that it "asks only about the weight of the burden on religious practice and the importance of the government's interest, without attending to the distribution of burdens within society."[157] They elaborate their distributive concern in an earlier article, in which they note that if religion is singled out for special benefit, the faithful "receive disproportionate authority over decisions about the use of collective authority." The objection to privileging religion is like one classic objection to welfare-driven measures of justice. Just as utilitarians must explain why their theory does not require the grant of disproportionate resources to "welfare monsters" whose utility curves demand more resources than anyone else, so those who would privilege religion must explain why such privileging does not license extravagant demands by the religious. It is unfair to "single out one of the ways that persons come to understand what is important in life, and grant those who choose that way a license to disregard legal norms that the rest of us are obliged to obey."[158]

The argument here cites Dworkin,[159] who argues that welfare-based ideas of equality will always have this defect. The problem with equality of welfare, Dworkin explains, is that under it "people are meant to decide what sorts of lives they want independently of information relevant to determining how much their choices will reduce or enhance the ability of others to have what they want." The consequence is to force everyone to unfairly subsidize those who have expensive tastes. Dworkin thinks that justice requires rather that "only an equal share of social resources be devoted to the lives of each of its members, as measured by the opportunity costs of such resources to others."[160] There obviously would be no room in this argument for giving religion any special status.

Dworkin is inconsistent in maintaining this position, however. When he considers the question of government subsidies for the arts, he rejects the view that the amount of art produced should be left to the free market. That rejection is not—or at least, Dworkin says it is not—based on what he calls the "lofty approach," which relies on the supposed intrinsic value of art. That approach is defective, Dworkin argues, because it "turns its back on what the people think they want" and instead aims at "what it is good for people to have." Instead, he thinks that subsidies can be justified as protecting "the diversity and innovative quality of the culture as a whole," which should be understood to be a public good. "We should try to define a rich cultural structure, one that multiplies distinct possibilities or opportunities of value, and count ourselves trustees for protecting the richness of our culture for those who will live their lives in it after us." The only value judgment that the state should make is that "it is better for people to have complexity and depth in the forms of life open to them."[161]

The attraction of this approach follows from Dworkin's first principles. Dworkin thinks that government fails to treat citizens with equal concern and respect whenever it restricts individual liberty on the ground that one citizen's conception of the good life is better than another's.[162] He therefore cannot rely on the lofty view. But he does not want to abandon subsidized art. He offers an alternative rationale for subsidies, one that purports to be consistent with neutrality. He claims that subsidy, on his rationale, merely "allows a greater rather than a lesser choice, for that is exactly the respect in which we believe people are better off with a richer than a poorer language."[163]

This rationale leaves us with a problem: which "distinct possibilities or opportunities of value" is it important to preserve? The state still has to decide that. The value of a large menu does not entail the presence on it of any item, or even of any class of items. Why support highbrow art, but not romance novels, kung fu movies, or pornography? These low cultural forms are not devoid of complexity, and some of that complexity will be lost if the state does not act to preserve it. If Dworkin is untroubled by the way in which the state picks and chooses, then it would seem that he is committed to the lofty view despite himself. If you reject the lofty view, then you ought to leave these matters to the market. The question of what forms of culture will survive would not be different in kind from the question of what forms of razor blade, or vacuum cleaner, or laundry detergent will survive.

One can similarly imagine a purely economic approach to the exemption question. Free exercise claims arise only because some valid laws will be able to achieve their purposes even if they are not uniformly enforced. Some draft exemptions are tolerable, for instance, so long as enough recruits are still drafted to stock the army. Exemptions should then be regarded as a scarce resource. And when they are so regarded, the question inevitably arises, why not just auction them off?[164]

Protection Is Privileging

In the same way that Dworkin implicitly relies on a lofty view of art, Eisgruber and Sager implicitly rely on a lofty view of religion. Religion is not the only possessor of the necessary loft. They reject claims "that religious convictions are more important or in some way more valuable than all others, that religious divisions are more dangerous than all others, or that religion is uniquely immune to political judgment and regulation."[165] But they are not Benthamite utilitarians who think that all preferences ought to be treated the same.

Some human desires, they think, are entitled to special treatment. In this their view differs revealingly from that of Brian Barry, another prominent opponent of judicially crafted exemptions. Barry thinks that exemption claims threaten us with "moral anarchy," because they imply that there exist "no overarching norms by which groups and communities can be judged—or at any rate no such judgements can legitimately form the basis for the exercise of political authority."[166] What liberalism offers to religion, Barry thinks, is "equal treatment, and equal treatment is what in this context is fair."[167] Unlike Barry, Eisgruber and Sager do not think that accommodations are anomalous per se. What they are not willing to do is give excessive weight to religious claims. But we still need to specify what counts as excessive weight.

Their claim really is that religion is one of these, and ought not to be privileged *relative to the others*: "[R]eligion does not exhaust the commitments and passions that move human beings in deep and valuable ways."[168] They offer several different formulations of the criteria for admission into this set of particularly important concerns: these are "deep" commitments;[169] religion should not be privileged "by comparison to comparably serious secular commitments";[170] other concerns are equally "important";[171] "religious practices enjoy a dignity equal to other deep human convictions (such as the love parents feel for their children)."[172] Eisgruber and Sager deny "that religion is a constitutional anomaly, a category of human experience that demands special benefits and/or necessitates special restrictions."[173] However, they have their own special class. It just happens to be larger than "religion."

Once it is stipulated that some human wants have a stronger claim than others, the distinction between the two models, of privilege and protection, disappears. What Eisgruber and Sager really advocate is that deep commitments be privileged relative to shallow ones, but protected from discrimination relative to one another.

To see how privilege and protection are intertwined, consider a familiar rule of law: all adults and no infants may vote in elections. Under this rule, adults A and B may vote, while infant C may not. A and B are thus privileged relative to C. If someone proposes to deny A the right to vote—say, because A is black, or female—this is discriminatory, and A is entitled to be protected from such a discriminatory rule. That rule would be wrong because it would impose an equality of the wrong sort: it would treat A as if she were (equal to) an infant. Guaranteeing the right to vote to both A and B protects each from discrimination relative to one another, but it also privileges both relative to C.

Thus, Eisgruber and Sager are too confident when they say that the Religious Freedom Restoration Act is unconstitutional because it singles out religion and treats it as more valuable than some other human activities, or relieves religious people from burdens others must bear. How can we know that the legislative regime of which RFRA is a part is giving unduly little weight to nonreligious concerns? RFRA alone cannot tell us that. We would have to know how those other concerns are in fact treated.

Eisgruber and Sager respond that all discrimination claims face a similar evidentiary problem: one always must find a comparator to show that discrimination is occurring.[174] But the real question is whether there is an intelligible analytic distinction between privileging and protection in this context. The difficulty is not merely evidentiary. It is that without further specification, we do not know what we are looking for evidence *of*.

Professor Eisgruber declares that this vagueness is "deliberate, because I mean the proposition to be neutral among various ways of filling out the concept—though I do mean to insist that there exist some 'comparably serious and fundamental' non-religious commitments."[175] But in order for the principle to have any bite, it is necessary to specify what those commitments are. Unless that is done, one cannot possibly tell whether they are unfairly being treated less favorably than comparable religious commitments.

Thomas Berg has shown that this is an intractable problem for Eisgruber and Sager. There are always multiple comparable commitments, and usually not all of them have been accommodated. Eisgruber and Sager argue, for example, that, where a police department allowed an officer to wear a beard for medical reasons, it also was appropriately required to allow a beard for religious reasons. Berg observes that the same police department did not allow beards "to mark an ethnic identity or follow the model of an honored father." So the requirement of equal regard is incoherent: "When some deeply-felt interests are accommodated and others are not, it is logically impossible to treat religion equally with all of them."[176]

Sometimes it is possible, without any general theory, to persuade courts that religion is being discriminated against by comparison with other comparably weighty human concerns. But how could this be done at the wholesale level at which RFRA and the mini-RFRAs operate? In order to show that RFRA is unfair, we would have to compare its treatment of religion with the law's treatment of all other equally deep commitments. What would the appropriate comparison set be for the whole universe of cases affected by RFRA or a mini-RFRA? Until this is specified, how could we know whether religion is being privileged unfairly? Even if a court in a particular case gives too much weight to a religious interest or too little weight to a secular interest, it is hard to see how this error could be blamed on the statute. As Eisgruber and Sager themselves note, there is no "sharp and recognizable difference between policies that remove a burden and those that provide a benefit."[177]

The unfairness that most concerns them is a case in which two persons who are otherwise *identically* situated are treated differently because one of them is religious and one is not. They hypothesize two women named Ms. Campbell, both of whom want to open soup kitchens to feed the homeless. Zoning restrictions ban both projects. If free exercise mandates specifically religious exemptions, "the first Ms. Campbell has a constitutional right to ignore the zoning ordinance while the second Ms. Campbell must obey the ordinance." That result "imposes a test of religious orthodoxy as a condition of constitutional entitlement."[178]

It would indeed be unfair to privilege Religious Campbell over Secular Campbell. But after the selective draft cases, which presented an almost identical problem, Secular Campbell could easily be deemed to be "religious" for free exercise purposes. The similarity between her and Religious Campbell seems to be of the same kind as the similarity between Welsh and a traditional Quaker objector. It is also relevant that cases like Secular Campbell do not arise often. The American regime privileges religion, but its vague definition of religion obviates much of Eisgruber and Sager's objection to privileging.

Eisgruber and Sager work remarkably hard to reconcile their account with accommodations specifically aimed at religion—laws that readers are unlikely to want to change, and in which religion does appear to get special benefits. (Here their argument resembles Dworkin's attempt to reconcile his own commitment to neutrality toward conceptions of the good with his desire to permit government support for the arts.) The state is generally not barred from endorsing divisive ideas, but it is barred from taking any position on religious matters. It may not conduct religious exercises in schools, though otherwise its discretion to mold the curriculum is unquestioned. The law insists on the institutional autonomy of religion, by making exceptions to the normal law of trusts, for example. Direct government aid to religion is much more heavily restricted than aid that passes through a beneficiary who gets to choose the ultimate recipient: such aid may not be used for direct religious indoctrination, and some monitoring is required to make sure this does not happen. Standing rules are unusually generous for religious liberty claimants. When school voucher programs are at issue, it matters—and Eisgruber and Sager concede that it matters, though they do not explain why—that there be a secular alternative. Eisgruber and Sager ignore some of these doctrines and try to subsume others under more general rules that do not treat religion as such as special. To do so, they sometimes distort existing law. For example, they try to rely on the constitutional freedom of association to explain why the Catholic Church is allowed to discriminate on the basis of sex in selecting priests,[179] but that freedom has in fact been read very narrowly, and only religious claimants have invoked it successfully.[180]

An easier way around these difficulties would be to say—and we have already seen that there is no reason in principle that they could not say—that although religion is entitled to equal regard with other deep beliefs, the special needs of religion entail unequal treatment in these areas. They "have no quarrel with accounts that emphasize that religion has distinct features that need to be taken account of."[181] This makes sense within a Dworkinian framework: treatment as an equal does not necessarily entail equal treatment. But of course, that kind of rationalization will then become available for any kind of special treatment of religion, and it will be impossible to violate the principle.

They deny "that religious obligations are more important or valuable to individuals than any others, or that God's commands (and God's commands alone) must trump the law, or that religion is uniquely generative of civic virtue."[182] These propositions should be rejected, but they are not necessarily inconsistent with equal regard. They could be true, and government could take them to be true, without denying equal respect to any citizen: "[I]f we thought that the government could identify the one, true faith, it would not be at all obvious why the government ought to accord Equal Liberty to all faiths."[183] The logic of equality can't take them to their conclusion. They need other premises. The fact that these propositions need not embarrass their argument is itself an embarrassment to their argument.

Strict in Theory

Is equal regard violated by the compelling interest test, which now governs federal law and the law of more than half the states? Here is the formulation that now governs federal law:

> Government may substantially burden a person's exercise of religion only if it demonstrates that application of the burden to the person is in furtherance of a compelling governmental interest; and is the least restrictive means of furthering that compelling governmental interest.[184]

This test sounds like, but obviously cannot be, the familiar compelling interest test that is strict in theory and fatal in fact. There are too many legitimate state interests that would be thwarted by exemptions.[185] It is a balancing test. The state often wins. What the "compelling interest" test requires in practice is that, when the balance is struck, the value of religion be given *some* weight. That is all the test can do. The verbal formulation conceals more than it informs.

Given the diversity of human goods, there is sometimes good reason to entrench respect for some of them by institutional mechanisms to ensure that certain specific goods retain their privileged status. Judicial protection is one such mechanism, and the proliferation of RFRAs reflects a widely shared judgment that it is an appropriate mechanism for protecting religion. But there are others. The intrinsic value of natural beauty and undisturbed ecological patterns are protected by the requirement that major federal projects be accompanied by environmental impact statements.[186] The Americans with Disabilities Act requires architects to consider the exercise of limited human powers in circumstances they might otherwise have overlooked.[187] Even efficiency is protected, for example by the dormant Commerce Clause doctrine, which requires judges to engage in just the kind of weighing of incommensurables that they do in religious exemption cases.[188] And so forth. Is this privilege or protection?

Eisgruber and Sager seem confident that privileging is going on if the task of carving out religious exemptions is given to judges (absent a legislative record showing systematic discrimination, as in the case of prisoners), but not if it is done by legislatures. This runs together two different concerns: when religion should be accommodated, and which institutional actor should decide. The problem appears to be that a rule giving presumptive accommodation to religion as a category reflects "blanket demands for special concessions to religious needs and interests." There is something special about forcing matters into court: they observe that RLUIPA "quite literally transforms any local zoning dispute into a federal case." The RFRAs, both state and federal, invoke the compelling interest test, which is "language of extraordinary special privilege." They acknowledge, however, that this language is so strong that "sensible judges were bound to find ways to avoid its directive," and that in practice it has been "strict in theory but feeble in fact."[189]

Any conceivable special treatment of religion in American law will confer, not an absolute immunity from legal regulation, but a judgment that sometimes upholds and sometimes rejects the religious liberty claim.[190] Eisgruber and Sager are right that some religious liberty claims are extravagant.[191] But this is not an objection to balancing as such. Balancing tests come in a variety of flavors. Some are deferential to asserted state interests,[192] while others are nearly impossible to satisfy.[193]

The decision whether to treat religion specially in any particular case requires the decision maker, whether it is a legislature or a court, to balance the good of religion against whatever good the generally applicable law seeks to pursue. That balancing is a matter of context-specific judgment.[194] It is not reducible to any legal formula.

There are at least two different ways in which religion can be unfairly privileged. One occurs if religious claims are made a basis for a colorable exemption claim when other, equally valuable concerns are not given similar weight. The other occurs if, after the balancing test is triggered, the exercise of religion is permitted to override other, equally valuable human concerns. The second of these is clearly unfair. But, once more, there is no way to decide in the abstract whether this is happening. It all depends on how the balance is struck in individual cases. All equally valuable concerns should be treated as equally valuable. This is tautologically true. But because it is a tautology, it cannot help us to resolve any actual case.

I cannot pretend to have dispelled the concern about unfairness. It will always be with us. Fairness cannot be guaranteed, but space can be created for its possibility. A mechanism for considering specifically religious exemptions is one means toward that end.

Because no single legal rule can protect all deeply valuable concerns, more specific rules are necessary. Accommodation of religion is one of these. The point is similar to the idea, in Hindu theology, that humans cannot comprehend the fullness of God, and so must look to multiple finite representations.[195] We can honor these representations only one at a time. Acknowledgment of the unique value of each human good is no insult to the others.

— 5 —

A Secular State?

American religious neutrality is one of the world's most successful legal strategies for coping with the fact of religious diversity. In the United States, a growing proliferation of remarkably different religious factions live together in peace and even some harmony. It is a spectacular achievement. Those on both the left and right who aim to dismantle this regime and replace it with a different one have a heavy burden of persuasion.

This is an academic book, primarily directed at scholars of law and political philosophy. The approach to religious diversity that it endorses, however, is not just for scholars. It is a regime of law, and so must be perceived as legitimate by nonspecialists. Rawls worried about what he called the problem of "stability": can a just society induce its citizens to freely endorse its principles and act accordingly?[1] No amount of normative theorizing can resolve the stability problem. It is a question of what principles can attract the allegiance of ordinary people.

The regime of American religious neutrality faces two opposing kinds of resistance, from those who think that it is not religion-friendly enough and from those who think that it is too religion-friendly. We considered their philosophical champions in the last chapter. Now focus on them as social groups in modern American society, each regarding the other with suspicion. These opponents, whom we can roughly denominate the "religious right" and the "militant atheists," have a common set of anxieties. Each group feels, for different reasons, that the regime excludes and stigmatizes them. Each feels threatened by the other. Each tends to view the other as intolerant and selfish.[2]

I will conclude by arguing that the regime I have described here has at least the potential to win the endorsement even of these bitterest of critics. This is so, in part, because the regime really does not take sides between them, and in part because the sense of threat on both sides rests on stereotypes that are demonstrably mistaken. They misperceive both the regime and each other. Both need to understand the common ground that we have been exploring here. American law bespeaks an aspiration that both can share.

Political philosophy has been deemed excessively fanciful and abstract ever since Machiavelli mocked those who imagined "states and princedoms such as nobody ever saw or knew in the real world."[3] What I have offered here, however, is not a proposal. It is a description. It is already the law in the United States. The normative question is not how to design an ideal commonwealth, but whether we should maintain what in fact we have inherited. The idea of "religion" that is at the center of that regime may seem esoteric. But if this body of law were comprehensible only to a specialized elite, it could not have lasted as long as it has.

In this concluding chapter, I will consider the stability of American religious neutrality. I will argue that the common ground is more robust than is commonly understood. That common ground emerges from common roots. This helps to explain the broadly ecumenical views which are held by most Americans, which we examined in Chapter 1. Here I will show that it also helps us to understand what is shared by the most bitterly opposed factions: the religious right and the militant atheists. American religious neutrality might be able to attract even greater support than it already has if the contending factions better understood themselves and each other.

Many issues of cultural politics in contemporary America, such as debates over abortion, gay rights, sex education, the roles of men and women, and, most pertinently here, the role of religion in public life, are rooted in different systems of moral understanding. At the root of these, James Davison Hunter observes, is the cleavage between what he calls the orthodox worldview, which views morality as obedience to the unchanging commands of a transcendent authority, and the progressive, which holds that understandings of (possibly divinely willed) morality in particular circumstances are revisable in light of experience. This cleavage cuts across old divisions between Protestants, Catholics, and Jews, because all three faiths are divided between orthodox and progressive factions.[4]

From the standpoint of Hunter's map of the political territory, contemporary Establishment Clause law appears emphatically not neutral, because it places the American regime on one side of the culture wars: for a secular and indeed antireligious conception of public life. It is therefore unsurprising that the law in this area elicits hostility from cultural conservatives.

As we have seen, this understanding of nonestablishment as hostile to religion is anachronistic and inaccurate. The Establishment Clause from the beginning has been religion-friendly and religion-protective. It facilitates religion by keeping the state's hands off of it, in the same way that free enterprise facilitates production.[5]

Some historical excavation helps to make clear that the warring sides have more common ground than they realize. In particular, modern atheism, which for many religious Americans symbolizes the selfish rejection of any basis for moral solidarity (a symbolic status once occupied by Jews and Catholics),[6] in fact has a common ancestry with theism, and many of the same commitments.

Charles Taylor's *A Secular Age* shows that modern Western secularism has its roots in Christian theology.[7] Secularism and Christianity share a commitment to human rights (a term I'll use here as shorthand, not just for the right to be free from torture and indefinite detention without trial, but more generally for the claim to decent treatment for all human beings).[8] That commitment does not follow from atheism.[9] The turn toward concern with the worldly flourishing of human beings had its roots in medieval movements of Church reform. Discontent with the division between the clergy and the laity, which had always been in tension with Christianity's universalizing aspirations, led to a sacralization of everyday life, which became a means of realizing God's benevolent intentions for mankind. This focus on the world, which coincided with growing technological control, eventually made it possible for God to drop out of the picture altogether, or even appear as an enemy of human fulfillment. Moreover, the problem of theodicy becomes more acute in a world in which the purposes of the world are understood to center around human flourishing: "The idea of blaming God gets a clearer sense and becomes much more salient in the modern era where people begin to think they know just what God was purposing in creating the world, and can check the results against the intention."[10] But the militant opposition to religion itself rests on a demand for universal justice, a demand that in no way follows from atheism as such.

What traditional religion and secularism have in common is what Taylor calls "strong evaluation"—discriminations of better and worse that are independent of our desires and offer standards by which those desires are to be judged. For many, Taylor observes, strong evaluation is inseparable from religion: "[T]heir highest sense of the good has been developed in a profoundly religious context," and "is inconceivable without God."[11] Their understanding that the world makes sense, that they live significant, morally intelligible lives in a significant, morally intelligible world, is closely tied to their religious beliefs and practices. That is not true of the secularists. But in the secular worldview, strong evaluation persists, and its objects bear a suspicious resemblance to those of the religious.

Taylor's history refutes what he calls the "subtraction view" of the movement toward secularism, according to which the decline of religious belief is simply the result of the falling away of superstition and the growth of knowledge. Rather, modern secularism is a religious worldview, with its own narrative of testing and redemption, and shares the vulnerabilities of such views. The news that secularists also live in glass houses has implications for ongoing stone-throwing operations.

WHAT CONTEMPORARY ATHEISTS are committed to might be called Naked Strong Evaluation: the idea, unsupported by any particular metaphysical claims, that the commitment to decent treatment for all human beings is a nonoptional criterion for judging our own desires and actions. It is difficult for many theists to imagine how such an atheist humanism can be coherent. Yet the nakedness of this commitment does not necessarily weaken it, as a basis for either morality or social solidarity.

Here I can offer some pertinent introspection. I'm a specimen of what Taylor is trying to explain: a modern secularist with a deep commitment to human rights. Since it's my worldview that he's anatomizing, I can offer some data as an anthropological informant.

I'm not prepared to claim, as Richard Rorty does, that there is no transcendent basis for my commitment, that it is a purely contingent historical formation.[12] Rorty is mighty sure of himself.[13] I just don't know. So there's what appears to be a permanent gap in my belief system. If I were a religious person, I guess I'd be entitled to call it a Mystery. It doesn't trouble me, because every belief system has Mysteries of its own. My agnosticism is the functional equivalent of atheism in many ways; I don't rely at all on a belief in God as the basis for any of my commitments. I don't think I have to. Naked Strong Evaluation works for me (although, as the existence of this book shows, religion exerts a continuing fascination nonetheless). There are a great many people for whom it wouldn't work.

The question about the relation between religion and human rights is chronically confused, because it is really four different questions:[14]

1. *Epistemic: how do we know that there are human rights?* The secularist commitment to human rights is curiously ungrounded. Religious revelation is one answer.

It would be implausible, however, to suggest that it is the only answer. Knowledge of God's existence has no more secure epistemic foundation than Naked Strong Evaluation. On the contrary, it raises new epistemic problems: remind me why you're so confident that the bush that Moses saw burned and was not consumed?[15]

2. *Justificatory: in a materialist universe, how can there be any compelling warrant for moral statements?* The question's implication is that moral obligations aren't the kind of thing that can be justified, or perhaps even be coherent, in a Godless universe.[16]

This one doesn't work, either. In order for this argument to be persuasive, it would have to be shown how God helps—how warranted moral claims can be dependent on God's existence. There are ancient and unresolved difficulties about whether morality is equivalent to whatever God commands, whether morality can be a constraint on God, whether evil deeds would become good if God did them, and so forth. Naked Strong Evaluation hasn't got these problems. The character of moral obligation remains mysterious, but at least it isn't chained to dubious claims of fact.

There certainly is something mysterious about strong evaluation in a materialistic universe. If there can be moral claims whose warrant transcends particular cultural formations, then what kind of warrant could this be? Utilitarian answers miss the point, since they themselves rest on some kind of strong evaluation that they cannot account for.

The Transcendent Something toward which all this points is, however, obscure.

3. *Sociological/psychological: can human beings sustain their allegiance to human rights if they don't believe in God?* It is sometimes suggested that the answer to this question must be no. But this claim is obviously silly.

It is an indisputable social fact that Naked Strong Evaluation and belief in human rights holds the allegiance of many. Different people manage, with varying degrees of success, to accomplish the psychological trick within themselves in different ways. Theists, of course, are susceptible to the same pathology of selective sympathy and indifference.

4. *Historical: did the idea of human rights, at least in the West, emerge from Christian doctrine?* The answer to this is yes, as Taylor has shown more thoroughly than anyone before him.

Some people have taken an affirmative answer to 4 to be evidence of an exclusively theistic answer to 1 or 2. This is a jejune error in logic. Our knowledge of the truth may be—often is—rooted in previous errors. Modern astronomy is rooted in astrology, but astrology is not a good epistemic path to knowledge of astronomy, nor does the data of astronomy need a justificatory basis in astrology.

Immanuel Kant argues that a person who acts morally is acting as if there were some reason to think that the aspirations of moral behavior—a world in which virtue is rewarded and vice punished—could be realized. And that implies a universe that is fundamentally orderly, which means, a universe presided over by a being who is omnipotent, omniscient, and infinitely good. But Kant is emphatically not endorsing a theistic answer to 1. For Kant, it's not that God implies human rights—there have been conceptions of God that haven't done that, and Kant has some harsh words about Abraham's willingness to sacrifice Isaac just on (someone who purported to be) God's say-so[17]—but that human rights implies God.

Kant also argues, however, that the relation of human rights and religion yields no information whatsoever about God, and certainly cannot be cited as evidence of God's existence. For Kant, God's existence isn't knowable; it is at best something that one assumes, from a practical standpoint, when one acts morally. The epistemic arrows don't work in either direction.

The fragmentation of religions is often, however, understood to conceal a deeper unity, as for example in the familiar American injunction to worship in the church of your choice.[18] The limits of tolerable diversity have shifted over time: Catholics were originally outside; by the mid-twentieth century, Jews and Catholics were included; the circle is widening again to include Muslims. Taylor's analysis of the origins of secularism implies that theists and atheists too have a deeper unity in something like the way that, we saw in the Introduction, Justice Scalia imagines: in some sense, they simply worship the same God in different ways. But what unifies them, *pace* Scalia, is not theism. It is something more abstract.

Religious fragmentation is an irresistible and ongoing trend, and so any attempt to define communal identity in any but the vaguest terms is a prescription for inevitable division. A persistent theme in all of the classic accounts of corruption was the idea that religion is individual, and that state interference distorts it. Modern developments have radicalized this individualistic tendency, although, as Milton and Roger Williams show, it was there from the beginning.

The broadening of the American civil religion is a sensible response to this trend. There are no longer any specific theological propositions that constitute the common ground. Rather, what unites the various religious views is a more generalized commitment to the humane treatment of every human being, the promotion of a culture of nonviolence and mutual respect.[19] The state should not discriminate among the citizens who share this common ground. Taylor's account also suggests that religious evolution is a delicate process in which the state is unlikely to have much to contribute. The ham-handedness of any contemporary intervention is the modern face of corrupting establishment.

There is a deep instability in the criticism of modern American law that is made by the conservative evangelical Protestants who are the most prominent and numerous opponents of American religious neutrality. They advocate prayer in the schools, the teaching of "creation science," and unrestricted state endorsement of theism. Yet in the 1960s, the school prayer cases tore apart the main Protestant organization advocating separation, Protestants and Other Americans United for Separation of Church and State.[20] Some of the membership had always strongly advocated separation, but shrank from the Supreme Court's conclusion, which was so at odds with state support for religion of a kind that seemed familiar and right. The rulings have sometimes been quietly defied.[21] In 1982, the Southern Baptist Convention formally endorsed a school prayer amendment to the Constitution.[22] Every Republican Party platform since 1972 has called for the restoration of prayer in schools. Yet despite the Supreme Court's growing conservatism, no justice has yet squarely repudiated the school prayer decisions.

The split here resembles that between the two most important separationist Baptist ministers at the time of the framing of the First Amendment, Isaac Backus and John Leland. As we have seen, Leland opposed any involvement of the state in religious matters. Backus began with similar separationist principles, but supported a law restricting public office holding to Christians, and official licensing of the publication of Bibles. He did not oppose official fast days, days of prayer, or even laws requiring church attendance. Backus's views were widely accepted, but inconsistent. Thomas Curry notes that he never confronted "the problem of how a government could maintain a Christian commonwealth without interfering in matters of religion or without defining Christianity."[23] Advocates of school prayer face a similar problem: why should they trust the state to decide what religious rituals are appropriate?[24]

If its ecumenism is one of the best things about American religiosity, one of the worst is its choice of where to draw the line. Atheists are perhaps the most disliked and distrusted group in contemporary America. Half of the public thinks that an atheist can't "be moral and have good values," and wouldn't vote for a political candidate who didn't believe in God even if he or she had been nominated by their own party.[25] That is about the number that was willing to vote for a Jew in 1936.[26] Family court judges have deprived parents of custody over their children because of the parents' atheism.[27] Unsurprisingly, religious conservatism predicts hostility to atheists: those who attend church regularly and those who are conservative Protestants are less likely to approve of intermarriage with atheists and more likely to say that atheists do not share their vision of American society.[28]

A survey of Americans' attitudes toward atheists found that two stereotypes predominate. Some associate atheism with social threats from the bottom of society's status hierarchy: drug use, prostitution, and similar deviance. Others see atheists as a threat from above: rich cultural elitists who make a lifestyle out of selfish consumption.[29] Both stereotypes have the same social function, and bear as much resemblance to reality, as the *Protocols of the Elders of Zion*. For all the reasons that Taylor's analysis would predict, self-professed atheists tend to be intensely idealistic and driven by urgent humanitarian concern. Real sociopaths tend to have little interest, positive or negative, in religious questions.

Militant atheists' unhappiness about the religion-friendliness of the regime is primarily driven by the fear that they will be thereby excluded or demoted to second-class status. They are increasingly reconciled to the fact that religion is not going away, and that they are not going to win over most Americans to their views. Their central concern has rather become protecting themselves from discrimination.[30] That is why the nonreligious conscientious objection cases, *Seeger* and *Welsh*, are so salient when secular political philosophers think about law's treatment of religion. Atheist conscientious objectors in fact rarely arise. "[U]nbelief entails no obligations and no observances," Michael McConnell observes. "Unbelief may be coupled with various sorts of moral conviction. . . . . But these convictions must necessarily be derived from some source other than unbelief itself."[31] In the conscientious objector cases, the direction of causation went the other way: it was moral conviction that generated the declaration of unbelief. But despite the rarity of these cases, they have enormous symbolic weight, because they test the status of atheists in the regime. The issue goes beyond fairness to individuals.

The American regime of religious neutrality does as much as constitutional law can do to guarantee full citizenship to atheists, and has done so since the Court held in 1961 that public officeholders could not be required to profess belief in God.[32] The *Seeger* and *Welsh* cases also show that in the present regime, the concept of religion is fluid enough to address the conscientious objection problem. Atheists will doubtless be uneasy with the law's treatment of religion as a good, but they can take comfort from the fact that this does not permit the state to endorse religious propositions except in the narrow, unexpandable category of ceremonial deism.

Vagueness has its virtues, particularly when one is not entitled to feel that one has precise knowledge. The ire directed at theists and atheists is in each case mistaken, because the targets are so heterogeneous. Arguments of the form "belief in God entails . . ." or "atheism entails . . ." treat these loose collections of worldviews as if they had some unique set of entailments. Thus, for instance, "belief in God produces oppression" or "atheism leads to immorality." Similarly with more particular views. Sam Harris's dunderheaded bestseller, *Letter to a Christian Nation*, summarily claims, on the basis of four biblical quotations, that Christianity rightly understood must support slavery, and that the abolitionists, who were a religious movement from the beginning, must have been "cherry-picking the Bible."[33] A particularly malign version of this has gotten a lot of play lately: "Islam is an intrinsically terrorist religion."

The problem with all of these claims is that belief in God, atheism, Christianity, and Islam each denote a large collection of views associated in various ways with a large collection of people, only some of which, and whom, are associated with the named pathology. Wilfred Cantwell Smith observes that "no man in one lifetime of study could possibly become sufficiently well informed on the history of either the Buddhist or the Hindu communities to be able to say that Buddhism or Hinduism is true, or alternatively it is false, and know what he was saying."[34] The same point can be made about other religions. Christians are centrally attached to Jesus Christ, but their idea of who that is has changed radically over the centuries.[35]

The same is true of some atheists' identification of religion with fanatical right-wing politics. In modern America, politics has become unusually polarized along religious lines. In the 2008 presidential election, for example, 55 percent of those attending church weekly or more voted for McCain, compared with 36 percent of those who attend services yearly or never; in 2004, the comparable numbers favoring Bush were 61 percent and 42 percent, respectively. In both years, the gap was 19 points.[36]

Robert Putnam and David Campbell have anatomized the peculiar set of circumstances that produced this unprecedented degree of religious political polarization. The liberalization of sexual mores in the 1960s mobilized religious conservatives against the change, and they soon aligned with the Republican Party. "[B]eginning in the 1980s and continuing into the first decade of the new century, conservative politics became the most visible aspect of religion in America."[37] This produced a counterbacklash, especially among those who came of age in the 1990s and who rejected traditional sexual morality. A liberal stance on homosexuality was a distinguishing mark of those who proclaimed no religious affiliation (even though, as noted in Chapter 1, most of them in fact believe in God and often pray). They are about 25 percent of those who came of age in the 1990s and 2000s, and overwhelmingly, they have aligned with the Democrats. The result is growing polarization: the sum of evangelicals plus the unaffiliated was 30 percent of the American population in 1973, but rose to 41 percent by 2008.[38]

This connection between religiosity and partisanship is driven primarily by two issues, abortion and homosexuality. Neither of these is likely to keep its partisan salience, because "while attitudes on same-sex marriage are moving sharply in a liberal direction, those on abortion are becoming somewhat more conservative—with both shifts most pronounced among young people."[39] As the divide on these issues narrows, the basis for religious/political polarization is likely to fade, and so religion will no longer be a marker for conservative politics. American politics is likely to return to its normal state, with religious people on both sides of whatever political divides there happen to be.

Before these developments, religion was often associated with the political left. The Social Gospel movement of the late nineteenth century fought alcoholism, sweatshops, decaying tenements, business monopolies, and foreign wars. Organized Catholics helped push the New Deal to the left.[40] In the 1960s, religious groups swung left on the most pressing issues, the civil rights movement and the Vietnam War.[41] The most important effect of politically mobilized religion in American public life, once more, is the abolition of slavery. Religion, in short, has been good for American democracy.[42] If history shows anything, it is that in this country the secular left can accomplish little without religious allies.[43] Attacks on religion in the name of the left, then, are spectacularly counterproductive. Militant atheism in contemporary America mistakes a historical blip for a permanent feature of the political world.

The promise of American religious neutrality is that we can prescind from our differences and unite around a common set of principles. Can the various factions unite around the conception of American identity that is implicit in the neutrality that I have described in this book?

In some respects, the common ground is already present. Rawls thought that, in the face of intractable disagreements about the good life, "we must find a new way of organizing familiar ideas and principles into a conception of political justice so that the claims in conflict, as previously understood, are seen in another light."[44] Historical excavation can offer resources for discovering common ground that Rawls's constructivist political philosophy lacks.

In another sense, however, the common ground will still have to be constructed. America today is often imagined as essentially a liberal democracy, dedicated to principles of liberty and equality. Yet this vision rests on a selective account of history: nativism, racism, and sexism have been equally important parts of American identity.[45] The liberal vision of American identity is an invention, albeit one that has done enormous good. Similarly, the consensus politics of the 1950s was the product of a deliberate project, carefully engineered by civic and business leaders, of reimagining America in a way that diminished the importance of class, racial, ethnic, and religious divisions.[46] The invention of "Judeo-Christian" religion, described in Chapter 1, was a manifestation of this. The consequence was to broaden membership in the American community, to recognize as Americans those who in fact had been here for a long time.[47]

The narrative I have offered here has a similar ambition. It reimagines American plurality to be even more inclusive than the Judeo-Christian unity of the 1950s. But because it is firmly rooted in present constitutional practice, it can also be understood as bringing to awareness the logic of that practice: to make us aware of what we are already doing, and thus to transform it into something more self-conscious and therefore more likely to endure.

Sebastian Castellio, one of the earliest proponents of religious toleration, in 1554 declared it senseless to penalize "those who differ from the mighty about matters hitherto unknown, for so many centuries disputed, and not yet cleared up."[48] The state is as incompetent to decide religious questions today as it was then.

The American regime of religious neutrality refuses to adjudicate those theological disputes. This very refusal, targeted at religious questions, implicitly recognizes the value of religion. The state reveals its reverence for the Absolute by omitting all reference to it in public decision making.

American religious neutrality demands that the state be silent about religious truth, but the silence is eloquent and highlights the importance of what is not articulated. It is like a rest in music.

Notes

Introduction

1. Both the statement and the ridicule are noted in Patrick Henry, *"And I Don't Care What It Is": The Tradition-History of a Civil Religion Proof-Text*, 49 J. Am. Acad. of Religion 35 (1981). Eisenhower's critics include Will Herberg and Robert Bellah.
2. See School Dist. of Abington v. Schempp, 374 U.S. 203, 218, 222, 225, 226 (1963).
3. See, e.g., Everson v. Bd. of Educ., 330 U.S. 1, 18 (1947); Zorach v. Clauson, 343 U.S. 306, 314 (1952); Walz v. Tax Comm'n, 397 U.S. 664, 676 (1970); Wallace v. Jaffree, 472 U.S. 38, 60 (1985); Rosenberger v. Rectors of University of Virginia, 515 U.S. 819, 839–846 (1995); McCreary County v. ACLU, 545 U.S. 844, 860, 874–881 (2005).
4. Steven D. Smith, Foreordained Failure: The Quest for a Constitutional Principle of Religious Freedom 77 (1995).
5. See, e.g., William A. Galston, Liberal Purposes: Goods, Virtues, and Diversity in the Liberal State 92–94 (1991); Smith, Foreordained Failure, at 77–97.
6. See, e.g., Edwards v. Aguillard, 482 U.S. 578, 616–618 (1987) (Scalia, J., dissenting); Michael W. McConnell, *Religious Freedom at a Crossroads*, 59 U. Chi. L. Rev. 115, 131 (1992).
7. George Sher, Beyond Neutrality: Perfectionism and Politics (1997).
8. Richard John Neuhaus, The Naked Public Square (2d ed. 1986).
9. Smith, Foreordained Failure, at 96.
10. Thomas Hurka, *Book Review: Sher, Beyond Neutrality*, 109 Ethics 190 (1998).
11. Mary Ann Glendon and Raul F. Yanes, *Structural Free Exercise*, 90 Mich. L. Rev. 477, 478 (1991); see also Mark V. Tushnet, Red, White, and Blue: A Critical Analysis of Constitutional Law 247 (1988) ("incoherent").
12. Vincent Phillip Muñoz, *Establishing Free Exercise*, 138 First Things 14 (Dec. 2003) ("If conservative and liberal church-state scholars agree on one thing, it is that the Supreme Court's religious liberty jurisprudence is a disaster.").

13. Steven D. Smith, *The Rise and Fall of Religious Freedom in Constitutional Discourse*, 140 U. Pa. L. Rev. 149, 149–150 (1991) ("It is by now notorious that legal doctrines and judicial decisions in the area of religious freedom are in serious disarray.").

14. Michael W. McConnell, *Neutrality, Separation and Accommodation: Tensions in American First Amendment Doctrine*, in Law and Religion 63, 64 (Rex J. Adhar, ed., 2000).

15. For a rare point of convergence between Justice Clarence Thomas, see Utah Highway Patrol Assn. v. American Atheists, 132 S.Ct. 12, 13 (2011) (Thomas, J., dissenting from denial of cert.), and Christopher L. Eisgruber & Lawrence G. Sager, *The Vulnerability of Conscience: The Constitutional Basis for Protecting Religious Conduct*, 61 U. Chi. L. Rev. 1245, 1246 (1994).

16. Ronald Y. Mykkeltvedt, *Souring on* Lemon: *The Supreme Court's Establishment Clause Doctrine in Transition*, 44 Mercer L. Rev. 881, 883 (1993).

17. Christopher L. Eisgruber & Lawrence G. Sager, *Unthinking Religious Freedom*, 74 Tex. L. Rev. 577, 578 (1996). Most of these quotations are drawn from Paul Horwitz, The Agnostic Age: Law, Religion, and the Constitution xii (2011).

18. Everson v. Bd. of Educ., 330 U.S. 1, 15 (1947).

19. Thomas v. Review Bd., 450 U.S. 707, 713 (1981).

20. I address this specific issue in *You Can't Hurry Love: Why Antidiscrimination Protections for Gay People Should Have Religious Exemptions*, 72 Brooklyn L. Rev. 125 (2006).

21. Michael W. McConnell, *Institutions and Interpretation: A Critique of City of Boerne v. Flores*, 111 Harv. L. Rev. 153, 160 (1997).

22. For a survey, see Douglas Laycock, *Theology Scholarships, the Pledge of Allegiance, and Religious Liberty: Avoiding the Extremes but Missing the Liberty*, 118 Harv. L. Rev. 155, 211–212 & nn.368–373 (2004).

23. 489 U.S. 1, 16 (1989) (plurality opinion by Brennan, J., joined by Marshall and Stevens, JJ.).

24. Id. at 27–28 (Blackmun, J., joined by O'Connor, J., concurring in the judgment).

25. See *Words and Phrases*, in 10 Gale Encyclopedia of American Law 448 (Donna Batten, ed., 3d ed. 2010).

26. *Abandonment*, 1 Words and Phrases 37–147, supp. 4-8 (2007 & Supp. 2011); *abuse of discretion*, id. at 323–462, supp. 2366.

27. *Religion*, 36C Words and Phrases 153–157, supp. 54-55 (2002 & supp. 2011).

28. See John R. Bowen, Why the French Don't Like Headscarves: Islam, the State, and Public Space (2008).

29. See Andrew Koppelman, *The New American Civil Religion: Lessons for Italy*, 41 Geo. Wash. Int'l L. Rev. 861, 872–874 (2010).

30. See John Rawls, A Theory of Justice 206 n./180 n. rev. (1971; revised ed., 1999); see also id. at 220/193 rev. Other exponents of liberal neutrality have described their project in similar terms. See Bruce Ackerman, Reconstructing American Law 99 (1984); Charles Larmore, The Morals of Modernity 144

(1996); Gerald F. Gaus, Justificatory Liberalism: An Essay on Epistemology and Political Theory 170 (1996).

31. John Rawls, *A Kantian Conception of Equality*, in Collected Papers 255 (Samuel Freeman, ed., 1999).

32. John Rawls, Political Liberalism 4 (expanded ed. 1996).

33. Rawls, A Theory of Justice, at 19/17 rev.

34. Rawls, Political Liberalism, at 12–13.

35. John Rawls, *Reply to Habermas*, 42 J. Phil. 132, 145 (1995). For similar formulations, see Political Liberalism, at xlvii; *The Idea of Public Reason Revisited*, in Collected Papers at 585; John Rawls, Justice as Fairness: A Restatement 37, 188–189 (2001).

36. *The Idea of Public Reason Revisited*, 579.

37. John Rawls, The Law of Peoples 32 (1999).

38. That the aim is to contain disagreement within a framework of mutual respect is particularly clear in T. M. Scanlon, *The Difficulty of Tolerance*, in Toleration: An Elusive Virtue 226–239 (David Heyd, ed., 1998), which is cited with approval in Rawls, *The Idea of Public Reason Revisited*, at 588 n.42.

39. T. M. Scanlon, *Rawls on Justification*, in The Cambridge Companion to Rawls 164 (Samuel Freeman, ed., 2003).

40. Lee v. Weisman, 505 U.S. 577, 646, 641 (1992) (Scalia, J., dissenting).

41. McCreary County v. ACLU, 545 U.S. 844, 893 (2005) (Scalia, J., joined by Rehnquist, C. J. and Thomas, J., dissenting).

42. Bd. of Educ. of Kiryas Joel v. Grumet, 512 U.S. 687, 748 (1994) (Scalia, J., dissenting).

43. Torcaso v. Watkins, 367 U.S. 488, 495 (1961).

44. Eugene Volokh, *A Common-Law Model for Religious Exemptions*, 46 UCLA L. Rev. 1465, 1474–1476 (1999). The limitations of courts are apparent in the fate of some of the mini-RFRAs (state laws that attempted to duplicate the effect of the federal RFRA), which have been construed so narrowly that they have little effect. See Christopher C. Lund, *Religious Liberty after* Gonzales: *A Look at State RFRAs*, 55 S.D. L. Rev. 466 (2010).

45. 530 U.S. 793 (2000).

46. 536 U.S. 639, 655 (2002).

47. Justice Sandra Day O'Connor, on the other hand, suggested that the test of constitutionality was whether a program in fact offered "genuine nonreligious options." Id. at 676 (O'Connor, J., concurring). She cast the deciding vote, but she is no longer on the Court.

1. The American Specification of Neutrality

1. On the definition of "perfectionism," see Andrew Koppelman, *The Fluidity of Neutrality*, 66 Rev. of Politics 633, 634 n.1 (2004).

2. John Rawls, A Theory of Justice 94/80–81 rev. (1971; revised ed., 1999); for similar claims, see Robert Nozick, Anarchy, State, and Utopia 33, 312 (1974); Bruce Ackerman, Social Justice in the Liberal State 11 (1980); Ronald Dworkin, *Liberalism*, in A Matter of Principle 191 (1985); Charles E. Larmore, Patterns of Moral Complexity 44 (1987); Gerald Gaus, *Liberal Neutrality: A Compelling and Radical Principle*, in Perfectionism and Neutrality: Essays in Liberal Theory 137 (Steven Wall & George Klosko, eds., 2003); Jonathan Quong, *Liberalism without Perfection* (2011). Rawls later expressly endorsed the idea of neutrality, citing with approval writings of Dworkin and Larmore. See John Rawls, Political Liberalism 190–195 (1993). At the same time, however, Rawls evidently did not endorse it in as strong a sense as these writers do. See John Rawls, Justice as Fairness: A Restatement 91 n.13 (2001) (arguing that basing all legislative decisions solely on purely political values is "neither attainable nor desirable"). See generally Steve Sheppard, *The Perfectionisms of John Rawls*, 11 Can. J. L. & Juris. 383 (1998).

3. Joseph Raz, The Morality of Freedom 220 (1986). Raz does not make the same point about neutrality, instead arguing that neutrality, in the form in which antiperfectionists have advocated it, is not an attractive political ideal. See id. at 110–162. He implicitly acknowledges that more modest forms of neutrality may sometimes be appropriate—see id. at 120–122—but his attention is focused elsewhere.

4. Peter Westen, *The Empty Idea of Equality*, 95 Harv. L. Rev. 537, 547 (1982). Other scholars have noted that Westen's deconstruction of "equality" also applies to the "neutrality" that is frequently invoked in religious freedom disputes. Douglas Laycock, *Formal, Substantive, and Disaggregated Neutrality toward Religion*, 39 DePaul L. Rev. 993, 995 (1990); Steven D. Smith, Foreordained Failure: The Quest for a Constitutional Principle of Religious Freedom 151–152 (1995); see also John T. Valauri, *The Concept of Neutrality in Establishment Clause Doctrine*, 48 U. Pitt. L. Rev. 83 (1986) (not relying on Westen, but making a similar objection to neutrality).

5. Westen made this claim at several points in his 1982 article. See *The Empty Idea of Equality* at 537, 542, 596. It was not repeated in his later book, but he did say there that his thesis would deprive equality of much of its rhetorical force. See Peter Westen, Speaking of Equality 287–288 (1990).

6. See Kenneth Karst, *Why Equality Matters*, 17 Ga. L. Rev. 245, 248 (1983).

7. See generally Andrew Koppelman, Antidiscrimination Law and Social Equality (1996).

8. The defense of neutrality and equality offered here applies with equal force to the idea of fairness, which is likewise so vague that it may appear empty. Stanley Fish makes a point analogous to Weston's by arguing that fairness "will have different meanings in relation to different assumptions and background conditions." Stanley Fish, *Introduction: "That's Not Fair,"* in There's

No Such Thing as Free Speech and It's a Good Thing, Too 4 (1994); see also Stanley Fish, *Mission Impossible: Settling the Just Bounds between Church and State*, 97 Colum. L. Rev. 2255 (1997). Fish is correct that it is impossible for any system of distribution to avoid some unfairness, and that absolute fairness is analytically impossible. It does not follow that the idea of fairness should be abandoned, or that claims of unfairness should be given no weight.

9. Frank S. Ravitch, Masters of Illusion: The Supreme Court and the Religion Clauses 38 (2007).

10. Id. at 19.

11. Ravitch is correct that neutrality depends on a baseline, and that it is often invoked in a conclusory way that conceals that baseline and so disguises the real basis for the result reached. See, e.g., Michael W. McConnell et al., Religion and the Constitution 377 (3d ed. 2011) (appropriating the label "neutrality" for the authors' favored approach to establishment clause litigation).

12. Thus, for example, the argument from character was overlooked in the article from which this chapter is adapted. See Koppelman, *The Fluidity of Neutrality*.

13. The dictionary definition of "fluid" applies here: "[a] substance that exists, or is regarded as existing, as a continuum characterized by low resistance to flow and the tendency to assume the shape of the container." American Heritage Dictionary of the English Language 505 (1976). By using this term, I do not, however, mean to imply that the version of neutrality that you adopt ought to shift over time. To the extent that your normative commitments and empirical beliefs remain stable, your neutrality will remain stable. On the other hand, American law's treatment of religion has been fluid and unstable precisely because its foundations have shifted over time.

14. See Richard Arneson, *Liberal Neutrality on the Good: An Autopsy*, in Perfectionism and Neutrality, supra, at 193. For a similar taxonomy, see William Galston, Liberal Purposes: Goods, Virtues, and Diversity in the Liberal State 100–101 (1991).

15. With each of these arguments, it is possible that the strength of the argument for neutrality may be greater for justification than for aim, or vice versa. Thus, for example, a moral pluralist might think that sound deliberation requires neutrality of justification, but that, because a little political hypocrisy is sometimes useful (say, professing a piety one does not feel), violations of neutrality of aim are less troubling.

16. John Locke, A Letter Concerning Toleration 36 (James H. Tully, ed.; William Popple, trans., 1983) (1689).

17. Id. at 27; cf. id. at 38–39.

18. Id. at 37.

19. Id. at 55.

20. Charles Larmore, The Morals of Modernity 123 (1996).

21. Rawls, Political Liberalism at 137. For an argument that this is a forlorn aspiration, see my *Respect and Contempt in Constitutional Law, Or, Is Jack Balkin Heartbreaking?*, 71 Md. L. Rev. 1126 (2012).

22. Larmore, Patterns of Moral Complexity, at 67; see also id. at 55.

23. John Milton, *Areopagitica* (1644), in Complete Poems and Major Prose 739, 728 (Merritt Y. Hughes, ed., 1957).

24. Id. at 730, 742.

25. See Vincent Blasi, *Milton's Areopagitica and the Modern First Amendment*, Yale Law School Occasional Papers (1995), available at http://lsr.nellco.org/yale/ylsop/papers/6 (visited June 18, 2008).

26. John Stuart Mill, *On Liberty*, in Mill 89–90, 68 (Alan Ryan, ed., 1997).

27. The resemblances between the arguments of Milton and Mill are further explored in Andrew Koppelman, *Veil of Ignorance: Tunnel Constructivism in Free Speech Theory*, Nw. L. Rev. (forthcoming 2013).

28. See Vincent Blasi, *Free Speech and Good Character: From Milton to Brandeis to the Present*, in Eternally Vigilant: Free Speech in the Modern Era 60 (Lee C. Bollinger & Geoffrey R. Stone, eds., 2002).

29. See, e.g., Dworkin, *Liberalism*.

30. See Gerald Dworkin, *Equal Respect and the Enforcement of Morality*, 7 Soc. Phil. & Pol'y 180 (1990).

31. For a catalogue of the ways in which this occurs, see Richard H. Thaler & Cass R. Sunstein, Nudge: Improving Decisions about Health, Wealth, and Happiness (2009).

32. George Sher, Beyond Neutrality: Perfectionism and Politics 73 (1997).

33. See Alan Wolfe, One Nation, After All (1999); Morris Fiorina et al., Culture War? The Myth of a Polarized America (2d ed. 2005).

34. This is noted by Smith, Foreordained Failure, at 78.

35. David Strauss, *The Myth of Colorblindness*, 1986 Sup. Ct. Rev. 99, 114.

36. See Comparative Secularisms in a Global Age (Linell E. Cady & Elizabeth Shakman Hurd, eds., 2010); Ahmet T. Kuru, Secularism and State Policies toward Religion: The United States, France, and Turkey (2009); Elizabeth Shakman Hurd, The Politics of Secularism in International Relations (2008); Charles Taylor, *Modes of Secularism*, in Secularism and Its Critics 33 (Rajeev Bhargava, ed., 1998); Talal Asad, Formations of the Secular: Christianity, Islam, Modernity (2003).

37. Kuru, Secularism and State Policies, at 14.

38. Bonnie Honig, Political Theory and the Displacement of Politics 2, 3, 6, 11 (1993).

39. Douglas Laycock, *Religious Liberty as Liberty*, 7 J. Contemp. Legal Issues 313, 314 (1996).

40. Will Herberg, Protestant, Catholic, Jew: An Essay in American Religious Sociology 99 (1955; rev. ed. 1960).

41. Thomas J. Curry, The First Freedoms: Church and State in America to the Passage of the First Amendment 123–124 (1986); see also id. at 218, 221; Donald L. Drakeman, Church, State, and Original Intent 253–256 (2010); Barry Alan Shain, *Eighteenth-Century Religious Liberty: The Founding Generation's Protestant-Derived Understanding*, in The Oxford Handbook of Church and State in the United States 42 (Derek H. Davis, ed., 2010); Douglas Laycock, *"Nonpreferential" Aid to Religion: A False Claim about Original Intent*, 27 Wm. & Mary L. Rev. 875, 918–919 (1986).

42. Morton Borden, Jews, Turks, and Infidels 4–5 (1984).

43. James Turner, Without God, without Creed: The Origins of Unbelief in America 23–25 (1985); Wilfred Cantwell Smith, The Meaning and End of Religion (1964). This conception of religion is shared by modern atheists, who understand religion to consist essentially of dubious factual claims. Indeed, as Turner shows, modern atheism was made possible by this conception of religion.

44. Diarmaid MacCulloch, The Reformation: A History 25 (2003).

45. Drakeman, Church, State, and Original Intent.

46. See Isaac Kramnick & R. Laurence Moore, The Godless Constitution: A Moral Defense of the Secular State 29–34 (rev. ed. 2005); Gerard V. Bradley, *The No Religious Test Clause and the Constitution of Religious Liberty: A Machine That Has Gone of Itself*, 37 Case W. L. Rev. 674, 681–683 (1987).

47. Quoted in Bradley, *The No Religious Test Clause*, at 683.

48. See Kramnick & Moore, The Godless Constitution, at 78–79; Ursula Henriques, Religious Toleration in England, 1787–1833, at 13–14 (1961).

49. Borden, Jews, Turks, and Infidels, at 11–15, 23–52. Kramnick & Moore, The Godless Constitution, at 79–83 claim that the framers of the First Amendment intended the abolition of all religious tests for office, and that "America's founding saw the triumph . . . of the privatization of religion, its removal from the public realm," id. at 83–84, but the views they cite are those of a minority and are inconsistent with the law that Americans in fact had on the books, and continued to have for many years afterward.

50. Borden, Jews, Turks, and Infidels, at 58–74; Philip Hamburger, Separation of Church and State 290–292 (2002).

51. 1824 Laws of Md., ch. 205. In the same spirit was an 1886 proposal by a group of New York rabbis to have the public schools teach the existence of God, the responsibility of man to his Maker, and the immortality of the soul. Hamburger, Separation of Church and State, at 392–393.

52. Curry, The First Freedoms, at 158.

53. People v. Ruggles, 8 Johns. 290, 295–296 (N.Y. 1811). Later, defending his decision, he relied again on the miniscule size of the remainder: "Are we not a christian people? Do not ninety-nine hundredths of our fellow citizens hold the general truths of the Bible to be dear and sacred?" Quoted in Borden, Jews,

Turks, and Infidels, at 31. The importance of religious convention for Kent becomes even clearer when it is considered that once, "in the privacy of his club, he had spoken of Christianity itself as a vulgar superstition from which cultivated men were free." Borden, Jews, Turks, and Infidels, at 138 n.27.

54. Sarah Barringer Gordon, *Blasphemy and the Law of Religious Liberty in Nineteenth-Century America*, 52 Am. Q. 682, 693, 695 (2000).

55. George M. Marsden, Religion and American Culture 63–65 (2d ed. 2001); Randall Balmer, The Making of Evangelicalism: From Revivalism to Politics and Beyond 19–23 (2010).

56. Sidney E. Mead, The Lively Experiment: The Shaping of Christianity in America 123 (1963).

57. Borden, Jews, Turks, and Infidels, at 30.

58. Bradley, *The No Religious Test Clause*, at 687.

59. Turner, Without God, without Creed, at 44.

60. This stereotyping persisted until the mid-twentieth century. See Robert Wuthnow, America and the Challenges of Religious Diversity 8–36 (2005).

61. Id. at 10–19.

62. Drakeman, Church, State, and Original Intent, at 305–314, 334.

63. Noah Feldman, Divided by God: America's Church-State Problem—and What We Should Do about It 60 (2005).

64. For further evidence of the pervasiveness of implicit Protestantism, see Tracy Fessenden, Culture and Redemption: Religion, the Secular, and American Literature (2007).

65. Quoted in John C. Jeffries Jr. & James E. Ryan, *A Political History of the Establishment Clause*, 100 Mich. L. Rev. 279, 298 (2001).

66. Id. at 299–300.

67. Jose Casanova, Public Religions in the Modern World 170 (1994).

68. Steven Macedo, Diversity and Distrust: Civic Education in a Multicultural Democracy 61 (2000).

69. Donahoe v. Richards, 38 Me. 379 (1854); Commonwealth v. Cooke, 7 Am. L. Reg. 417 (Mass. Police Ct. 1859).

70. A. James Reichley, Religion in American Public Life 186–187 (1985); John T. McGreevy, Catholicism and American Freedom: A History (2003); Sydney E. Ahlstrom, A Religious History of the American People 555–568 (1972).

71. James M. McPherson, Battle Cry of Freedom: The Civil War Era 135–141 (1988).

72. George C. Lorimer, The Great Conflict: A Discourse, Concerning Baptists, and Religious Liberty 116 (1877), quoted in Hamburger, Separation of Church and State, at 284.

73. Hamburger, Separation of Church and State, at 364.

74. Josiah Strong, Our Country: Its Possible Future and Its Present Crisis 101 (1886; 1912 ed.), quoted in Macedo, Diversity and Distrust, at 79.

75. Jeffries and Ryan, *A Political History of the Establishment Clause*, at 301–305.

76. See generally Turner, Without God, without Creed.

77. Its story is told in Hamburger, Separation of Church and State, at 287–334. Hamburger exaggerates its importance, however. See Douglas Laycock, *The Many Meanings of Separation*, 70 U. Chi. L. Rev. 1667, 1695–1697 (2003).

78. Vidal v. Gerard's Executors, 43 U.S. 127, 200 (1844).

79. Davis v. Beason, 133 U.S. 333, 343 (1890). In the same year, the Court also called polygamy "contrary to the spirit of Christianity, and of the civilization which Christianity has produced in the western world." Mormon Church v. United States, 136 U.S. 1, 49 (1890).

80. Holy Trinity Church v. U.S., 143 U.S. 457, 471 (1892).

81. Irving Howe, World of Our Fathers: The Journey of the East European Jews to America and the Life They Found and Made (1976).

82. Ahlstrom, A Religious History, at 573, 969.

83. See George M. Marsden, The Soul of the Modern University: From Protestant Establishment to Established Nonbelief (1994); Dorothy Ross, The Origins of American Social Science (1992).

84. Sarah Barringer Gordon, The Spirit of the Law: Religious Voices and the Constitution in Modern America 34–35, 38–39 (2010). This ecumenism was hardly unanimous; other Protestants deplored it.

85. Kevin Schultz, Tri-Faith America: How Catholics and Jews Held Postwar America to Its Protestant Promise (2011).

86. Herberg, Protestant, Catholic, Jew, at 87, 65 n.2. It is at this time that the first reliable polls of public opinion concerning religion were conducted. Martin E. Marty, Modern American Religion, v. 3: Under God, Indivisible, 1941–1960, at 278–280 (1996).

87. Herberg, Protestant, Catholic, Jew, at 260. Herberg observed that in the 1950s, it was "quite inconceivable" that an atheist like Robert G. Ingersoll, who went around the country making antireligious speeches, could be so respected in American politics that he was called upon to make a nominating speech at the 1876 Republican convention. Id. at 52, 68. Marty observes that a "state of the art" poll in 1952 found that "only about 1 percent called themselves atheists or made the point to interviewers that they did not believe in God." Marty, Modern American Religion, at 280. For other data on the exceptionally high religiosity of the 1950s, see Robert D. Putnam & David E. Campbell, American Grace: How Religion Divides and Unites Us 82–90 (2010).

88. Charles Oakman, R-Mich., quoted in Gordon, The Spirit of the Law, at 54.

89. These are only a few examples of a broader outpouring of official declarations of theism, days of national prayer, and the like. Jeremy Gunn, Spiritual Weapons: The Cold War and the Forging of an American National Religion 50–74 (2009).

90. Zorach v. Clauson, 343 U.S. 306 (1952).

91. Schultz, Tri-Faith America, at 179–197.

92. Torcaso v. Watkins, 367 U.S. 488, 495 (1961).

93. William K. Muir Jr., Prayer in the Public Schools: Law and Attitude Change 13 (1967).

94. Abington School Dist. v. Schempp, 374 U.S. 203 (1963).

95. Engel v. Vitale, 370 U.S. 421 (1962).

96. Jeffries and Ryan at 313. A resurgence of distrust of Catholicism certainly played a role in the persistence of the "no-aid" view of the Establishment Clause, and as that distrust dissipated, the no-aid view relaxed. See Thomas C. Berg, *Anti-Catholicism and Modern Church-State Relations*, 33 Loy. U. Chi. L.J. 121 (2001).

97. Jeffries and Ryan, *A Political History*, at 316–317.

98. Sherbert v. Verner, 374 U.S. 398 (1963); Wisconsin v. Yoder, 406 U.S. 205 (1972).

99. Claude S. Fischer & Michael Hout, Century of Difference: How America Changed in the Last One Hundred Years 187 (2006).

100. Frank Newport, *This Easter, Smaller Percentage of Americans Are Christian*, Gallup Poll, Apr. 10, 2009, available at http://www.gallup.com/poll/117409/ easter-smaller-percentage-americans-christian.aspx (visited June 15, 2009).

101. Wuthnow, America and the Challenges of Religious Diversity, at 202–203.

102. Diana Eck, A New Religious America: How a "Christian Country" Has Become the World's Most Religiously Diverse Nation 4 (2001).

103. Wuthnow, America and the Challenges of Religious Diversity, at 190–191.

104. Fischer & Hout, Century of Difference, at 192; see also Putnam & Campbell, American Grace, at 534–540 (89 percent of Americans think that those not of their faith can get into heaven).

105. Putnam & Campbell, American Grace, at 520.

106. Joseph Gremillion & Jim Castelli, The Emerging Parish: The Notre Dame Study of Catholic Life since Vatican II 132 (1987). For an argument that this feeling of connection is central to modern American Catholic practice, see Andrew Greeley, The Catholic Imagination (2001).

107. Alan Wolfe, The Transformation of American Religion: How We Actually Live Our Faith 41 (2003).

108. Id. at 35–36.

109. Edwards v. Aguillard, 482 U.S. 578, 617 (1987) (Scalia, J., dissenting).

110. Lee v. Weisman, 505 U.S. 577, 641 (1992) (Scalia, J., dissenting).

111. McCreary County v. ACLU, 545 U.S. 844, 909 (2005) (Scalia, J., joined by Rehnquist, C.J. and Thomas, J., dissenting). There is a delicious ambiguity, which I won't pursue further here, about what it means to be "associated with a single religious belief." If the Ten Commandments are not so associated, then neither is the divinity of Christ, since Protestants and Catholics who violently disagree on many religious issues are nonetheless in agreement

about that. On the protean variety of forms of Christianity, see Steven D. Smith, Barnette's *Big Blunder*, 78 Chi.-Kent L. Rev. 625, 650–651 (2003).

112. Van Orden v. Perry, 545 U.S. 677, 717–718 (2005) (Stevens, J., dissenting), citing Steven Lubet, *The Ten Commandments in Alabama*, 15 Const. Commentary 471, 474–476 (Fall 1998).

113. *McCreary*, 545 U.S. at 909 n.12 (Scalia, J., joined by Rehnquist, C.J., Kennedy, J., and Thomas, J., dissenting).

114. Wallace v. Jaffree, 472 U.S. 38, 113 (1985) (Rehnquist, J., dissenting).

115. Bd. of Educ. of Kiryas Joel v. Grumet, 512 U.S. 687, 748 (1994) (Scalia, J., dissenting).

116. *McCreary*, 545 U.S. at 894 (Scalia, J., dissenting).

117. U.S. Census Bureau, Statistical Abstract of the United States: 2004–2005 (124th ed. 2004), at 55; cited in id. Further data on the number of people Scalia is leaving out are compiled in Frederick Mark Gedicks and Roger Hendrix, *Uncivil Religion: Judeo-Christianity and the Ten Commandments*, 110 W. Va. L. Rev. 275, 284–285 (2007). The data on which the Census Bureau relies are described in detail in Barry A. Kosmin & Ariela Keysar, Religion in a Free Market (2006).

The numbers are more complicated than the Statistical Abstract suggests. The proportion of Americans who report having no religious preference doubled in the 1990s, from 7 percent in 1991 (which had been its level for almost twenty years) to 14 percent in 1998, to about 17 percent in 2008. However, most of the members of this category are in fact religious. More than half believe in God, more than half believe in life after death, about a third believe in heaven and hell, and 93 percent sometimes pray. The most careful study of this group concludes that the newer members of this group are mostly "unchurched believers" who declare no religious preference in an effort to express their distance from the religious right. Michael Hout & Claude S. Fischer, *Why More Americans Have No Religious Preference: Politics and Generations*, 67 Am. Sociological Rev. 165 (2002); Putnam & Campbell, American Grace, at 120–132. They are disproportionately represented among the young, including about 25 percent of those who came of age in the 1990s and 2000s. Putnam & Campbell at 123. Scalia's remainder is thus likely to grow.

118. Steven G. Gey, *Life after the Establishment Clause*, 110 W. Va. L. Rev. 1, 20 (2007).

119. City of Boerne v. Flores, 521 U.S. 507 (1997).

120. Gonzales v. O Centro Espirita Beneficente Uniao do Vegetal, 546 U.S. 418 (2006).

121. Michael W. McConnell, *The Problem of Singling Out Religion*, 50 DePaul L. Rev. 1, 3–6, 19–21 (2000).

122. Michael W. McConnell, *Institutions and Interpretation: A Critique of City of Boerne v. Flores*, 111 Harv. L. Rev. 153, 160 (1997).

123. United States v. Seeger, 380 U.S. 163, 166 (1965).

124. Id. at 188–193 (Douglas, J., concurring); Welsh v. United States, 398 U.S. 333, 344–367 (1970) (Harlan, J., concurring in the result).

125. Henry Fielding, The History of Tom Jones, A Foundling 82 (Modern Library ed. 1940) (1749).

126. Davis v. Beason, 133 U.S. 333, 342 (1890).

127. United States v. McIntosh, 283 U.S. 605, 633–634 (1931).

128. See William P. Alston, *Religion*, in 7 Encyclopedia of Philosophy 142 (Paul Edwards, ed., 1967); George C. Freeman III, *The Misguided Search for the Constitutional Definition of "Religion,"* 71 Geo. L.J. 1519 (1983); Kent Greenawalt, *Religion as a Concept in Constitutional Law*, 72 Cal. L. Rev. 753 (1984); Laurence Tribe, American Constitutional Law 1181–1183 (2d ed. 1988); Eduardo Peñalver, Note, *The Concept of Religion*, 107 Yale L.J. 791 (1997); 1 Kent Greenawalt, Religion and the Constitution: Free Exercise and Fairness 124–156 (2006); William T. Cavanaugh, The Myth of Religious Violence: Secular Ideology and the Roots of Modern Conflict 57–122 (2009). Courts in Europe have done no better in devising a definition. Rex Ahdar and Ian Leigh, Religious Freedom in the Liberal State 110–126 (2005). Indeed, it appears that no jurisdiction in the world has managed to solve this problem. See T. Jeremy Gunn, *The Complexity of Religion and the Definition of "Religion" in International Law*, 16 Harv. Hum. Rts. J. 189 (2003). Lest one think that the neo-Wittgensteinian approach advocated here is an artifact of academic preciousness, note that an analogical criterion is also used by that singularly hardheaded entity, the Internal Revenue Service. See *Defining "Religious Organization" and "Church,"* 868 Est., Gifts & Tr. Portfolios (BNA) ch. III (2007), available at http://taxandaccounting. bna.com/btac/.

129. Ludwig Wittgenstein, Philosophical Investigations 20, 31, 33 (G. E. M. Anscombe, trans., 3d ed. 1958).

130. Charles Taylor, *To Follow a Rule*, in Philosophical Arguments 178 (1995).

131. See Al Yankovic, Another One Rides the Bus (Placebo Records 1981).

132. Jonathan Z. Smith, *Religion, Religions, Religious*, in Critical Terms for Religious Studies 269 (Mark C. Taylor, ed., 1998); Talal Asad, Genealogies of Religion: Discipline and Reasons of Power in Christianity and Islam (1993).

133. Cavanaugh, The Myth of Religious Violence, at 192.

134. Martin Riesebrodt, The Promise of Salvation: A Theory of Religion (2010).

135. This stability may not last forever. Those draft cases placed pressure on the definition of religion that was becoming fairly unendurable by the time the Vietnam War ended: in 1972, more young men successfully claimed exemption from the draft than were inducted. Andrew Koppelman, *The Story of Welsh v. United States: Elliott Welsh's Two Religious Tests*, in First Amendment Stories 314–315 (Richard Garnett and Andrew Koppelman, eds., 2011). But this disintegration ended with the war, and has not been a problem since.

136. Cavanaugh's attack, in *The Myth of Religious Violence*, on the coherence of the concept of religion thus has no bite against the practice of treating religion as special in the way that American law does. One need not (and, Cavanaugh shows, one had better not) regard religion as a natural kind in order to defend American practices in this area.

2. Corruption of Religion and the Establishment Clause

1. See Kent Greenawalt, 2 Religion and the Constitution: Establishment and Fairness 6–13 (2008); Steven H. Shiffrin, The Religious Left and Church-State Relations (2009).
2. Lemon v. Kurtzman, 403 U.S. 602, 622, 623 (1971).
3. For a thorough catalogue of examples, see Richard W. Garnett, *Religion, Division, and the First Amendment*, 94 Geo. L. J. 1667 (2006). The argument has a large scholarly following. See, e.g., Robert Audi, Religious Commitment and Secular Reason (2000); Douglas Laycock, *Religious Liberty as Liberty*, 7 J. Contemp. Legal Issues 313 (1996); Ira C. Lupu, *To Control Faction and Protect Liberty: A General Theory of the Religion Clauses*, 7 J. Contemp. Legal Issues 357 (1996); Kathleen M. Sullivan, *Religion and Liberal Democracy*, 59 U. Chi. L. Rev. 195 (1992).
4. Religious division has been a basis for political division throughout American history. See A. James Reichley, Religion in American Public Life (1985). These divisions have remained manageable, not because of judicial intervention, but because the proliferation of religious factions has prevented any of them from gaining ascendancy. See Anthony Gill, The Political Origins of Religious Liberty 60–113 (2008).
5. Laurence Tribe, American Constitutional Law 1278–1284 (2d ed. 1988). Some have suggested that courts should focus on protecting religious minorities. Thomas Berg has shown that this criterion is similarly unworkable in *Minority Religions and the Religion Clauses*, 82 Wash. U. L. Q. 919 (2004). Autonomy is another unsuccessful candidate. See my *Religious Establishment and Autonomy*, 25 Const. Comm. 291 (2008).
6. Steven D. Smith, Foreordained Failure: The Quest for a Constitutional Principle of Religious Freedom 106–109 (1995).
7. Lynch v. Donnelly, 465 U.S. 668, 687, 688 (1984) (O'Connor, J., concurring).
8. County of Allegheny v. ACLU, 492 U.S. 573, 627 (1989) (O'Connor, J., concurring in part and concurring in the judgment). This argument also has a large scholarly following. See, e.g., Christopher L. Eisgruber & Lawrence G. Sager, Religious Freedom and the Constitution 61–62, 122 (2007); Steven G. Gey, *Life after the Establishment Clause*, 110 W. Va. L. Rev. 1 (2007); Steven B. Epstein, *Rethinking the Constitutionality of Ceremonial Deism*, 96 Colum. L. Rev. 2083 (1996). Many writers draw on both arguments. Thus, for example,

Noah Feldman relies on the danger of political division to argue for an absolute rule against public funding for religious activities, while he relies on an alienation rationale for permitting government-sponsored religious displays and prayers. See Noah Feldman, Divided by God: America's Church-State Problem—and What We Should Do about It 14–16 (2005). He is aware that his proposals present their own dangers of division and alienation, but does not explain how he knows how to quantify the magnitudes on each side— how, for example, he knows that secularists' "concerns over exclusion cannot effectively trump the sense of exclusion shared by the many Americans who want to express their religious values through politics." Id. at 16.

9. Smith, Foreordained Failure, at 109–115.

10. Steven D. Smith, *Symbols, Perceptions, and Doctrinal Illusions: Establishment Neutrality and the "No Endorsement" Test,* 86 Mich. L. Rev. 266, 300 (1987).

11. Neil R. Feigenson, *Political Standing and Governmental Endorsement of Religion: An Alternative to Current Establishment Clause Doctrine,* 40 DePaul L. Rev. 53, 87 (1990).

12. See Frederick Mark Gedicks, The Rhetoric of Church and State: A Critical Analysis of Religion Clause Jurisprudence (1995).

13. Feldman draws a similar contrast, between the legal views of "legal secularists" and "values evangelicals." Divided by God, at 6–8. His omission of religiously based separatism from his diagnosis is noted in Perry Dane, *Separation Anxiety,* 22 J. L. & Religion 545 (2007), and Darryl Hart, A Secular Faith: Why Christianity Favors the Separation of Church and State 14–15 (2006).

14. The description of their views below is drawn from my more detailed analysis of each in *Corruption of Religion and the Establishment Clause,* 50 Wm. & Mary L. Rev. 1831 (2009).

15. Engel v. Vitale, 370 U.S. 421, 431–432 (1962) (quoting James Madison, Memorial and Remonstrance against Religious Assessments [1785], in 2 The Writings of James Madison 183, 187 [1901]).

16. See, e.g., Lee v. Weisman, 505 U.S. 577, 589 (1992) ("The First Amendment's Religion Clauses mean that religious beliefs and religious expression are too precious to be either proscribed or prescribed by the State."); id. at 608 (Blackmun, J., concurring) ("The favored religion may be compromised as political figures reshape the religion's beliefs for their own purposes; it may be reformed as government largesse brings government regulation."); County of Allegheny v. ACLU, 492 U.S. 573, 645 (1989) (Brennan, J., concurring in part and dissenting in part) ("The government-sponsored display of the menorah alongside a Christmas tree also works a distortion of the Jewish religious calendar.... [T]he city's erection alongside the Christmas tree of the symbol of a relatively minor Jewish religious holiday . . . has the effect of promoting a Christianized version of Judaism."); Bowen v. Kendrick, 487 U.S. 589,

640 n.10 (1988) (Blackmun, J., dissenting) ("The First Amendment protects not only the State from being captured by the Church, but also protects the Church from being corrupted by the State and adopted for its purposes."); Aguilar v. Felton, 473 U.S. 402, 409–410 (1985) ("When the state becomes enmeshed with a given denomination in matters of religious significance . . . the freedom of even the adherents of the denomination is limited by the governmental intrusion into sacred matters."); Sch. Dist. of Grand Rapids v. Ball, 473 U.S. 373, 385 (1985) (favored religions may be "taint[ed] . . . with a corrosive secularism"); Marsh v. Chambers, 463 U.S. 783, 804 (1983) (Brennan, J., dissenting) (stating that one "purpose of separation and neutrality is to prevent the trivialization and degradation of religion by too close an attachment to the organs of government"); Roemer v. Bd. of Pub. Works, 426 U.S. 736, 775 (1976) (Stevens, J., dissenting) (noting "the pernicious tendency of a state subsidy to tempt religious schools to compromise their religious mission without wholly abandoning it"); Sch. Dist. of Abingdon v. Schempp, 374 U.S. 203, 259 (1963) (Brennan, J., concurring) ("It is not only the nonbeliever who fears the injection of sectarian doctrines and controversies into the civil polity, but in as high degree it is the devout believer who fears the secularization of a creed which becomes too deeply involved with and dependent upon the government."); Everson v. Bd. of Educ., 330 U.S. 1, 59 (1947) (Rutledge, J., dissenting) ("[W]e have staked the very existence of our country on the faith that complete separation between the state and religion is best for the state and best for religion.").

17. See Mark 12:17; Matthew 22:21; Luke 20:25. Other early Christian formulations of the separation claim are surveyed in E. Gregory Wallace, *Justifying Religious Freedom: The Western Tradition*, 114 Penn St. L. Rev. 485 (2009); and, more briefly, Philip Hamburger, Separation of Church and State 21–38 (2002), and John Witte Jr., *That Serpentine Wall of Separation*, 101 Mich. L. Rev. 1869, 1876–1886 (2003). For earlier English and American Protestant formulations, see Thomas G. Sanders, Protestant Concepts of Church and State: Historical Backgrounds and Approaches for the Future 184–202 (1964).

18. See generally Michael W. McConnell, *Establishment and Disestablishment at the Founding, Part I: Establishment of Religion*, 44 Wm. & Mary L. Rev. 2105 (2003).

19. See Leonard W. Levy, Emergence of a Free Press 6 (1985).

20. John Milton, Areopagitica (1644), *reprinted in* John Milton: Complete Poems and Major Prose 748, 739, 728, 727 (Merritt Y. Hughes, ed., 1957).

21. Id. at 742, 733.

22. Id. at 747–748.

23. Christopher Hill, Milton and the English Revolution 268–278 (1977).

24. Id. at 306.

25. See id. at 233–337. His religious views rested on a reading of biblical authority that was equally idiosyncratic. See Regina M. Schwartz, *Milton on the Bible*, in A Companion to Milton 37 (Thomas N. Corns, ed., 2001).

26. See William Haller, Liberty and Reformation in the Puritan Revolution 56–64 (1955).

27. John Milton, Considerations Touching the Likeliest Means to Remove Hirelings out of the Church (1659), reprinted in Complete Poems and Major Prose, at 870, 866.

28. Id. at 872.

29. See, e.g Van Orden v. Perry, 545 U.S. 677, 693–694 (2005) (Thomas, J., concurring); Michael W. McConnell, *Coercion: The Lost Element of Establishment*, 27 Wm. & Mary L. Rev. 933, 938–939 (1986). For a critique of claims that this was the original meaning of the Establishment Clause, see Douglas Laycock, *"Noncoercive" Support for Religion: Another False Claim about the Establishment Clause*, 26 Val. U. L. Rev. 37 (1991).

30. Timothy L. Hall, Separating Church and State: Roger Williams and Religious Liberty 6, 18 (1998).

31. Hall notes this and uses the term on pp. 8–10, 147, and 165. The parallel between Williams and Rawls is developed in Martha Nussbaum, Liberty of Conscience: In Defense of America's Tradition of Religious Equality 57–63 (2008). See also Edmund S. Morgan, Roger Williams: The Church and the State 115–126 (1967) (discussing Williams's political philosophy).

32. Nussbaum claims that Williams "nowhere alludes to these beliefs in arguing for liberty of conscience—nor should he, since it is his considered position that political principles should not be based on sectarian religious views of any sort." Nussbaum, Liberty of Conscience, at 43. This is true of some of Williams's arguments. It is not, however, true of his argument that establishment corrupts religion.

33. Morgan, Roger Williams, at 17, 22–23, 15–17, 20, 37, 27.

34. Id. at 70–72, 74–76.

35. Roger Williams, The Bloudy Tenent of Persecution (1644), reprinted in 3 The Complete Writings of Roger Williams 1, 12, 64 (Samuel L. Caldwell, ed., 1963).

36. Morgan, Roger Williams, at 32, 139, 89.

37. Williams, The Bloudy Tenent, at 250.

38. Perry Miller, Roger Williams: His Contribution to the American Tradition 29 (1962).

39. See Morgan, Roger Williams, at 130–142.

40. William G. McLoughlin, *Isaac Backus and the Separation of Church and State in America*, 73 Am. Hist. Rev. 1392, 1408 (1968).

41. Jean-Jacques Rousseau, On The Social Contract 131 (Roger D. Masters, ed.; Judith R. Masters, trans., 1978) (1762).

42. Mark DeWolfe Howe, The Garden and the Wilderness: Religion and Government in American Constitutional History (1965) appropriates Williams

in a strange way. Howe, throughout the book, draws a contrast between the Jeffersonian, secularist view of separation, which he disfavors, and that of Williams, who feared "the worldly corruptions which might consume the churches if sturdy fences against the wilderness were not maintained." Id. at 6. He takes as evidence that the Williams view better represents our traditions, what he calls the "*de facto* establishment," which embraces "a host of favoring tributes to faith" such as Sunday closing laws, the use of God on the currency, legislative prayers, Thanksgiving proclamations, and so forth. Id. at 11. He uses the term because "this social reality, in its technical independence from law, bears legally some analogy to that ugly actuality known as *de facto* segregation." Id.

This gives rise to several puzzles. What Howe describes is not de facto at all, but de jure. De facto segregation is segregation in which the state does not officially give recognition to race at all, or even silently but intentionally take race into account. What Howe calls de facto establishment is a set of practices in which the state behaves in overtly religious ways and proclaims religious truth. "Ceremonial Deism" would be a better term for these practices. (The Court has never used "de facto establishment," but there have been a few references to "ceremonial Deism" in the opinions.) When Justice Brennan introduced that term, he wrote:

> [S]uch practices as the designation of "In God We Trust" as our national motto, or the references to God contained in the Pledge of Allegiance . . . can best be understood, in Dean Rostow's apt phrase, as a form of "ceremonial deism," protected from Establishment Clause scrutiny chiefly because they have lost through rote repetition any significant religious content.

Lynch v. Donnelly, 465 U.S. 668, 716 (1984) (Brennan, J., dissenting) (citation omitted).

Perhaps ceremonial Deism can be justified. But Williams would be a strange authority to invoke on its behalf. Williams's suspicion of state control over religion would appear logically to extend to any degree of ceremonial support for religion. The draining of religious meaning through rote repetition is just the kind of degradation of religion of which Williams was afraid. That is why Rhode Island did not have an established church. If the state is incompetent to adjudicate religious matters, then why should it be authorized to declare that there is one God, and that the Hindus, Buddhists, and atheists are mistaken about this? This question never occurs to Howe. One can imagine what Williams would have thought of the modern Christmas display, paid for by tax dollars secured through the influence of the local merchants association, reminding us that Christ suffered and died on the cross so that we could enjoy great holiday shopping.

43. John Locke, A Letter Concerning Toleration 26 (James H. Tully, ed.; William Popple, trans., 1983) (1689).

44. Id. at 27.

45. This is emphasized in Smith, Foreordained Failure, at 64–67; Jeremy Waldron, God, Locke, and Equality: Christian Foundations of John Locke's Political Thought 208–211 (2002); Micah Schwartzman, *The Relevance of Locke's Religious Arguments for Toleration*, 33 Pol. Theory 678 (2005); and Stanley Fish, *Mission Impossible: Settling the Just Bounds between Church and State*, 97 Colum. L. Rev. 2255, 2259–2260 (1997).

46. Samuel Pufendorf, Of the Nature and Qualification of Religion in Reference to Civil Society 13, 33 (Simone Zurbuchen, ed.; Jodocus Crull, trans., 2002) (1689).

47. Elisha Williams, The Essential Rights and Liberties of Protestants (1774), reprinted in Political Sermons of the Founding Era, 1730–1805, at 51, 61, 62, 77 (Ellis Sandoz, ed., 2d ed. 1998).

48. Id. at 73.

49. Thomas J. Curry, The First Freedoms: Church and State in America to the Passage of the First Amendment 118 (1986).

50. See, e.g., id. at 130, 144, 156, 168; Hamburger, Separation of Church and State, at 5 n.7, 55, 74–75, 121–122, 124, 170–171; Leonard W. Levy, The Establishment Clause: Religion and the First Amendment 64–67, 124 (2d ed. 1994).

51. William G. McLoughlin, *Introduction* to Isaac Backus on Church, State, and Calvinism: Pamphlets, 1754–1789, at 1, 41–42 (William G. McLoughlin, ed., 1968) [hereinafter *Introduction*].

52. Isaac Backus, An Appeal to the Public for Religious Liberty (1773), reprinted in Isaac Backus on Church, State, and Calvinism, at 303, 334.

53. McLoughlin, *Introduction*, at 31. "Though [Backus was] never imprisoned himself, he was several times in imminent danger of it." Id. at n.11.

54. Isaac Backus, Isaac Backus' Draft for a Bill of Rights for the Massachusetts Constitution (1779), reprinted in Isaac Backus on Church, State, and Calvinism, *supra* note , at 487. Put another way, "[I]n religion each one has an equal right to judge for himself, for we must all appear before the judgment seat of Christ." An Appeal, at 332. William McLoughlin notes that the individualism here is different from that of a Deist such as George Mason, who wrote in the Virginia Declaration of Rights that religion "can be directed only by reason and conviction, not by force or violence." *Introduction,* at 47. "The pietist wanted religious freedom so that men may follow the Truth of Revelation; the deist wanted it so men might seek the Truth wherever reason may lead." Id. at 48. See also 2 William G. McLoughlin, New England Dissent, 1630–1883: The Baptists and the Separation of Church and State 1403–1404 (1971) (drawing a similar contrast with Jefferson).

55. McLoughlin, *Introduction*, at 8–9.

56. Id. at 29.

57. Isaac Backus, Policy as Well as Honesty (1779), reprinted in Isaac Backus on Church, State, and Calvinism, at 367, 373.

58. Backus, An Appeal, at 314, 315.

59. McLoughlin, *Introduction*, at 50–57; Curry, The First Freedoms, at 217.

60. Curry, The First Freedoms, at 170.

61. McLoughlin, New England Dissent, at 931.

62. McLoughlin, *Introduction*, at 50.

63. John Witte Jr., *"A Most Mild and Equitable Establishment of Religion": John Adams and the Massachusetts Experiment*, 41 J. Church & St. 213, 217 (1999). This inconsistency weakened the Baptists' position politically. "Congregationalists found it difficult to believe that Baptist preoccupation with ministerial maintenance was anything more than a rationalization of self-interest on the part of people who wanted to avoid spending money." Curry, The First Freedoms, at 176.

64. See L. H. Butterfield, *Elder John Leland, Jeffersonian Itinerant*, 62 Proc. Am. Antiquarian Soc. 154, 172–176 (1952).

65. See Curry, The First Freedoms, at 176.

66. See Butterfield, *Elder John Leland*, at 155, 183–184.

67. Id. at 183–196; Paul Finkelman, *James Madison and the Bill of Rights: A Reluctant Paternity*, 1990 Sup. Ct. Rev. 301, 323–324. The evidence that the meeting did take place is marshaled in detail in Mark Scarberry, *John Leland and James Madison: Religious Influence on the Ratification of the Constitution and on the Proposal of the Bill of Rights*, 113 Penn. St. L. Rev. 733 (2009).

68. John Leland, The Rights of Conscience Inalienable (1791), *reprinted in* 2 Political Sermons of the Founding Era, 1730–1805, at 1079, 1085 (Ellis Sandoz, ed., 2d ed. 1998).

69. Butterfield, *Elder John Leland*, at 199.

70. Leland, The Rights of Conscience Inalienable, at 1087.

71. See Curry, The First Freedoms, at 176.

72. McLoughlin, New England Dissent, at 932; The Writings of Elder John Leland 561–570 (L. F. Greene, ed., 1845).

73. Butterfield, *Elder John Leland*, at 235.

74. Id. at 205–206.

75. Sanders, Protestant Concepts of Church and State, at 193.

76. Mark A. Noll, America's God: From Jonathan Edwards to Abraham Lincoln 11 (2002).

77. Butterfield, *Elder John Leland*, at 239.

78. See Hamburger, Separation of Church and State, at 156–157.

79. McLoughlin, New England Dissent, at 931.

80. Id.

81. See Butterfield, *Elder John Leland*, at 158.

82. At Baptist revivals, he wrote:

> Such a heavenly confusion among the preachers, and such a celestial discord among the people, destroy all articulation, so that the understanding is not edified; but the awful echo, sounding in the ears, and the

objects in great distress, and great raptures before the eyes, raise great emotion in the heart.

Id. at 170.

83. Id. at 242.

84. On the place of Deism in eighteenth-century America, see David L. Holmes, The Faiths of the Founding Fathers 1–51 (2006).

85. See id. at 56, 65–68.

86. Thomas Paine, The Age of Reason (1795), reprinted in The Thomas Paine Reader 395, 400 (Michael Foot & Isaac Kramnick, eds., 1987).

87. Id. at 417.

88. Id. at 442.

89. Id. at 401. Benjamin Franklin held a similar view of "the essentials of every religion," which were unfortunately, in many religions, "more or less mix'd with other articles, which, without any tendency to inspire, promote, or confirm morality, serv'd principally to divide us, and make us unfriendly to one another." Sidney E. Mead, The Lively Experiment: The Shaping of Christianity in America 64 (1963).

90. Joseph Priestley, A History of the Corruptions of Christianity (1782).

91. He wrote to Adams that he had read the book "over and over again." Holmes, The Faiths of the Founding Fathers, at 82. He "recommended it for students at the University of Virginia as the work most likely to wean them from sectarian narrowness." Mead, The Lively Experiment, at 48.

92. See Jaroslav Pelikan, Jesus through the Centuries: His Place in the History of Culture 189–193 (1985).

93. Mead, The Lively Experiment, at 46 (quoting Letter from Thomas Jefferson to Mrs. M. Harrison Smith [Aug. 6, 1816]). This letter was written late in Jefferson's life. Jefferson became more radical about religious matters as he grew older, but even in his early career he sometimes expressed anticlerical views in private. Feldman, Divided by God, at 39.

94. The contrast between Jefferson and Backus is nicely laid out in J. Judd Owen, The Struggle between "Religion and Nonreligion": Jefferson, Backus, and the Dissonance of America's Founding Principles, 101 Am. Pol. Sci. Rev. 493 (2007).

95. Thomas Jefferson, Bill for Establishing Religious Freedom (1777), in Thomas Jefferson: Writings 346 (Merrill D. Peterson, ed., 1984).

96. Id. at 347. Jefferson reported drafting the bill in 1777; it was enacted, with some deletions, in 1786. Id. at 1554.

97. Id. at 346–347. That the prevention of corruption is the dominant theme in Jefferson's bill is argued in Garry Wills, Head and Heart: American Christianities 191–197 (2007).

98. Bill for Establishing Religious Freedom, at 347.

99. Notes on the State of Virginia (1788), reprinted in Thomas Jefferson: Writings, at 283, 285, 286.

100. Letter from Thomas Jefferson to Messrs. Nehemiah Dodge and Others, a Committee of the Danbury Baptist Association (Jan. 1, 1802), in Thomas Jefferson: Writings, at 510.

101. Thomas E. Buckley, Church and State in Revolutionary Virginia, 1776–1787, at 62–65 (1977); Levy, The Establishment Clause, at 70–75.

102. A Bill Establishing a Provision for Teachers of the Christian Religion (1784), reprinted in Everson v. Bd. of Educ., 330 U.S. 1 app. at 72–74 (1947).

103. Letter from James Madison to Thomas Jefferson (Oct. 24, 1787), in The Republic of Letters: The Correspondence between Thomas Jefferson and James Madison, 1776–1826, at 495, 501 (James Morton Smith, ed., 1995).

104. Buckley, Church and State in Revolutionary Virginia, at 179–180.

105. Memorial and Remonstrance at 184–185, 187. The importance of the corruption theme in the *Memorial and Remonstrance* is further elaborated in Wills, Head and Heart, at 207–222.

106. See Holmes, The Faiths of the Founding Fathers, at 91–98. For some evidence that Madison was, at least early in his life, sincere in holding the religious views stated in the *Memorial*, see John T. Noonan Jr., The Lustre of Our Country: The American Experience of Religious Freedom 64–91 (1998). The specific claims about corruption in the *Memorial* are also made in his private correspondence, both early and late in his life. See The Mind of the Founder: Sources of the Political Thought of James Madison 2–5, 341 (Marvin Meyers, ed., rev. ed. 1981).

107. On the variety of religious positions to which Madison was appealing, see Buckley, Church and State in Revolutionary Virginia, at 179–180, and John Witte Jr., Religion and the American Constitutional Experiment 21–35 (2d ed. 2005). Vincent Phillip Muñoz observes that "Madison leaves it unclear whether the 'Memorial's' argument is theological, strictly rational, or both." Vincent Phillip Muñoz, *James Madison's Principle of Religious Liberty*, 97 Am. Pol. Sci. Rev. 17, 22 n.13 (2003).

108. Douglas Laycock has explained why an originalist might focus on the Virginia debate in which Madison's was the most important document:

> The state debates help show how the concept of establishment was understood in the Framers' generation. Learning how that generation understood the concept may be more informative than the brief and unfocused debate in the House [on the First Amendment. The Senate debate was not recorded]. If the Framers generally understood the concept in a certain way, and if nothing indicates that they used the word in an unusual sense in the first amendment, then we can fairly assume that the Framers used the word in accordance with their general understanding of the concept. . . .
>
> For several reasons, the debates in Virginia were most important. First, the arguments were developed most fully in Virginia. Second,

Madison led the winning coalition, and he played a dominant role in the adoption of the establishment clause three years later. Third, the debates in Virginia may have been the best known.

Douglas Laycock, *"Nonpreferential" Aid to Religion: A False Claim about Original Intent*, 27 Wm. & Mary L. Rev. 875, 895 (1986).

109. Sanders, Protestant Concepts of Church and State, at 211–212.

110. James Madison, *Detached Memorandum* (ca. 1820), with accompanying notes, in Michael W. McConnell, John H. Garvey, & Thomas C. Berg, Religion and the Constitution 67–69 (2d ed. 2006).

111. Kurt Lash, *The Second Adoption of the Establishment Clause: The Rise of the Non-Establishment Principle*, 27 Ariz. St. L.J. 1085, 1154 (1995). For a similar view on the incorporation question, see Greenawalt, Establishment and Fairness at 14–15, 26–39.

112. Bd. of Educ. v. Minor, 23 Ohio St. 211, 250–251 (1872), quoted in Lash, *The Second Adoption*, at 1129.

113. Samuel Fleischacker, *Adam Smith's Reception among the American Founders, 1776–1790*, 59 Wm. & Mary Q. 897, 901 (2002).

114. Id. at 907.

115. Adam Smith, An Inquiry into the Nature and Causes of the Wealth of Nations 788 (R. H. Campbell & A. S. Skinner, eds., 1981) (1776).

116. Id. at 792.

117. Id. at 793.

118. Id. at 795–796.

119. James Madison, *Federalist No. 10, in* The Federalist Papers 45 (Clinton Rossiter, ed., 1951).

120. See Fleischacker, *Adam Smith's Reception*, at 907. Smith also influenced the rather different view of Friedrich Hayek, who thought that competition would produce a prevalence of religious views that promoted good capitalist behavior. See the discussion in Koppelman, *Corruption of Religion*, at 1880–1882.

121. See Hamburger, Separation of Church and State, at 130–132.

122. Alexis de Tocqueville, Democracy in America 526, 527 (George Lawrence, trans.; J. P. Mayer, ed., 1969) (1835–1840).

123. Id. at 448, 294.

124. Id. at 296, 297.

125. Id. at 297, 295.

126. Id. at 445.

127. Marvin Zetterbaum, *Alexis de Tocqueville, in* History of Political Philosophy 761, 778 (Leo Strauss & Joseph Cropsey, eds., 3d ed. 1987).

128. On the psychological and sociological forces inherent in religion that sometimes produce intolerance and persecution, see William P. Marshall, *The Other Side of Religion*, 44 Hastings L.J. 843, 853–859 (1993).

129. Smith, Foreordained Failure, at 102.
130. The following discussion is heavily indebted to Perry Dane, *Separation Anxiety*, 22 J. L. & Religion 545, 568–570 (2007).
131. Everson v. Bd. of Educ., 330 U.S. 1 (1947).
132. Illinois *ex rel.* McCollum v. Bd. of Educ., 333 U.S. 203 (1948).
133. Torcaso v. Watkins, 367 U.S. 488 (1961).
134. Engel v. Vitale, 370 U.S. 421 (1962).
135. Id. at 431–432 (quoting Memorial and Remonstrance at 187).
136. Roger K. Newman, Hugo Black: A Biography 523 (2d ed. 1994).
137. Id. at 523–524. He reportedly cited the same passage in other correspondence concerning *Engel*. *See* Mr. Justice and Mrs. Black: The Memoirs of Hugo L. Black and Elizabeth Black 95 (1986). His son recalls him saying in response to the protest against *Engel*: "Most of these people who are complaining, Son, are pure hypocrites who never pray anywhere but in public for the credit of it. Prayer ought to be a private thing, just like religion for a truly religious person." Hugo Black Jr., My Father: A Remembrance 176 (1975).
138. 343 U.S. 306, 319–320 (1952).
139. Id. at 320.
140. The exception is his concurrence in *Epperson v. Arkansas*, 393 U.S. 97 (1968) (Black, J., concurring), in which he argued that a statute barring the teaching of evolution in the public schools should be invalidated on grounds of vagueness rather than as an Establishment Clause violation. He there suggested that, because both Darwin and the Bible were excluded from the curriculum, it was arguable that the exclusion "leave[s] the State in a neutral position toward these supposedly competing religious and anti-religious doctrines." Id. at 113.
141. Engel v. Vitale, 370 U.S. 421, 431–434 (1962); Everson v. Bd. of Educ. of Ewing, 330 U.S. 1, 12–13 (1947).
142. *Everson*, 330 U.S. at 15–16. He fought with Justice Felix Frankfurter over whether this opinion ought to be cited in subsequent Supreme Court opinions. See James F. Simon, The Antagonists: Hugo Black, Felix Frankfurter and Civil Liberties in Modern America 180–183 (1989); Samuel A. Alito, Note, *The "Released Time" Cases Revisited: A Study of Group Decisionmaking by the Supreme Court*, 83 Yale L.J. 1202, 1210–1222 (1974). Black repeated this entire passage in *Illinois* ex rel. *McCollum v. Board of Education*, 333 U.S. 203, 210–211 (1948), *Torcaso v. Watkins*, 367 U.S. 488, 492–493 (1961), and his dissent in *Board of Education v. Allen*, 392 U.S. 236, 250–251 (1968) (Black, J., dissenting).
143. *McCollum*, 333 U.S. at 212.
144. *Torcaso*, 367 U.S. at 490, 494 (quoting *McCollum*, 333 U.S. at 232 [Frankfurter, J., concurring], which in turn was quoting *Everson*, 330 U.S. at 59 [Rutledge, J., dissenting]).

145. Engel v. Vitale, 370 U.S. 421, 425 (1962).
146. Id. at 430.
147. Id. at 435.
148. See Donald L. Drakeman, Church, State, and Original Intent 79–81 (2010); Hamburger, Separation of Church and State, at 422–434, 461–463; John T. McGreevy, Catholicism and American Freedom: A History 184–186 (2003); Lucas A. Powe Jr., The Warren Court and American Politics 182, 190, 368–369 (2000); Thomas C. Berg, *Anti-Catholicism and Modern Church-State Relations*, 33 Loy. U. Chi. L.J. 121, 127–129 (2001). A different psychological explanation is offered by Feldman, who speculates that Black was reacting to the atrocities of World War II. Divided by God, at 173–175. Black was not innocent of anti-Catholic bigotry. There is no excuse for his dissent in *Board of Education v. Allen*, 392 U.S. 236, 250–254 (1968), which hysterically claims that Catholic schools seeking to borrow textbooks from the state are "looking toward complete domination and supremacy of their particular brand of religion." Id. at 251.
149. He occasionally attended services at a Unitarian church. Newman, Hugo Black, at 521.
150. See Black, My Father, at 172.
151. He also had a typically Baptist view of the primacy of individual conscience. See *Welsh v. United States*, 398 U.S. 333, 344 (1970).
152. John Courtney Murray, *Law or Prepossessions?*, 14 L. & Contemp. Probs. 23, 29, 31, 30 (1949).
153. Everson v. Bd. of Educ., 330 U.S. 1, 59 (1947) (Rutledge, J., dissenting).
154. Murray, *Law or Prepossessions?*, at 30 n.33. Murray was on shakier ground when he claimed that "Madison's radically individualistic concept of religion" was "today quite passé." Id. at 29 n.29.
155. The only extended treatment of the problem of which I am aware is Murray, *Law or Prepossessions?* It is noted in Kent Greenawalt, 2 Religion and the Constitution: Establishment and Fairness 493 (2008), and Kent Greenawalt, *Fundamental Questions about the Religion Clauses: Reflections on Some Critiques*, 47 San Diego L. Rev. 1131, 1138–1142 (2010), and may explain the caution with which he deploys the corruption argument. It is also discussed by Douglas Laycock, *Religious Liberty as Liberty*, 7 J. Contemp. Legal Issues 313, 324–326 (1996), who eschews reliance on it because "these religious beliefs cannot be imputed to the Constitution without abandoning government neutrality on religious questions." Id. at 324.
156. Justice Stevens is another important proponent of the argument. See my *Justice Stevens, Religious Enthusiast*, 106 Nw. U. L. Rev. 567 (2012). Most revealingly, he has twice quoted with approval the following statement by Clarence Darrow:

The realm of religion . . . is where knowledge leaves off, and where faith begins, and it never has needed the arm of the State for support, and wherever it has received it, it has harmed both the public and the religion that it would pretend to serve.

Tr. of Oral Arg. 7, Scopes v. State, 154 Tenn. 105, 289 S.W. 363 (1927) (on file with Clarence Darrow Papers, Library of Congress) (punctuation corrected); quoted in Wolman v. Walter, 433 U.S. 229, 264 (1977) (Stevens, J., dissenting), and Capitol Square Review and Advisory Board v. Pinette, 515 U.S. 753, 812 n.19 (1995) (Stevens, J., dissenting).

157. Justice Black never did. Black's influence on Souter is sometimes direct, as when Souter quoted with approval Black's declaration that the framers thought "that individual religious liberty could be achieved best under a government which was stripped of all power to tax, to support, or otherwise to assist any or all religions." Hein v. Freedom From Religion Found., 551 U.S. 587, 643 (2007) (Souter, J., dissenting) (quoting Everson v. Bd. of Educ., 330 U.S. 1, 11 [1947]).

158. 536 U.S. 639, 711–713 (2002) (Souter, J., dissenting).

159. Kevin Pybas, *Does the Establishment Clause Require Religion to Be Confined to the Private Sphere?*, 40 Val. U. L. Rev. 71, 101–102 (2005).

160. I borrow this distinction from Eugene Volokh, The First Amendment and Related Statutes: Problems, Cases and Policy Arguments 723 (4th ed. 2011).

161. *Zelman*, 536 U.S. at 713 (Souter, J., dissenting).

162. See United States v. Ballard, 322 U.S. 78 (1944).

163. See 2A Norman J. Singer & J. D. Shambie Singer, Statutes and Statutory Construction § 45:11 (7th ed. 2007).

164. See Railroad Comm'n v. Pullman Co., 312 U.S. 496 (1941).

165. This is elegantly argued by Gedicks, The Rhetoric of Church and State, at 62–80.

166. In *Hall v. Bradshaw*, 630 F.2d 1018 (4th Cir. 1980), the court noted that ceremonial references to the Deity on coinage and the like

> may be treated as "grandfathered" exceptions to the general prohibition against officially composed theological statements. Present at the very foundations, few in number, fixed and invariable in form, confined in display and utterance to a limited set of official occasions and objects, they can safely occupy their own small, unexpandable niche in Establishment Clause doctrine. Their singular quality of being rooted in our history and their incapacity to tempt competing or complementary theological formulations by contemporary agencies of government sufficiently cabin them in and distinguish then [*sic*] from new, open-form theological expressions published under the aegis of the state.

Id. at 1023 n.2.

167. See McCreary County v. ACLU, 545 U.S. 844 (2005) (invalidating recently erected display); Van Orden v. Perry, 545 U.S. 677 (2005) (upholding forty-year-old display).

168. Elk Grove Unified School Dist. v. Newdow, 542 U.S. 1, 37 (2004) (O'Connor, J., concurring in the judgment).

169. See Russell Korobkin, *The Endowment Effect and Legal Analysis*, 97 Nw. U. L. Rev. 1227 (2003).

170. Douglas Laycock, *Theology Scholarships, the Pledge of Allegiance, and Religious Liberty: Avoiding the Extremes but Missing the Liberty*, 118 Harv. L. Rev. 155, 232 (2004).

171. As with the Ten Commandments, this can sometimes be true of the same text in different contexts. For example, placing "In God We Trust" on all American currency was a manifestation of generic ecumenism and anticommunism in 1956, but when Indiana in 2006 placed the same words on its license plates, it was taking sides in the culture wars.

172. See Jeffrey James Poelvoorde, *The American Civil Religion and the American Constitution*, in How Does the Constitution Protect Religious Freedom? 141 (Robert A. Goldwin & Art Kaufman, eds., 1987). For recent examples of the latter unattractive effect, see Andrew Koppelman, *Reading Lolita at Guantanamo*, 53 Dissent 64 (2006).

173. See Eisgruber & Sager, Religious Freedom and the Constitution, at 27–28; Greenawalt, Establishment and Fairness, at 451–456. This is why the corruption argument has so much more bite when government tries to affect religion as such than when it engages in facially neutral action that has a religious impact, such as providing education vouchers that can be used at religious schools.

174. 465 U.S. 668 (1984).

175. 492 U.S. 573 (1989).

176. Michael W. McConnell, *Religious Freedom at a Crossroads*, 59 U. Chi. L. Rev. 115, 127 (1992).

177. Id. at 193.

178. Another, the object of similar litigation, is the Mount Soledad cross in San Diego. See Trunk v. City of San Diego, 629 F.3d 1099 (2011).

179. Salazar v. Buono, 130 S.Ct. 1803, 1816 (2010) (plurality opinion).

180. Id. at 1817.

181. 463 U.S. 783 (1983).

182. Christopher C. Lund, *Legislative Prayer and the Secret Costs of Religious Endorsements*, 94 Minn. L. Rev. 972, 978, 1025–1028, 1045–1046, 1044 (2010).

183. H. Jefferson Powell, *The Earthly Peace of the Liberal Republic*, in Christian Perspectives on Legal Thought 91 (Michael W. McConnell et al., eds., 2001).

184. See Anthony Kenny, *Worshipping an Unknown God*, 19 Ratio (n.s.) 441 (2006).

3. Religion Clause Doctrine Explained

1. Richard H. Fallon Jr., Implementing the Constitution (2001).

2. Philip Bobbitt, Constitutional Fate: Theory of the Constitution (1982).

3. For a wealth of illustrations, see Donald L. Drakeman, Church, State, and Original Intent (2010).

4. The argument that follows is more fully stated in Andrew Koppelman, *Originalism, Abortion, and the Thirteenth Amendment*, Colum. L. Rev. (forthcoming 2012).

5. See Mitchell N. Berman, *Originalism Is Bunk*, 84 N.Y.U. L. Rev. 1 (2009).

6. See the catalogue in Thomas B. Colby, *The Sacrifice of the New Originalism*, 99 Georgetown L.J. 713, 716–736 (2011).

7. See the sources cited in id. at 716–717, 769–776, and Berman, *Originalism Is Bunk,* at 9–16.

8. See id.; Peter J. Smith, *How Different Are Originalism and Non-Originalism?*, 62 Hastings L. J. 707 (2011); Thomas B. Colby & Peter J. Smith, *Living Originalism*, 59 Duke L. J. 239 (2008).

9. Jamal Greene, *On the Origins of Originalism*, 88 Tex. L. Rev. 1, 62–81 (2009).

10. Jed Rubenfeld, Freedom and Time: A Theory of Constitutional Self-Government 145–159 (2001).

11. This conclusion reinforces Jack Balkin's argument that the United States has multiple Constitutions, rooted in the ideals of its multiple interpreters. See Andrew Koppelman, *Respect and Contempt in Constitutional Law, Or, Is Jack Balkin Heartbreaking?*, 71 Md. L. Rev. 1126 (2012).

12. See generally Theodore Brantner Wilson, The Black Codes of the South (1965).

13. Rubenfeld, Freedom and Time, at 183.

14. Rubenfeld briefly discusses the interpretation of the Establishment Clause in Revolution by Judiciary: The Structure of American Constitutional Law 29–30 (2005).

15. See Thomas J. Curry, The First Freedoms: Church and State in America to the Passage of the First Amendment 211 (1986). The Court has similarly observed that the purpose of the framers of the First Amendment "was to state an objective, not to write a statute." Walz v. Tax Comm'n, 397 U.S. 664, 668 (1970).

16. The Supreme Court has sometimes responded to this difficulty by seizing on a few texts and exaggerating their importance. Thus, for example, the Court justified its reliance on Jefferson's letter to the Danbury Baptists, with its famous "wall of separation" metaphor, by declaring that "it may be accepted almost as an authoritative declaration of the scope and effect of the amendment." Reynolds v. United States, 98 U.S. 145, 164 (1879). This metaphor, which has been the focus of enormous contestation, does not entail any particular set of legal rules. Its useless indeterminacy is also noted in Christopher L. Eisgruber & Lawrence G. Sager, Religious Freedom and the Constitution 17–18 (2007).

17. He also shows that the instability is present even within the work of a single scholar, since he disavows the conclusions of his own earlier work. Drakeman,

Church, State, and Original Intent, at 343 n.24. Drakeman's argument is further critiqued in Michael I. Meyerson, Endowed By Our Creator: The Birth of Religious Freedom in America 238–240 (2012).

18. See Andrew Koppelman, *Phony Originalism and the Establishment Clause*, 103 Nw. U. L. Rev. 727 (2009).

19. Sch. Dist. of Abington Twp. v. Schempp, 374 U.S. 203, 236, 241 (1963) (Brennan, J., concurring).

20. 403 U.S. 602, 612–613 (citation and internal quotes omitted) (1971).

21. For those unacquainted with legal terms of art, the parts of a multipart legal test are typically referred to as "prongs," using a metaphor drawn from the prongs of a fork.

22. Lower courts have also relied upon the secular purpose prong many times. See Andrew Koppelman, *Secular Purpose*, 88 Va. L. Rev. 87, 95 n. 12 (2002) (collecting cases).

23. 393 U.S. 97, 107, 103 (1968).

24. 449 U.S. 39, 41–42 (1980).

25. 472 U.S. 38, 40, 56, 58–59 (1985).

26. 482 U.S. 578, 590, 592 (1987).

27. 530 U.S. 290, 306 (2000).

28. 545 U.S. 844 (2005).

29. 366 U.S. 420, 445 (1961).

30. 465 U.S. 668, 691 (1984).

31. *Wallace*, 472 U.S. at 108 (Rehnquist, J., dissenting).

32. *Aguillard*, 482 U.S. at 636 (Scalia, J., dissenting). No summary can do justice to Justice Scalia's extensive and richly entertaining catalogue of difficulties. See id. at 636–640.

33. I draw the name from the Supreme Court's opinion in *Zorach v. Clauson*, 343 U.S. 306, 314 (1952) (warning against a reading of the Constitution that would require "that the government show a callous indifference to religious groups"), quoted in Corp. of the Presiding Bishop v. Amos, 483 U.S. 327, 335 (1987).

34. *Aguillard*, 482 U.S. at 616–617 (Scalia, J., dissenting).

35. *Wallace*, 472 U.S. at 69 (O'Connor, J., concurring in the judgment) (citation omitted).

36. *Aguillard*, 482 U.S. at 585, 587; *Santa Fe*, 530 U.S. at 305.

37. *Wallace*, 472 U.S. at 76, 74 (O'Connor, J., concurring in the judgment).

38. Id. at 82–83 (citation omitted).

39. Justice O'Connor thought that religious accommodations are sometimes required by the Free Exercise Clause. See Employment Division v. Smith, 494 U.S. 872, 891–907 (1990) (O'Connor, J., concurring in the judgment).

40. *Wallace*, 477 U.S. at 82, 83 (O'Connor, J., concurring in the judgment) (quoting Walz v. Tax Commission, 397 U.S. 664, 668–669 [1970]).

41. See Steven D. Smith, *Symbols, Perceptions, and Doctrinal Illusions: Establishment Neutrality and the "No Endorsement" Test*, 86 Mich. L. Rev. 266 (1987); see also Michael W. McConnell, *Religious Freedom at a Crossroads*, 59 U. Chi. L. Rev. 115, 148–151, 192–193 (1992) (expressing similar objections).

42. Corp. of the Presiding Bishop v. Amos, 483 U.S. 327, 348–349 (1987) (O'Connor, J., concurring in the judgment).

43. McConnell, *Religious Freedom at a Crossroads*, at 151.

44. Smith, *Symbols, Perceptions*, at 282.

45. Id. at 279–281 (footnotes omitted).

46. 393 U.S. 97, 103–104 (1968).

47. See, e.g., United States v. Eichman, 496 U.S. 310 (1990) (holding that the First Amendment protects the burning of a United States flag).

48. On these prohibitions in Jewish law, see 14 Encyclopaedia Judaica 567 (1971).

49. Steven D. Smith, *Barnette's Big Blunder*, 78 Chi.-Kent L. Rev. 625, 656 (2003); see also Steven D. Smith, Foreordained Failure: The Quest for a Constitutional Principle of Religious Freedom 81–90 (1995).

50. Religious Commitment and Secular Reason 89 (2000).

51. Christopher Eberle has objected, in conversation, that this understanding of the Establishment Clause puts great weight on a distinction between morally equivalent actions. Laws such as the Sabbath statute are unconstitutional because they communicate religious messages, even though the government has not made any explicit religious statement at all. But the teaching of evolution is permissible even though it logically implies the falsity of certain specific religious beliefs, beliefs that are salient for many citizens. In both cases, everyone understands that a religious message is being communicated.

Eberle's concern must bypass the stop sign case, in which a religious view is implicit but not salient. That would distend the secular purpose requirement to the point of absurdity, because there would be no way to engage in any intentional action whatever without violating it. Rather, the claim is that, if the principles extend to the Sabbath law, it should (must logically?) also extend to the science curriculum, forbidding any state action that is understood by some subset (how small?) of citizens to imply a religious message, even if that message is unlikely to have been salient to anyone else. This is, of course, an optional expansion of the requirement, but it could destroy the capacity of the state to pursue legitimate and perhaps urgent secular purposes. It is not incoherent to make the secular purpose requirement easier to satisfy than this, so that a law will not be invalidated unless the case for it manifestly satisfies Audi's condition. This is what contemporary American law does, robustly and intelligibly. The problem is not purely one of moral philosophy. It is how to implement the Establishment Clause with workable rules of law.

52. Santa Fe Independent School Dist. v. Doe, 530 U.S. 290, 315 (2000), quoting Lynch v. Donnelly, 465 U.S. 668, 694 (1984) (O'Connor, J., concurring).

53. The meaning that the natives do in fact ascribe to it is, of course, probative. See Shari Seidman Diamond & Andrew Koppelman, *Measured Endorsement*, 60 Md. L. Rev. 713 (2001).

54. See Wallace v. Jaffree, 472 U.S. 38, 75 (1985) (O'Connor, J., concurring in the judgment). The mere fact that some citizens support a law for religious reasons will not, therefore, make a law unconstitutional. See Harris v. McRae, 448 U.S. 297 (1980).

55. 545 U.S. 844, 861–863 (2005).

56. Edwards v. Aguillard, 482 U.S. 578, 636 (1987) (Scalia, J., dissenting).

57. Andrew Koppelman, Romer v. Evans *and Invidious Intent*, 6 Wm. & Mary Bill Rts. J. 89, 103–111 (1997).

58. Andrew Koppelman, Antidiscrimination Law and Social Equality 13–56 (1996); Koppelman, Romer v. Evans *and Invidious Intent*, at 98–101.

59. See Christopher J. Eberle, Religious Conviction in Liberal Politics (2002).

60. Epperson v. Arkansas, 393 U.S. 97, 104 (1968).

61. Michael W. McConnell, *The Problem of Singling Out Religion*, 50 DePaul L. Rev. 1, 31, 42 (2000).

62. 517 U.S. 620, 632, 634 (1996).

63. Daniel A. Crane, *Faith, Reason, and Bare Animosity*, 21 Campbell L. Rev. 125, 146, 162, 169, 156 (1999).

64. Some judges have explicitly invoked sectarian teachings as a basis for their decisions. See Scott C. Idleman, Note, *The Role of Religious Values in Judicial Decision Making*, 68 Ind. L.J. 433, 475–477 (1993) (citing cases). But such behavior is not to be found in modern majority opinions of the U.S. Supreme Court, and it is inappropriate in any American court.

65. 388 U.S. 1, 3 (1967) (quoting trial court opinion).

66. Examples are collected in Koppelman, *Secular Purpose*, at 164 n.285.

67. *Loving*, 388 U.S. at 11, 12.

68. Courts are faced with the same dilemma when the state attempts to defend a statute on the basis of bare assertions of public morality. Peter M. Cicchino, *Reason and the Rule of Law: Should Bare Assertions of "Public Morality" Qualify as Legitimate Government Interests for the Purposes of Equal Protection Review?*, 87 Geo. L.J. 139 (1998).

69. See, e.g., Bradwell v. Illinois, 83 U.S. (16 Wall.) 130, 141 (1872) (Bradley, J., concurring in the judgment).

70. William P. Marshall, *"We Know It When We See It": The Supreme Court and Establishment*, 59 S. Cal. L. Rev. 495, 501 (1986).

71. See Erika King, *Tax Exemptions and the Establishment Clause*, 49 Syracuse L. Rev. 971, 981–83 (1999).

72. 397 U.S. 664, 666–667, 673 (1970).

73. See also Tex. Monthly v. Bullock, 489 U.S. 1, 14–15 (1989) (plurality opinion) (holding that Texas's sales tax exemption for religious faith periodicals lacked sufficient breadth to pass scrutiny under the Establishment Clause);

Comm. for Pub. Educ. & Religious Liberty v. Nyquist, 413 U.S. 756, 794 (1973) (invalidating grants to religious schools and contrasting the exemption in *Walz*, which "was not restricted to a class composed exclusively or even predominantly of religious institutions").

74. For this reason, it will not do to argue that religions get tax exemptions because they are nonprofit organizations. See, e.g., Boris I. Bittker & George K. Rahdert, *The Exemption of Nonprofit Organizations from Federal Income Taxation*, 85 Yale L.J. 299, 342–345 (1976); John M. Swomley, *The Impact of Tax Exemption and Deductibility on Churches and Public Policy*, 22 Cumb. L. Rev. 595 (1991–1992). Such an argument cannot explain why "religion," rather than "nonprofit organization," is the operative category for the exemption.

75. 463 U.S. 388, 396 (1983).

76. Marshall, *"We Know It When We See It,"* at 501 n.38. This fact renders problematic McConnell's preferred interpretation of the endorsement test, under which government "favoritism or preference" for religion would be prohibited. McConnell, *Religious Freedom at a Crossroads*, at 156. A tax exemption for which only religions qualify does "prefer religion . . . over the alternatives." Id. at 157 (internal quotes omitted).

Another basis for permitting exemptions that has been suggested in some of the Court's opinions is the distinction between a tax exemption and a subsidy. See Edward A. Zelinsky, *Are Tax "Benefits" Constitutionally Equivalent to Direct Expenditures?*, 112 Harv. L. Rev. 379, 392–399 (1998) (collecting cases). This distinction is crude, however. It would invalidate permanent entitlement programs to which religious entities are incidental beneficiaries, while it would tolerate tax exemptions that are functionally equivalent to direct outlays, such as "a one-time economic development tax abatement designed to attract an out-of-state religious entity to relocate." Id. at 425.

77. 489 U.S. 1, 33, 37 (1989) (Scalia, J., dissenting).

78. *Walz*, 397 U.S. at 689 (Brennan, J., concurring).

79. *Texas Monthly*, 489 U.S. at 37 (Scalia, J., dissenting).

80. See Andrew Koppelman, *The New U.S. Civil Religion: Lessons for Italy*, 41 George Washington Int'l L. Rev. 861 (2010).

81. *Walz*, 397 U.S. at 690 n.9 (Brennan, J., concurring).

82. 393 U.S. at 112–113 (Black, J., concurring).

83. 449 U.S. at 45 (Rehnquist, J., dissenting).

84. Id. at 42 (majority opinion).

85. As the Court did (with Justice Scalia voting with the majority!) in *Church of the Lukumi Babalu Aye v. City of Hialeah*, 508 U.S. 520, 525–528, 535–540 (1993). See Andrew Koppelman, The Gay Rights Question in Contemporary American Law 15–16 (2002) (discussing the role of context in *Lukumi*).

86. Frederick Mark Gedicks, *Motivation, Rationality, and Secular Purpose in Establishment Clause Review*, 1985 Ariz. St. L.J. 677, 700–701.

87. 530 U.S. at 315.

88. 472 U.S. 58–59; id. at 88 (Burger, C.J., dissenting).

89. President Bill Clinton noted several years later that "some students in America have been prohibited from reading the Bible silently in study hall. Some student religious groups haven't been allowed to publicize their meetings in the same way that nonreligious groups can. Some students have been prevented even from saying grace before lunch." *Remarks at James Madison High School in Vienna, Virginia* (July 12, 1995), in 31 Weekly Compilation of Presidential Documents 1220, 1225 (1995).

90. It is also possible that the evanescence objection is raised by this problem, in the following way. Legislative purpose is not knowable, but the secular purpose requirement demands that one treat it as if it were knowable, so that courts tend to hunt through the legislative history for any guilty trace of participation by religious people—and any such trace will then invalidate the law. (Arguably this is what happened in *Wallace v. Jaffree*.) Thus the evanescence objection and the participation objection can work in tandem, as they typically do in the opinions of Justice Scalia.

91. See *Aguillard*, 482 U.S. at 612 (Scalia, J., dissenting), 604 (Powell, J., concurring), 581–582. Perhaps the best argument for the result the Court reached is that suggested by Justice White: The district court and the court of appeals below had both construed the statute to be religious in purpose, and "[w]e usually defer to courts of appeals on the meaning of a state statute, especially when a district court has the same view." Id. at 609 (White, J., concurring in the judgment).

92. 400 F.Supp. 2d 707 (2005).

93. For an exhaustive survey of possible secular justifications of the Sunday laws, which concludes that none of the justifications are persuasive, see Gedicks, *Motivation, Rationality*, at 694–697.

94. See Daniel A. Farber, The First Amendment 20–30 (3d ed. 2010).

95. Everson v. Bd. of Educ., 330 U.S. 1, 15 (1947).

96. See, e.g., Mitchell v. Helms, 530 U.S. 793 (2000); Rosenberger v. Rector & Visitors of Univ. of Va., 515 U.S. 819 (1995).

97. There is the possibly embarrassing case of military and prison chaplains, but this exception is limited to cases where government participation is necessary if religious exercise is to be possible at all. Even in this context, denominational discrimination is prohibited. See Cruz v. Beto, 405 U.S. 319 (1972); Katcoff v. Marsh, 755 F.2d 223 (2d Cir. 1985). Like many of the exceptions to these general rules, this one is firmly confined to its facts. Any new attempt to put ministers, as such, on the public payroll would certainly be invalidated.

98. Engel v. Vitale, 370 U.S. 421 (1962); Abington v. Schempp, 374 U.S. 203 (1963); Lee v. Weisman, 505 U.S. 577 (1992).

99. Board of Education v. Mergens, 496 U.S. 226 (1990); Good News Club v. Milford Central School, 533 U.S. 98 (2001).

100. Santa Fe Independent School District v. Doe, 530 U.S. 290 (2000).

101. McDaniel v. Paty, 435 U.S. 618 (1978).

102. Church of the Lukumi Babalu Aye, Inc. v. Hialeah, 508 U.S. 520, 543 (1993).

103. See, e.g., County of Allegheny v. ACLU, 492 U.S. 573 (1989).

104. Larson v. Valente, 456 U.S. 228 (1982).

105. Torcaso v. Watkins, 367 U.S. 488 (1961).

106. U.S. Const., art. VI, cl. 3.

107. United States v. Ballard, 322 U.S. 78, 87 (1944).

108. Presbyterian Church v. Mary Elizabeth Blue Hull Mem'l Presbyterian Church, 393 U.S. 440, 449, 450 (1969).

109. Jones v. Wolf, 443 U.S. 595, 603 (1979) (quoting Md. & Va. Eldership v. Church of God, 396 U.S. 367, 368 (1970) (Brennan, J., concurring)).

110. *Md. & Va. Eldership*, 396 U.S at 368 (Brennan, J., concurring).

111. *Ballard*, 322 U.S. at 87.

112. Larkin v. Grendel's Den, 459 U.S. 116 (1982).

113. See Santa Fe Independent School District v. Doe, 530 U.S. 290 (2000).

114. Lee v. Weisman, 505 U.S. 577, 587 (1992).

115. County of Allegheny v. ACLU, 492 U.S. 573, 661 (1989) (Kennedy, J., concurring in the judgment in part and dissenting in part) (footnote omitted), quoted in part with approval in Salazar v. Buono, 130 S.Ct. 1803, 1816 (2010) (Kennedy, J., joined by Roberts, C.J. and Alito, J.). Roberts and Alito, the justices who have joined the Court since O'Connor's retirement, have thus signed onto something like the endorsement test.

116. Lee v. Weisman, 505 U.S. 577 (1992).

117. *Salazar*, 130 S.Ct. at 1816.

118. Lund observes: "If the endorsement test is abandoned, it will probably be replaced by something that looks a heck of a lot like it." Christopher Lund, Salazar v. Buono *and the Future of the Establishment Clause*, 105 Nw. U. L. Rev. Colloquy 60, 70 (2010).

119. Laurence Tribe, American Constitutional Law 1232–1242 (2d ed. 1988).

120. See Presbyterian Church v. Mary Elizabeth Blue Hull Mem'l Presbyterian Church, 393 U.S. 440 (1969); Serbian Orthodox Diocese v. Milivojevich, 426 U.S. 696 (1976).

121. Hosanna-Tabor Evangelical Lutheran Church and School v. EEOC, 2012 WL 75047 (2012).

122. See Tribe, American Constitutional Law, at 1241–1242.

123. Jared A. Goldstein, *Is There a "Religious Question" Doctrine? Judicial Authority to Examine Religious Practices and Beliefs*, 54 Catholic U. L. Rev. 497 (2005). A similar concern underlies Samuel J. Levine, *Rethinking the Supreme Court's Hands-Off Approach to Questions of Religious Practice and Belief*, 25 Fordham Urban L. J. 85 (1997).

124. 406 U.S. 205 (1972).

125. Marci A. Hamilton, God vs. the Gavel: Religion and the Rule of Law 44–46 (2005).
126. The classic citation is Ronald Dworkin, *Rights as Trumps*, in Theories of Rights 153 (Jeremy Waldron, ed., 1984).
127. See Thomas C. Berg, *Minority Religions and the Religion Clauses*, 82 Wash. U. L. Q. 919, 968–970 (2004).
128. Before *Employment Division v. Smith*, 494 U.S. 872 (1990), held that there is no right to religious exemptions from laws of general applicability, free exercise claims had a success rate of 39.5 percent. Afterward, that success rate dropped to 28.4 percent. More importantly, the number of filed claims plunged after *Smith*, from 310 decided in the nine and a quarter years before the decision to 38 in the three and a half years after it. Under the Religious Freedom Restoration Act, 42 U.S.C. § 2000bb, which temporarily (until the Supreme Court struck it down in *City of Boerne v. Flores*, 521 U.S. 507 [1997]) restored the "compelling interest" test, success rates rose to 45.2 percent and the number of filed claims in that three-year period rose to 114, perhaps in response to the strong legislative signal that courts should take religious impact very seriously. See Amy Adamczyk, John Wibraniec, & Roger Finke, *Religious Regulation and the Courts: Documenting the Effects of* Smith *and* RFRA, 46 J. Church & State 237, 250 tbl. 1 (2004).

    Eisgruber and Sager claim that when religious exemption claims were brought in federal courts before Smith, "almost everybody lost." Religious Freedom and the Constitution, at 100. They acknowledge the Adamczyk data, but note its limitations: the authors did not control for changes in courts' receptivity to civil rights claims in general, and free exercise claims were *less* likely to succeed when the compelling interest test was invoked. Id. at 299 n.35. These concerns, while reasonable, do not vindicate Eisgruber and Sager's overbroad generalization about the fate of exemption claims. The victory rate in the Adamczyk data is considerably in excess of zero.
129. Eugene Volokh, *A Common-Law Model for Religious Exemptions*, 46 UCLA L. Rev. 1465 (1999).
130. Eisgruber and Sager are unconvinced by Volokh's defense of mini-RFRAs. But they also concede that a sensible jurisprudence of religious freedom may emerge, because a presumptive right to disobey the laws is so anomalous that "sensible judges were bound to find ways to avoid its directive." Id. at 280. In fact, some of the mini-RFRAs have been construed remarkably narrowly. See Christopher C. Lund, *Religious Liberty after* Gonzales: *A Look at State RFRAs*, 55 S.D. L. Rev. 466 (2010).
131. Locke v. Davey, 540 U.S. 712 (2004).
132. Winnifred Fallers Sullivan, Prison Religion: Faith-Based Reform and the Constitution 95, 19–21 (2009).

133. Walter Kautzky, Iowa DOC director, 1997–2000, quoted in id. at 21–22.

134. Sullivan observes that, in considering recidivism rates, one should note IFI's selectivity in recruiting participants and its ability to eliminate participants at any time. Id. at 33–34.

135. Id. at 26, 39.

136. Id. at 28, 31, 198.

137. Id. at 52, 53, 201, 40, 51, 222.

138. Id. at 47–48, 129, 150.

139. See id. at 28, 62, 185–203.

140. Id. at 199, 35, 190, 46.

141. Americans United for Separation of Church and State v. Prison Fellowship Ministries, 432 F.Supp. 2d 862 (S.D. Iowa 2006), aff'd in pertinent part, 509 F.3d 406 (8th Cir. 2007).

142. Id. at 117; see also id. at 139. Sullivan is, however, doubtful about the salience of the religious/secular distinction in this context. "The modern state is . . . perhaps at its most religious when it exerts total control over its citizens and attempts to coercively remake them into new human beings. . . . Even when explicitly religious language is absent, the sacred haunts the prison and all who work there." Id. at 6. The point is accurate, but for constitutional purposes it matters a great deal whether explicitly religious language is absent.

143. 530 U.S. 793, 794, 810, 813, 820 (2000).

144. Samuel Freeman, *Illiberal Libertarians: Why Libertarianism Is Not a Liberal View*, 30 Phil. & Pub. Aff. 105 (2001).

145. 377 U.S. 218 (1964).

146. San Antonio v. Rodriguez, 411 U.S. 1, 37 (1973). If, on the other hand, the state did have such an obligation, then it might perhaps be obligated to make sure that such education was available on nonreligious terms. See Eisgruber and Sager, Religious Freedom and the Constitution, at 204–221. But the antecedent is disputable, at least for judicial purposes. Eisgruber and Sager admit that the obligation, if there is one, is judicially underenforced. Id. at 209.

147. These are reviewed in the first two chapters of Koppelman, Antidiscrimination Law and Social Equality.

148. Washington v. Davis, 426 U.S. 229 (1976).

149. DeShaney v. Winnebago County Dept. of Social Services, 489 U.S. 189, 195 (1989); accord Town of Castle Rock v. Gonzales, 545 U.S. 748 (2005).

150. See *DeShaney* at 203.

151. See Hunt v. Cromartie, 526 U.S. 541, 547 n.3, 548–549 (1999).

152. See Walter F. Murphy, Constitutional Democracy: Creating and Maintaining a Just Political Order 489–490 (2006).

153. See Larry Kramer, *Putting the Politics Back into the Political Safeguards of Federalism*, 100 Colum. L. Rev. 215 (2000), reviewing a large literature.
154. 551 U.S. 587 (2007).
155. 131 S.Ct. 1436 (2011).
156. Ira C. Lupu & Robert W. Tuttle, *Ball on a Needle:* Hein v. Freedom from Religion Foundation, Inc. *and the Future of Establishment Clause Adjudication*, 2008 B.Y.U. L. Rev. 115, 152.
157. 131 S.Ct. at 1449.
158. Id. at 1450–1463 (Kagan, J., dissenting).

4. Why Single Out Religion?

1. Christopher Hitchens, god Is Not Great: How Religion Poisons Everything (2007).
2. Peter L. Berger, The Sacred Canopy: Elements of a Sociological Theory of Religion 112–121 (Anchor ed. 1969).
3. See, e.g., Robert Orsi, *"Mildred, Is It Fun to Be a Cripple?" The Culture of Suffering in Mid-Twentieth Century American Catholicism*, in Between Heaven and Earth: The Religious Worlds People Make and the Scholars Who Study Them 19 (2005).
4. When Eisenhower declared, "Our form of government has no sense unless it is founded in a deeply felt religious faith, and I don't care what it is," he less famously made clear in the next sentence that he was not talking about just any religion at all: "With us of course it is the Judeo-Christian concept but it must be a religion that all men are created equal." Patrick Henry, *"And I Don't Care What It Is": The Tradition-History of a Civil Religion Proof-Text*, 49 J. Am. Acad. of Religion 35 (1981).
5. Under the contemporary state and federal RFRAs, a religion demanding, say, the killing of nonadherents would be entitled to judicial scrutiny of the burden that the homicide laws place upon its exercise. That burden would nominally be invalid unless necessary to a compelling interest. To that extent, even this religion would be treated as presumptively valuable. These laws so obviously survive such scrutiny that no one has bothered to test them.
6. Berger, The Sacred Canopy, at 37.
7. I have always been fond of the following two-line joke:
    Q. Do you swear to tell the truth, the whole truth, and nothing but the truth, so help you God?
    A. If I knew the truth, the whole truth, and nothing but the truth, I would *be* God.
8. See, e.g., Joseph Cardinal Ratzinger, Introduction to Christianity 40–41 (rev. ed. 2004).
9. Paul Tillich's description of God as one's "ultimate concern," which the Supreme Court quoted with approval in United States v. Seeger, 380 U.S. 163,

187 (1965), goes on to say that the deep concern of which he speaks should perhaps be called "hope, simply hope." Paul Tillich, The Shaking of the Foundations 59 (1948).

10. See Phil Zuckerman, Society without God: What the Least Religious Nations Can Tell Us about Contentment (2008).

11. Charles Taylor, A Secular Age (2007); Regina Mara Schwartz, Sacramental Poetics at the Dawn of Secularism: When God Left the World (2008).

12. See Steven D. Smith, The Disenchantment of Secular Discourse (2010); Jürgen Habermas, An Awareness of What Is Missing: Faith and Reason in a Post-Secular Age (2010).

13. David J. Garrow, Bearing the Cross: Martin Luther King, Jr., and the Southern Christian Leadership Conference 56–58 (1986).

14. A contrary view appears in Daniel C. Dennett, Breaking the Spell: Religion as a Natural Phenomenon 54–56 (2006).

15. Paul J. Weithman, Religion and the Obligations of Citizenship 41–66 (2002).

16. Robert D. Putnam & David E. Campbell, American Grace: How Religion Divides and Unites Us 443–492 (2010).

17. Paul Horwitz, The Agnostic Age: Law, Religion, and the Constitution 83, 86 (2011).

18. John M. Finnis, Natural Law and Natural Rights 89–90 (1980).

19. Keith E. Yandell, Philosophy of Religion: A Contemporary Introduction 17–34 (1999).

20. Paul Tillich, The Courage to Be (1952).

21. Immanuel Kant, Critique of Practical Reason (1788; Cambridge: Cambridge University Press, 1997); Religion within the Limits of Reason Alone (1794; New York: Harper, 1960).

22. Rudolf Otto, The Idea of the Holy (2d ed. 1950).

23. It goes unmentioned in the opinions of Justices Scalia and Thomas, who claim to be originalists. See my *Phony Originalism and the Establishment Clause*, 103 Nw. U. L. Rev. 727 (2009).

24. *Foundations of Religious Liberty: Toleration or Respect?*, 47 San Diego L. Rev. 935 (2010); *Why Tolerate Religion?*, 25 Const. Comm. 1 (2008).

25. *Why Tolerate Religion?*, at 25.

26. *Foundations*, at 957. The following discussion is drawn from a fuller critique of these papers in *How Shall I Praise Thee? Brian Leiter on Respect for Religion*, 47 San Diego L. Rev. 961 (2010).

27. In the United States, quite a lot of the time. Only 39 percent of Americans believe in the theory of evolution, smaller than the roughly 44 percent who think that God created humans within the last ten thousand years. This superstition divides on party lines, affecting 60 percent of Republicans and 38 percent of Democrats. See Frank Newport, *On Darwin's Birthday, Only 4 in 10 Believe in Evolution*, Gallup Poll, Feb. 11, 2009, available at http://www.gallup.com/poll/114544/darwin-birthday-believe-evolution.aspx   (visited

Sept. 30, 2009); Frank Newport, *Republicans, Democrats Differ on Creationism: Republicans Much More Likely Than Democrats to Believe Humans Created As-Is 10,000 Years Ago*, Gallup Poll, June 20, 2008, available at http://www.gallup.com/poll/108226/Republicans-Democrats-Differ-Creationism.aspx (visited Sept. 30, 2009).

28. For a photograph, see *Creation Museum*, Wikipedia, available at http://en.wikipedia.org/wiki/Creation_Museum (visited Oct. 1, 2009).

29. Leiter, *Foundations*, at 955.

30. *Why Tolerate Religion?*, at 23.

31. Id.at 20.

32. Id.at 20–21; *Foundations*, at 950–951.

33. Simon Blackburn, *Religion and Respect*, in Philosophers without Gods: Meditations on Atheism and the Secular Life 179, 186, 193 (Louise M. Anthony, ed., 2007). Like Leiter, Blackburn deplores the tendency of the religious to believe dubious propositions of fact. Many modern theologians, he observes, try to rescue their position by rejecting such propositional claims as "onto-religion" and instead adopting an "expressive interpretation" in which religion merely expresses an emotional stance toward the world. In order for this expressive stance to be psychologically sustainable, Blackburn objects, the ontological bit has to persist; without it the emotional part would lose its force. Id. at 185. He is probably right about this, but why presume that the amplification comes from *certainty* about the ontological part? Once more, hope may be enough to do the job.

34. Joseph Raz, The Morality of Freedom (1986); Joseph Raz, *Facing Diversity: The Case of Epistemic Abstinence*, in Ethics in the Public Domain: Essays in the Morality of Law and Politics 60 (1994).

35. See Timothy Macklem, Independence of Mind 120–126 (2006). David Richards similarly argues that commonsense conceptions of religion "hopelessly track often unprincipled and ad hoc majoritarian intuitions of 'proper' or 'real' religion." See David A. J. Richards, Toleration and the Constitution 142 (1986).

36. Macklem, Independence of Mind, at 140. Macklem's view of religion is nonetheless condescending: he writes that "for some people the nature of life and the content of morality are unknowable on the basis of reason alone," id. at 139–140, implying that he is one of the smart ones who has the nature of life all figured out. Lucky him.

37. Id. at 140.

38. Cf. Shel Silverstein, *What's in the Sack?*, in Where the Sidewalk Ends 111 (1974).

39. Macklem, Independence of Mind, at 142.

40. Id.

41. *Autonomy, Toleration, and the Harm Principle*, in Justifying Toleration: Conceptual and Historical Perspectives 155, 164 (Susan Mendus, ed., 1988).

42. Macklem, Independence of Mind, at 145.

43. *Why Tolerate Religion?*, at 16; *Foundations*, at 946.

44. See, e.g., Blackburn, *Religion and Respect*, at 190–192.

45. See, e.g., Richard Dawkins's suggestion that those who share his views label themselves "brights." See The God Delusion (2006).

46. See, e.g., Amy Gutmann, Identity in Democracy 151–191 (2003); William Galston, The Practice of Liberal Pluralism 45–71 (2005); Kwame Anthony Appiah, The Ethics of Identity 98 (2005); Michael J. Sandel, Democracy's Discontent: America in Search of a Public Philosophy 65–71 (1996); Martha Nussbaum, Liberty of Conscience: In Defense of America's Tradition of Religious Equality (2008); Jocelyn Maclure & Charles Taylor, Secularism and Freedom of Conscience (2011); Rogers M. Smith, *"Equal" Treatment? A Liberal Separationist View*, in Equal Treatment of Religion in a Pluralistic Society 190–194 (Steven V. Monsma & J. Christopher Soper, eds., 1998); Ira C. Lupu, *The Trouble with Accommodation*, 60 Geo. Wash. L. Rev. 743 (1992); Rodney K. Smith, *Conscience, Coercion and the Establishment of Religion: The Beginning of an End to the Wanderings of a Wayward Judiciary?*, 43 Case W. Res. L. Rev. 917 (1993); Rodney K. Smith, *Converting the Religious Equality Amendment into a Statute with a Little "Conscience,"* 1996 BYU L. Rev. 645. The Supreme Court cases are discussed below.

47. Thomas E. Hill Jr., *Four Conceptions of Conscience*, in Nomos XL: Integrity and Conscience 14 (Ian Shapiro & Robert Adams, eds., 1998). My analysis of multiple conceptions of conscience is in some ways similar to Hill's, but he is concerned about different accounts of the role of conscience in morality, while I am interested in different accounts of the role of conscience in the law's treatment of persons.

48. Quoted in United States v. Seeger, 326 F.2d 846, 848 (2d Cir. 1964), aff'd, 380 U.S. 163 (1965).

49. Quoted in Peter Irons, The Courage of Their Convictions: Sixteen Americans Who Fought Their Way to the Supreme Court 169 (1988).

50. *Seeger*, 326 F.2d at 848–849.

51. Id. at 847, quoting 50 U.S.C.A. § 456(j) (rev. 1948).

52. Id. at 853.

53. United States v. Seeger, 380 U.S. 163, 166, 187 (1965).

54. Interview with Elliott Ashton Welsh II, December 2009. For further details of Welsh's story, see my *The Story of* Welsh v. United States: *Elliott Welsh's Two Religious Tests*, in First Amendment Stories 293 (Richard Garnett & Andrew Koppelman, eds., 2011).

55. Welsh v. United States, 398 U.S. 333, 344 (1970). The author was Hugo Black, and his implicit Protestantism, which we explored in Chapter 2, appears to have been operative here as well.

56. Id. at 351, 348, 360 n.12, 358 (Harlan, J., concurring in the result).

57. Welsh v. United States, 404 F.2d 1078, 1092 (9th Cir. 1968) (Hamley, J., dissenting).

58. The problem is a long-familiar one. See, e.g., G. W. F. Hegel, Philosophy of Right 90–92 (T. M. Knox., trans., 1952).

59. 494 U.S. 872 (1990). This result was reversed, with respect to federal law, by statute, which the Court has followed. See Gonzales v. O Centro Espirita Beneficente Uniao do Vegetal, 546 U.S. 418 (2006).

60. Christopher L. Eisgruber & Lawrence G. Sager, Religious Freedom and the Constitution 243 (2007).

61. See Garrett Epps, *To an Unknown God: The Hidden History of* Employment Division v. Smith, 30 Ariz. St. L. Rev. 953, 959–965, 978–985 (1998).

62. 42 U.S.C. § 2000cc-5(7)(A). Some of the state statutes mandating religious accommodation have similar language. See Ariz. Rev. Stat. Ann. §41–1493 (West 2004); Fla. Stat. Ann. §761.02 (West Supp. 2004); Idaho Code §73–401 (Michie Supp. 2004); 775 Ill. Comp. Stat. Ann. 35/5 (West 2001 & Supp. 2004); Mo. Ann. Stat. §§1.302 (West Supp. 2004); Tex. Civ. Prac. & Rem. Code Ann. §§110.001 (West Supp. 2004). But see 71 Pa. Cons. Stat. Ann. §§2403 (West Supp. 2004) (adopting a more restrictive definition of a substantial burden).

63. 521 U.S. 507 (1997).

64. 485 U.S. 439, 451, 450 (1988).

65. Eisgruber & Sager, Religious Freedom and the Constitution, at 243–244.

66. See Jeremy Bentham, *The Psychology of Economic Man*, in 3 Jeremy Bentham's Economic Writings 435 (W. Stark, ed., 1954).

67. Immanuel Kant famously heaped scorn on this conception of religion in Religion within the Limits of Reason Alone (1794).

68. See Richard Sorabji, *Graeco-Roman Origins of the Idea of Moral Conscience*, 44 Studia Patristica 361 (2010).

69. Michael G. Baylor, Action and Person: Conscience in Late Scholasticism and the Young Luther 24–25 (1977). For earlier uses of the concept, see Linda Hogan, Confronting the Truth: Conscience in the Catholic Tradition 36–42 (2000).

70. For overviews of Catholic uses of the term, see Hogan, Confronting the Truth; Charles E. Curran, *Conscience in the Light of the Catholic Moral Tradition*, in Conscience: Readings in Moral Theology 3–24 (Charles E. Curran, ed., 2004).

71. Peter Abelard, *Ethics*, in Ethical Writings 24, 29 (Paul Vincent Spade, trans., 1995); Baylor, Action and Person, at 27–28; Hogan, Confronting the Truth, at 73–75.

72. Thomas Aquinas, Summa Theologiae, IaIIae, q. 19, a. 5, v. 18, at 63 (Cambridge: McGraw-Hill/Blackfriars, 1966).

73. Brian Tierney, *Religious Rights: An Historical Perspective*, in Religious Human Rights in Global Perspective 25 (John Witte Jr. & Johan D. van der Vyver, eds., 1996) (quoting Ordinary Gloss to the Decretals, which explained two

judgments by Innocent). "Aquinas did not make clear whether he believed that a well informed conscience could ever be in conflict with ecclesiastical authority." Baylor, Action and Person, at 57 n.138. That problem, of course, came to a head with Martin Luther. I do not discuss Luther because his pertinent ideas about conscience resemble those of Aquinas. See id. at 261–262. Luther's most important innovation in this area was his view that invincible ignorance does not excuse: One is obligated to follow conscience, but doing so is not the path to salvation. Absent faith and grace, all action is sinful. See id. at 152–153, 243–244.

74. Noah Feldman, *The Intellectual Origins of the Establishment Clause*, 77 N.Y.U. L. Rev. 346, 357 (2002).

75. St. Thomas Aquinas, Selected Political Writings 77–79 (A. P. D'Entreves, ed., 1981).

76. Thus, John Finnis thinks that the sounder inference from Aquinas's premises is that faith must be "voluntary and free from coercive pressures." John Finnis, Aquinas 293 (1998); for a similar view, see Vatican Council II, *Declaration on Religious Freedom* (1965): "[T]he exercise of religion, of its very nature, consists before all else in those internal, voluntary and free acts whereby man sets the course of his life directly toward God. No merely human power can either command or prohibit acts of this kind." This forbids laws that aim at religious coercion, but does not entail exemption from otherwise valid, generally applicable laws. See, e.g., Gerard V. Bradley, *Beguiled: Free Exercise Exemptions and the Siren Song of Liberalism*, 20 Hofstra L. Rev. 245 (1991).

77. John Locke, A Letter Concerning Toleration 38 (1689; James H. Tully, ed., 1983).

78. The shifting meaning of the term is noted in William Lee Miller, The First Liberty: Religion and the American Republic (1986), at 122–123.

79. James Madison, Memorial and Remonstrance against Religious Assessments (1785), in 2 The Writings of James Madison 184–185 [1901]).

80. When he presents his argument for exemptions, he frequently begins by quoting this passage from Madison. See Michael W. McConnell, *The Origins and Historical Understanding of Free Exercise of Religion*, 103 Harv. L. Rev. 1409, 1453, 1497 (1990); Michael W. McConnell, *The Problem of Singling Out Religion*, 50 DePaul L. Rev. 1, 29 (2000); Michael W. McConnell, *Why Is Religious Liberty the 'First Freedom'?*, 21 Cardozo L. Rev. 1243, 1246–1247 (2000).

81. *The Origins and Historical Understanding*, at 1453.

82. *The Problem of Singling Out Religion*, at 30; see also Michael W. McConnell, *Free Exercise Revisionism and the* Smith *Decision*, 57 U. Chi. L. Rev. 1109, 1151–1152 (1990).

83. *The Problem of Singling Out Religion*, at 30. Note here the appeal to the intensity of the desire to disobey the law (as opposed to the soundness of the

conscientious objection). McConnell here comes dangerously close to Harlan's position.

84. McConnell offers it as an interpretation of the original sources, but none of them state this general principle as clearly as he does, so his originality here should be admitted. Perhaps the principle was inchoate in some early practice, but that is different from saying that it was consciously adopted and followed. See Philip A. Hamburger, *A Constitutional Right of Religious Exemption: An Historical Perspective*, 60 Geo. Wash. L. Rev. 915 (1992). Vincent Phillip Muñoz reads the same text to *preclude* religious accommodation. See his God and the Founders: Madison, Washington, and Jefferson 25–26, 39–40 (2009). Both McConnell and Muñoz offer creative glosses on texts ambiguous enough to be consistent with both.

85. This coinage is offered with acknowledgment of the many other scholars who have also defended religious exemptions. McConnell's defense is, in my view, the most thoroughly worked out of these.

86. McConnell emphasizes that government is forbidden to declare religious truth—see McConnell, *The Problem of Singling Out Religion*, at 23–28—but he does not resolve the tension between this idea and the idea that religious exercise is privileged because it is a duty to God.

87. Sandel, Democracy's Discontent, at 68, 67. Sandel inconsistently insists both on the primacy of conscience because of its importance to individual identity and on the value of religion because of "its place in a good life or, from a political point of view, its tendency to promote the habits and dispositions that make good citizens." Id. at 66. These are obviously not the same thing: conscience as Sandel describes it refers only to the internal mental state of the possessor, while the habits-and-dispositions argument rests on external contingencies.

88. Sandel, id. at 68 & n.66, quotes *Seeger* with approval.

89. Harry Frankfurt, *Duty and Love*, 1 Phil. Explorations 4 (Jan. 1998).

90. Harry G. Frankfurt, The Reasons of Love 46 (2004).

91. He probably never said it. See Diarmaid MacCulloch, The Reformation: A History 127 (2004).

92. Harry G. Frankfurt, *The Importance of What We Care About*, in The Importance of What We Care About 86 (1988).

93. Id. at 87; see also Harry G. Frankfurt, Taking Ourselves Seriously and Getting It Right 43–45 (Debra Satz, ed., 2006).

94. Harry G. Frankfurt, *Rationality and the Unthinkable*, in The Importance of What We Care About, at 188.

95. For elaboration, see Harry G. Frankfurt, *Autonomy, Necessity, and Love*, in Necessity, Volition, and Love, at 138–139.

96. The Reasons of Love, at 98.

97. Gerhard L. Weinberg, A World at Arms: A Global History of World War II 45–46 (1994).

98. See Gutmann, Identity in Democracy, at 171.

99. See Jonathan Bennett, *The Conscience of Huckleberry Finn*, 49 Philosophy 123 (1974).

100. Welsh v. United States, 398 U.S. 333, 340 (1970).

101. *Seeger*, 380 U.S. at 183, 187, quoting David Saville Muzzey, Ethics as a Religion 95 (1951), and Paul Tillich, The Shaking of the Foundations 57 (1948). Both of these formulations denote ideas more capacious than "conscience," even though *Seeger* is often cited for the proposition that conscience is what the Court is protecting.

102. For a discussion that emphasizes this, see John Rawls's defense of accommodation of conscientious objectors to the draft in A Theory of Justice 370–371/325–326 rev. (1971; revised ed., 1999).

103. Another factor that helps to account for the result in these cases is that, if the statute were construed as requiring theism, it would be drawing its lines in an impermissible way by discriminating among religions. So in order to save the statute, the Court had to broaden it.

104. Not least of these is that, if religion promises salvation, one can object that "religion" is an overinclusive category, because only the true religion can do this. See Larry Alexander, *Good God, Garvey! The Inevitability and Impossibility of a Religious Justification of Free Exercise Exemptions*, 47 Drake L. Rev. 35 (1998).

105. John Rawls, *A Kantian Conception of Equality*, in Collected Papers 255 (Samuel Freeman, ed., 1999).

106. See John Rawls, Political Liberalism 144–150 (expanded ed. 1996).

107. John Rawls, A Theory of Justice 207/181 rev.

108. Other writers have expanded on this Rawlsian point, and the rejoinder offered here is by implication directed at them as well. See Gerald Gaus, The Order of Public Reason: A Theory of Freedom and Morality in a Diverse and Bounded World (2011); Robert Audi, Democratic Authority and the Separation of Church and State (2011).

109. Rawls, Political Liberalism, at 49 n.2; 224.

110. Id. at 215, 214.

111. John Rawls, Justice as Fairness: A Restatement 152 (2001).

112. Id. at 152 n.26; see also Political Liberalism at 214–215.

113. Samuel Freeman, Rawls 80 (2007).

114. Chad Flanders, *The Mutability of Public Reason*, 25 Ratio Juris 180 (2012).

115. It would certainly permit them if they were grounded on political values, such as the need to reinforce morality and social solidarity. See *The Idea of Public Reason Revisited*, in Collected Papers at 601–602.

116. Political Liberalism, at 49 n.2.

117. Samuel Freeman, Justice and the Social Contract: Essays on Rawlsian Political Philosophy 201 (2007); see also id. at 200, 220, 224.

118. Id. at 204.
119. Freeman, Rawls, at 383.It is unclear how much work is being done here by the fact that Saudi Arabia does not respect the basic liberties of its citizens.
120. Rawls, Political Liberalism, at 231, 236.
121. American religious neutrality is an instance of what Jonathan Quong calls "comprehensive antiperfectionism," in which the state is neutral between competing conceptions of the good life, but the ultimate justification for this neutrality is not itself neutral in this sense, depending instead on some contestable ultimate value. Liberalism Without Perfection 19 (2011).
122. See Andrew Koppelman, *The Limits of Constructivism: Can Rawls Condemn Female Genital Mutilation?*, 71 Rev. Pol. 459 (2009).
123. Jeffrey Stout, Democracy and Tradition 72–73, 92–117 (2004).
124. Kwame Anthony Appiah similarly suggests that "Rawlsian structures about the ideal of public reason are perhaps best interpreted as debating tips: as rhetorical advice about how best, within a plural polity, to win adherents and influence policies." The Ethics of Identity 81 (2007). Rawls sometimes endorses a similar view. *The Idea of Public Reason Revisited*, in Collected Papers at 592.
125. Gerald Gaus argues with impressive care and thoroughness that those who do not enter into a strictly neutralist liberal social contract are unreasonable, because they have conclusive reasons from within their own evidentiary set to do so. Justificatory Liberalism: An Essay on Epistemology and Political Theory (1996). One may still wonder whether this demonstration advances the cause of social unity.
126. Political Liberalism, at 58, 13, 61.
127. Id. at 13.
128. Bruce Ackerman, *Should Opera Be Subsidized?*, 46 Dissent 89 (Summer 1999).
129. Beginning in the 1980s, Americans became increasingly hostile to the involvement of religious leaders in politics, and this hostility was strongest among those who did not identify with any religion. Putnam & Campbell, American Grace, at 120–121.
130. The substantive arguments for the claim are elegantly rebutted in Christopher J. Eberle, Religious Conviction in Liberal Politics (2002).
131. Martha Nussbaum, Liberty of Conscience: In Defense of America's Tradition of Religious Equality 168 (2008).
132. Id. at 168–169.
133. The list appears in many of Nussbaum's writings. One recent version is Martha C. Nussbaum, Creating Capabilities: The Human Development Approach 33–34 (2011).
134. Martha Nussbaum, *Aristotelian Social Democracy*, in Liberalism and the Good 236 (R. Bruce Douglass et al., eds., 1990).

135. Martha C. Nussbaum, Women and Human Development: The Capabilities Approach 179, 180 (2000)

136. Id. at 209.

137. Liberty of Conscience at 19; see also id. at 37.

138. Id. at 102, 165, 171, 172.

139. Its canonical statement is their book, *Religious Freedom and the Constitution.* Because some details of the argument are stated more fully in their earlier articles, which aim at a more specialized readership, I will draw upon them as well as the book. The response to them offered here is elaborated upon and more fully documented in *Justice Stevens, Religious Enthusiast,* 106 Nw. U. L. Rev. 567 (2012), and *Is It Fair to Give Religion Special Treatment?,* 2006 U. of Ill. L. Rev. 571.

140. Religious Freedom and the Constitution, at 24.

141. Id. at 52. Recall from Chapter 2 that this is also the foundational premise of Justice O'Connor's interpretation of the Establishment Clause. Eisgruber has noted the affinity between his view and O'Connor's. Christopher L. Eisgruber, *Justice Stevens, Religious Freedom, and the Value of Equal Membership,* 74 Fordham L. Rev. 2177 (2006).

142. Religious Freedom and the Constitution at 52–53, 245.

143. Christopher L. Eisgruber & Lawrence G. Sager, *Congressional Power and Religious Liberty after* City of Boerne v. Flores, 1997 Sup. Ct. Rev. 79, 106; see also Religious Freedom and the Constitution at 203 (in providing any kind of subsidy, government must "avoid preferring, endorsing, or affiliating itself with a particular viewpoint about religion").

144. *Congressional Power,* at 107. In many religious exemption cases, notably zoning cases, "the burdens upon religious exercise reduce to considerations of cost and convenience." Id.

145. Religious Freedom and the Constitution, at 58.

146. Id. at 9, 13, 92–93; Christopher L. Eisgruber & Lawrence G. Sager, *The Vulnerability of Conscience: The Constitutional Basis for Protecting Religious Conduct,* 61 U. Chi. L. Rev. 1245, 1290 (1994).

    This approach, they claim, accounts for all the case law on exemptions. See Religious Freedom and the Constitution at 13–14, 78–120; *The Vulnerability of Conscience* at 1277–1282.

147. Religious Freedom and the Constitution, at 19, 127, 163–164.

148. Id. at 125, 126.

149. Christopher L. Eisgruber & Lawrence G. Sager, *Chips Off Our Block? A Reply to Berg, Greenawalt, Lupu and Tuttle,* 85 Tex. L. Rev. 1271, 1281–1282 (2007).

150. Religious Freedom and the Constitution, at 264, 267, 269–275.

151. For a summary of process-based theories of discrimination, see Andrew Koppelman, Antidiscrimination Law and Social Equality 13–56 (1996).

152. Religious Freedom and the Constitution, at 102, 106; see also id. at 300 n.37.

153. Id. at 52, 69, 97, 112, 219; *Chips Off Our Block?* at 1274, 1276, 1280, 1282; see also Religious Freedom and the Constitution at 279 (government must not be "hostile or insensitive to the needs or interests of minority faiths"); id. at 102 (The question a court should ask itself "is whether a government that was alert and sympathetic in principle to the religiously inspired interests of a particular minority faith could have fashioned the contested disparity in accommodation.").

154. Religious Freedom and the Constitution at 93.

155. Paul Brest, *The Supreme Court 1975 Term, Foreword: In Defense of the Anti-discrimination Principle*, 90 Harv. L. Rev. 1, 7–8 (1976).

156. Ronald Dworkin, Taking Rights Seriously 227 (rev. ed. 1978).

157. Religious Freedom and the Constitution at 89–90; see also *Chips Off Our Block?*, at 1278.

158. *The Vulnerability of Conscience*, at 1257, 1315.

159. Id. at 1256 n.30. This argument by Dworkin is not referenced in the later book, Religious Freedom and the Constitution, but the argument about distributive justice just quoted still implicitly relies on his claim, or at least substitutes nothing else in its place. Eisgruber and Sager's implicit reliance on antiperfectionist liberalism like Dworkin's is further explored in Chad Flanders, *The Possibility of a Secular First Amendment*, 26 Quinnipiac L. Rev. 257 (2008).

160. Ronald Dworkin, Sovereign Virtue: The Theory and Practice of Equality 69, 112 (2000).

161. Ronald Dworkin, *Can a Liberal State Support Art?, in* A Matter of Principle 221, 233, 229 (1985).

162. *See* id. at 222. This claim is more fully developed in *Liberalism*, in id. at 181–204. The argument does not work, because respect for a person is not the same as respect for his ends. There is a gap between the premise of equal concern and respect and the conclusion of neutrality. Preferences based on *who* people are necessarily violate equal concern and respect; views of *how* people ought to behave do not. See Gerald Dworkin, *Equal Respect and the Enforcement of Morality*, 7 Soc. Phil. & Pol'y 180, 193 (1990). As we have seen, Eisgruber and Sager seek to fill this gap by invoking the social meaning of religion.

163. Dworkin, *Can a Liberal State Support Art?*, at 230.

164. Or, if one is concerned about the unfairness of initial distributions of cash, give each person tradable exemption credits.

165. *Chips Off Our Block?*, at 1275.

166. Brian Barry, Culture and Equality: An Egalitarian Critique of Multiculturalism 133 (2001).

167. Id. at 28.

168. Eisgruber & Sager, *The Vulnerability of Conscience,* at 1245 n.††.

169. Religious Freedom and the Constitution at 87, 89, 95, 101, 197, 241, 246, 252.

170. Eisgruber & Sager, *The Vulnerability of Conscience*, at 1271; see also Eisgruber & Sager, *Congressional Power*, at 104 (referring to "other, comparably serious commitments"); Religious Freedom and the Constitution at 90, 101, 103, 108, 300 ("serious").
171. Religious Freedom and the Constitution, at 6, 9, 15, 52, 95, 96.
172. Eisgruber & Sager, *Congressional Power*, at 114.
173. Religious Freedom and the Constitution, at 6.
174. Id. at 100–108 (responding to earlier criticisms of mine).
175. E-mail from Christopher L. Eisgruber to Andrew Koppelman (July 10, 2005).
176. Thomas C. Berg, *Can Religious Liberty Be Protected as Equality?*, 85 Tex. L. Rev. 1185, 1194, 1195 (2007).
177. Religious Freedom and the Constitution, at 25.
178. Id. at 11.
179. Id. at 203, 64–65.
180. On the freedom of association doctrine, see generally Andrew Koppelman with Tobias Barrington Wolff, A Right to Discriminate? How the Case of *Boy Scouts of America v. James Dale* Warped the Law of Free Association (2009). It is possible that they are proposing to expand freedom of association beyond its current limits, but given the pitfalls involved in that endeavor— see id.—they need to say more about what new rules of law they propose.
181. *Chips Off Our Block?*, at 1275.
182. Religious Freedom and the Constitution, at 5.
183. Id. at 1283.
184. Religious Freedom Restoration Act of 1993, 42 U.S.C. § 2000bb-1(b) (2000) (subsection numbers omitted). Congress was attempting to codify earlier Supreme Court decisions that nominally adopted the same test, though in fact the Court had shown a range of different levels of deference in different contexts. See Marci A. Hamilton, *The Religious Freedom Restoration Act Is Unconstitutional, Period*, 1 U. Pa. J. Const. L. 1, 6–7 (1998).
185. Religious Freedom and the Constitution, at 40–44.
186. See 42 U.S.C. § 4332(C) (2000).
187. 42 U.S.C. § 12112(b)(5)(A).
188. See, e.g., Pike v. Bruce Church, Inc., 397 U.S. 137, 142 (1970).
189. Religious Freedom and the Constitution, at 279, 270, 274–75, 280, 43. For evidence that some of the mini-RFRAs have been construed very narrowly, sometimes in ways that gutted their meaning, see Christopher C. Lund, *Religious Liberty after* Gonzales: *A Look at State RFRAs*, 55 S.D. L. Rev. 466 (2010). Eisgruber and Sager acknowledge that religious claimants often prevail in court, but claim that this is consistent with Equal Liberty. Religious Freedom and the Constitution, at 299 n.35. Because of the malleability of the counterfactual Equal Liberty test, it is impossible to show that they are wrong, but a rule that is frequently invoked with success is not feeble in fact.

190. The Court has recently suggested that a balancing test, which gives religion some but not absolute weight, may be the most that the Establishment Clause permits. It noted that it had earlier invalidated a law giving Sabbatarians an absolute right not to work on their Sabbath because the law "'unyielding[ly] weigh[ted]' the interests of Sabbatarians 'over all other interests,'" while the RLUIPA, which it upheld, would likely "be applied in an appropriately balanced way." Cutter v. Wilkinson, 544 U.S. 709, 722 (2005) (quoting Thornton v. Caldor, 472 U.S. 703, 710 [1985]).

191. Religious Freedom and the Constitution, at 78–120, 262; *Congressional Power*, at 105–109.

192. See, e.g Ward v. Rock Against Racism, 491 U.S. 781, 791 (1989) (deferential balancing test for content-neutral regulations of the time, place, and manner of speech); United States v. O'Brien, 391 U.S. 367, 376–382 (1968) (deferential balancing test for governmental regulation of conduct that incidentally burdens freedom of expression).

193. See, e.g Loving v. Virginia, 388 U.S. 1, 11–12 (1967) (racial classifications presumptively unconstitutional). *But see* Grutter v. Bollinger, 539 U.S. 306 (2003) (effectively relaxing that presumption).

194. Just how context-specific was not clear to me until I read 1 Kent Greenawalt, Religion and Fairness: Free Exercise (2006), which carefully treats, seriatim, the full range of typical free exercise situations and thus brings forth just how heterogeneous they are.

195. See, e.g Sarvepalli Radhakrishnan, The Hindu View of Life 11–25 (1927). For an attempt to adapt the same insight to the Christian tradition, see Diana L. Eck, Encountering God: A Spiritual Journey from Bozeman to Banaras (1993).

5. A Secular State?

1. See Samuel Freeman, Rawls 243–283 (2007).

2. Robert D. Putnam & David E. Campbell, American Grace: How Religion Divides and Unites Us 495–501 (2010).

3. Niccolo Machiavelli, The Prince 44 (Robert M. Adams, trans., 1977).

4. James Davison Hunter, Culture Wars: The Struggle to Define America (1991).

5. I owe the analogy to Michael W. McConnell, *Religion and Its Relation to Limited Government*, 33 Harv. J. L. & Pub. Pol'y 943, 952 (2010).

6. Penny Edgell, Joseph Gerteis, & Douglas Hartmann, *Atheists as "Other": Moral Boundaries and Cultural Membership in American Society*, 71 Am. Soc. Rev. 211, 230 (2006).

7. Its relation to other religious traditions is not explored by Taylor, and I will not attempt that here. In the context of the overwhelmingly Christian United States, this is the linkage that matters historically.

8. I acknowledge that this commonly used shorthand is the product of a very recent historical moment and bespeaks a truncated and chastened political

aspiration. That aspiration is nonetheless utopian, and its power across religious lines is revealing. See Samuel Moyn, The Last Utopia: Human Rights in History (2010). Thanks to Nancy Koppelman for directing my attention to this book.

9. In the speech quoted in the Introduction, Eisenhower recalled being reproached by his friend, Russian Field Marshal Georgy Zhukov, for capitalism's "appeal to all that is materialistic and selfish," as contrasted with the Soviet Union's "appeal to something higher and nobler." *Text of Eisenhower Speech*, N.Y. Times, Dec. 23, 1952, at 16. Eisenhower focused on Zhukov's atheism, but atheism did not generate Zhukov's aspirations.

10. Charles Taylor, A Secular Age 388 (2007). For a similar analysis, with American illustrations, see James Turner, Without God, without Creed: The Origins of Unbelief in America 204–207 (1985). Turner's history parallels Taylor's to a remarkable extent while drawing on an almost completely different set of primary sources.

11. Taylor, A Secular Age, at 544. The overwhelming majority of Americans believe that right and wrong should be based on God's laws. Putnam & Campbell, American Grace, at 495–496.

12. Richard Rorty, Contingency, Irony, and Solidarity (1989).

13. Astoundingly sure, given that he understands that his view is itself merely a contingent cultural formation. See J. Judd Owen, Religion and the Demise of Liberal Rationalism: The Foundational Crisis of the Separation of Church and State 56, 60–61, 65–66 (2001).

14. Thanks to Christopher Green for clarification on these matters.

15. Jeremy Waldron claims that "a commitment to human equality is most coherent and attractive when it is grounded in theological truth, truths associated particularly with the Christian heritage." God, Locke, and Equality: Christian Foundations in Locke's Political Thought 236 (2002). He convincingly shows that Locke's argument for equality was thus grounded, but Waldron's case for its attractiveness is underdeveloped. Locke thought people needed to be told their duties by "one manifestly sent from God, and coming with visible authority from him." John Locke, The Reasonableness of Christianity 139 (1794), quoted with approval in God, Locke, and Equality at 103. The divine authority of Jesus Christ is less manifest and visible than Locke thought.

16. This is emphasized by Henri de Lubac, The Drama of Atheist Humanism (1944; rev. English ed. 1995), who argues that atheism has no basis for attributing any absolute value to the human individual, and no warrant for universal respect for persons. As atheist humanism conceives man, there is

> nothing to prevent his being used as material or as a tool either for the preparation of some future society or for ensuring, here and now, the dominance of one privileged group. There is not even anything to prevent his being cast aside as useless.

Id. at 66; see also id. at 70, 263–264. The same view is implicit in Steven D. Smith, The Disenchantment of Secular Discourse (2010), who critiques modern secularists such as Ronald Dworkin, Martha Nussbaum, and John Rawls in the same spirit as de Lubac dissects Feuerbach, Marx, Nietzsche, Comte, and the atheists depicted in Dostoyevsky. There is, however, a notable distance between the two studies: de Lubac's targets in fact betray the humanism to which they are nominally committed, while Smith's merely fail to justify theirs to his satisfaction.

17. Immanuel Kant, Religion within the Limits of Reason Alone 82, 175 (1794; Theodore M. Greene & Hoyt Hudson, trans., 1960).

18. Taylor, A Secular Age, at 453–454.

19. See A Global Ethic: The Declaration of the Parliament of the World's Religions (1993).

20. Sarah Barringer Gordon, The Spirit of the Law: Religious Voices and the Constitution in Modern America 89–93 (2010).

21. Bruce Dierenfield, The Battle over School Prayer: How Engel v. Vitale Changed America 187–212 (2007); Rob Boston, Forever and Ever Amen: The 30 Years' War over Prayer and Bible Reading in the Public School, 46 Church and State 10 (June 1993); Kenneth Dolbeare & Phillip Hammond, The School Prayer Decisions: From Court Policy to Local Practice (1971).

22. Gordon, The Spirit of the Law, at 91.

23. Thomas Curry, The First Freedoms: Church and State in America to the Passage of the First Amendment 177 (1986).

24. For a thoughtful modern articulation of Leland's separationist ideal, see Randall Balmer, The Making of Evangelicalism: From Revivalism to Politics and Beyond (2010).

25. Edgell et al., Atheists as "Other."

26. Claude S. Fischer & Michael Hout, Century of Difference: How America Changed in the Last One Hundred Years 200, 222 (2006).

27. See Eugene Volokh, Parent-Child Speech and Child Custody Speech Restrictions, 81 NYU L. Rev. 631, 633–635 (2006).

28. Edgell et al., Atheists as "Other," at 218.

29. Id. at 225–227.

30. Richard Cimino & Christopher Smith, Secular Humanism and Atheism beyond Progressive Secularism, 68 Sociology of Rel. 407 (2007).

31. Michael McConnell, Accommodation of Religion, 1985 Sup. Ct. Rev. 1, 10–11.

32. Torcaso v. Watkins, 367 U.S. 488 (1961).

33. Sam Harris, Letter to a Christian Nation 14–18 (rev. ed. 2008). Harris offers a similarly bold leap of logic when he claims that the question of slavery can be resolved by observation of fact: "The moment a person recognizes that slaves are human beings like himself, enjoying the same capacity for suffering and happiness, he will understand that it is patently evil to own them and treat

them like farm equipment." Id. at 18–19. Not only is the logic fallacious, but the claim is inconsistent with the observed facts: many Southern slaveholders understood the humanity of their slaves perfectly well. Harris is remarkably unreflective about the Naked Strong Evaluation that drives him.

34. Wilfred Cantwell Smith, Questions of Religious Truth 74 (1967).

35. See Jaroslav Pelikan, Jesus through the Centuries: His Place in the History of Culture (1985).

36. Pew Forum on Religion and Public Life, Much Hope, Modest Change for Democrats: Religion in the 2008 Presidential Election, Aug. 11, 2010.

37. Putnam & Campbell, American Grace, at 81. Relevantly here, Putnam and Campbell find little evidence that Supreme Court decisions, such as the school prayer cases, contributed much to the rise of the religious right. Id. at 115–118.

38. Id. at 129, 123, 106.

39. Id. at 370.

40. See A. James Reichley, Religion in American Public Life (1985).

41. Robert Wuthnow, The Restructuring of American Religion 218–222 (1988).

42. Robert Audi elaborates upon the dangers of religion in politics, while almost completely ignoring the other column of the ledger, in Religious Commitment and Secular Reason (2000).

43. The continuing existence of a large religious left is often overlooked. See Steven H. Shiffrin, The Religious Left and Church-State Relations (2009); Gordon, The Spirit of the Law.

44. John Rawls, *Justice as Fairness: Political Not Metaphysical,* in Collected Papers 393 (1999).

45. Rogers M. Smith, Civic Ideals: Conflicting Visions of Citizenship in U.S. History (1997).

46. Wendy L. Wall, Inventing the "American Way": The Politics of Consensus from the New Deal to the Civil Rights Movement (2008); Kevin Schultz, Tri-Faith America: How Catholics and Jews Held Postwar America to Its Protestant Promise (2011).

47. Another invention, undertaken in a similarly entrepreneurial spirit, is Susan Jacoby's category of "freethinkers," in which she tries, anachronistically, to enlist the eighteenth-century Deists as allies of contemporary atheists. Susan Jacoby, Freethinkers: A History of American Secularists (2004).

48. Sebastian Castellio, Concerning Heretics; Whether They are to be Persecuted and How They are to be Treated 123 (1554; Roland H. Bainton, trans., 1935).

Acknowledgements

Michael Perry and Steven D. Smith generously organized a private conference at Emory University in March, 2011, at which the participants, who also included Thomas Berg, Fred Gedicks, Rick Garnett, Judd Owen, and Robert Schapiro, tore the manuscript apart chapter by chapter. The philosophical section was also the object of an enlightening discussion with Kyla Ebels Duggan, Anne Eaton, Samuel Fleischacker, Richard Kraut, and Mark Rosen. Dean Lawrence Sager responded to the manuscript at the University of Texas Conference on The Future of Equality. I also received helpful reactions from four philosophy graduate students in my winter 2011 seminar on political neutrality in the Northwestern Philosophy Dept., Cristina Carillo-Canas, Chelsea Egbert, Seth Mayer, and Tyler Zimmer. Critical comments on chapters were also provided by Robert Audi, Robert Bennett, Mary Jean Dolan, Donald Drakeman, John Inazu, Josh Kleinfeld, Erica Landsberg, Martha Nussbaum, John Ohlendorf, Robert Orsi, Stephen Presser, Frank Ravitch, Martin Redish, Kevin Schultz, Steven Shiffrin, Richard Sorabji, Winnifred Fallers Sullivan, Alexander Tsesis, and audiences at the 2010 and 2011 Annual Law and Religion Roundtables. An incisive edit by Elizabeth Knoll made the book shorter and clearer. Marcia Lehr provided characteristically fabulous research assistance, and Jane Brock helped prepare the manuscript.

This book originated while I was a fellow in the Harvard Program in Ethics and the Professions, which gave me the freedom to poke around in unfamiliar territory.

I owe a special debt of gratitude to John Finnis, from whom I first got the basic idea for this book while reading his suggestion in *Natural Law and Natural Rights* (New York: Oxford University Press 1980), 89–90, that religion, broadly understood, can be shown to be a basic human good. I have always admired his work, but our public exchanges have consisted exclusively of vigorous debates about the gay rights issue. I am pleased to be able to acknowledge what I have learned from him. Needless to say, he is in no way to blame for the use to which I have put his ideas.

The Northwestern University School of Law has been a wonderful place to work on this project. I am grateful to my Deans, David Van Zandt and Daniel Rodriguez, for their support.

My wife, Valerie Quinn, and children, Miles, Gina, and Emme, have patiently endured this book's slow progress.

Various pieces of this book have appeared previously in print. I would like to thank the following publications for their permission to use those materials here: *The Fluidity of Neutrality*, 66 Review of Politics 633 (2004), in Chapter 1; *Corruption of Religion and the Establishment Clause*, 50 Wm. & Mary L. Rev. 1831 (2009), in Chapter 2; *Secular Purpose*, 88 Va. L. Rev. 87 (2002), in Chapter 3; *Is it Fair to Give Religion Special Treatment?*, 2006 U. of Ill. L. Rev. 571, *Conscience, Volitional Necessity, and Religious Exemptions*, 15 Legal Theory 215 (2009), *The Limits of Constructivism: Can Rawls Condemn Female Genital Mutilation?*, 71 Rev. Politics 459 (2009), and *How Shall I Praise Thee? Brian Leiter on Respect for Religion*, 47 San Diego L. Rev. 961 (2010), in Chapter 4; and *Naked Strong Evaluation*, 56 Dissent 105 (Winter 2009), in Chapter 5.

Index

Abelard, Peter, 137
abortion, 16, 167, 176
Abraham, 171
accommodation, 5–6, 11, 38, 42, 43, 87,
    88, 90, 106, 107–119, 121, 131, 134, 135,
    140–143, 152–156, 159, 161, 164, 165,
    218n62, 220n84, 221n102, 224n153;
    boundaries of, 98–101
Ackerman, Bruce, 149
Adamczyk, Amy, 212n128
Adams, John, 57, 198n91
affirmative action, 156
African Americans, 123
agnosticism, 6, 100, 124, 170
agnostics, 34, 101
Alabama, 85
Alito, Samuel, 118, 211n115
American identity, 26, 36, 80, 176–177;
    assimilationist tendencies in, 80; as
    Judeo-Christian, 37, 39, 177, 214n4; as
    Protestant, 39
American Revolution, 29, 33, 59, 62, 80
Americans with Disabilities Act, 163
Amish, 108
Anglican Church, 51, 53, 63
anti-Catholics, 33–34, 36, 202n148
antiperfectionism, 16, 18, 20, 21, 24, 26, 30,
    182n3, 222n121, 224n159
anti-Semitism, 8
apartheid, 130
Appiah, Kwame Anthony, 222n124
Aquinas, Thomas, 219n73, 219n76
Aquinas-conscience, 136–142
Areopagitica (Milton), 22–23, 50–53

Aristotle, 29
*Arizona Christian School Tuition Organi-
    zation v. Winn,* 118
Arkansas, 85
Arminianism, 31, 51
Arneson, Richard, 18–19
Asad, Talal, 44
association: freedom of, 162, 225n180
atheism, 6, 95, 100, 168–170, 173–176,
    185n43, 227n9, 227n16
atheists, 32, 37, 41, 130, 150, 166, 167,
    169, 172–175, 185n43, 187n87, 195n42,
    228n16, 229n47; population growth of,
    35, 41
Audi, Robert, 92, 207n51, 229n42
Australia, 80
autonomy: argument from, 24, 131, 138,
    144, 191n5. *See also* dignity, argument
    from

Bach, Johann Sebastian, 127
Backus, Isaac, 48, 56–58, 62, 67, 70, 173,
    196nn53–54, 198n94
Balkin, Jack, 205n11
Ballard, Edna and Donald, 72–73
Balmer, Randall, 228n24
Baptists, 34, 41, 42, 56, 57–59, 61, 70,
    197n63, 197n82, 202n151; coalition with
    Presbyterians, 62; Danbury, 28, 205n16;
    dissenters, 67; school prayer amend-
    ment, 173
Barry, Brian, 159
Bellah, Robert, 179n1
Bentham, Jeremy, 135–136, 159

233